The Tastes of Ayurveda

More Healthful, Healing Recipes for the Modern Ayurvedic

Amrita Sondhi

ARSENAL
PULP PRESS

VANCOUVER

THE TASTES OF AYURVEDA

ARSENAL PULP PRESS
Suite 101, 211 East Georgia St.
Vancouver, BC
Canada V6A 1Z6
arsenalpulp.com

The publisher gratefully acknowledges the support of the Government of Canada (through the Canada Book Fund) and the Government of British Columbia (through the Book Publishing Tax Credit Program) for its publishing activities.

The author and publisher assert that the information contained in this book is true and complete to the best of their knowledge. All recommendations are made without guarantee on the part of the author and publisher. The author and publisher disclaim any liability in connection with the use of this information. For more information, contact the publisher.

Note for our UK readers: measurements for non-liquids are for volume, not weight.

Book design by Electra Design Group

Printed and bound in Canada

Food photography by Tracey Kusiewicz (*foodiephotography.com*) with props supplied by Dream Designs Yoga photography by Alasdair Benson Photography (*alasdairbensonphotography.com*) Yoga Studio courtesy of Yogapod (yogapod.com). Clothing courtesy of Movementglobal (*movementglobal.com*). Models are: Yogi Todd Inouye (Kapha body type) of *yogapod.com*; Padma (Marla Stewart) of *padmayoga.ca* (Pitta body type); and Clara Roberts-Oss of *pixieyoga.net* (Vata body type).

Library and Archives Canada Cataloguing in Publication:

Sondhi, Amrita, 1959-

    The tastes of Ayurveda : more healthful, healing recipes for the

modern Ayurvedic / Amrita Sondhi.

Includes index.

Also issued in electronic format.

ISBN 978-1-55152-438-2

    1. Vegetarian cooking. 2. Medicine, Ayurvedic. 3. Cookbooks.

I. Title.

TX837.S663 2012   641.5'636   C2011-908407-4

I dedicate this book to all my invaluable comrades, students, and teachers, the "fringe dwellers" who keep pushing the edge on the "new normal" by practicing and regenerating the ancient healing arts; to those who pursue and create breakthroughs in health through being shining, living examples of vitality; and to the community of yogis and yoginis—locally and globally—who keep connecting to the source and transmitting the light.

To all the people who want to get the most nutrition and blissful flavor and balance (*ananda*) from the food they eat and live wonderful lives while they contribute to the communities and environment around them.

Table of Contents

Acknowledgments

I would like to thank the readers who told me over and over again how much they loved using *The Modern Ayurvedic Cookbook*; how much they (you) enjoyed the simple and straightforward recipes made up of wholesome ingredients, and who shared the joy of using the book with friends near and far.

I would also like to thank the television and radio stations, webzines, and print magazines, including *LA Yoga* and *Yogi Times*, for featuring our recipes for Thanksgiving dinners and daily fare. I would like to thank Jessica Romp and Randall Mark and Joy TV for asking me to write and co-host our now twenty-six-episode program, *The Ayurvedic Way*, featuring recipes from *The Modern Ayurvedic Cookbook* and encouraging me to write the next book so we could do more episodes!

Once again, I would like to thank all my friends and family and the Bowen Islanders who ceaselessly encouraged me, helped me test recipes, and made it fun when it sometimes seemed daunting to write another 400-page book!

And finally, I would like to express my deep gratitude for the wonderful team at Arsenal Pulp Press for their enthusiastic support of my work and helping birth my second book, *The Tastes of Ayurveda*.

Introduction

When I was writing *The Modern Ayurvedic Cookbook* in 2006, I kept coming up with more ideas and recipes to add to the book. Brian and the staff at Arsenal finally said, "Save it for the next book; we have to get this one to the press!" And that's how *The Tastes of Ayurveda* began. Since then I have maintained my curiosity about food, yoga, and living life to the fullest. I have continued to collect recipes from my own inspiration, family, friends, fellow yogis and yoginis, backyard gardeners, and people who have returned to and/or never stopped following ancient traditions and maintain a zest for food, life, and contributing to both their local and global communities.

I was inspired to start the Pamoja Foundation (*pamoja.org*) when I climbed Mount Kilimanjaro, the highest mountain in Africa, for my fortieth birthday. I learned that I could help raise money for the foundation through directing my passions and gifts; I got off the yogic mountaintop and started living the yoga. I donate ten percent of the profits from Movementglobal (*movementglobal.com*), my sustainable eco-yoga/ fashion line, and both of my books to the Pamoja Foundation, which raises money to sustainably alleviate poverty in east Africa and in Kenya (where I was born) through micro-financing. All of the donations go directly to grassroots borrowers (not to administrative costs), who then repay the loans so they can be lent to others in need.

People often tell me that they have no idea how I accomplish all that I do in my life (I also teach three yoga classes a week). I tell them that I am sustained and energized by my continual practice of yoga and my Ayurvedic diet. I have always believed we must be, in large part, what we eat—what we nourish ourselves with, on both physical and emotional levels. This is what motivated me to write this book.

Like its predecessor, *The Tastes of Ayurveda* includes an explanation of what the doshas are (p. 14) and the dosha questionnaire (p. 16), which lets readers determine their own primary dosha. If you've already completed the questionnaire, it is a great idea to do it again, as your constitution can change slightly over time. A section on the six essential tastes of Ayurveda follows, which explains how food, specifically the taste of food, affects people's personal constitutions. This book also offers basic tips on using herbs and spices, and recipes for staples such as ghee and paneer, which are traditional to Ayurvedic cooking, and information about sprouting.

Over 200 easy-to-follow vegetarian recipes make up the major portion of this book. Each recipe has symbols to indicate how it affects your dosha (p. 15). Many recipes also include variations for different doshas. Most recipes use whole grains and fresh foods (although I make reference to some recipes that freeze well if desired). There's a new interest in raw food diets since *The Modern Ayurvedic Cookbook* was published, so I've included a short introduction to Ayurvedic raw food principles in the Appendix, and each raw recipe is marked with a symbol (p. 358). Vegan options and vegan recipes are also marked with a symbol (p. 33). And since more people are interested in wanting to take control of their food sources, I've also included a section in the Appendix on how easy it is to start a simple balcony garden.

If the principles of Ayurveda are new to you, let's start by looking briefly at its long history and traditions.

History of Ayurveda

Originating in India more than 5,000 years ago, Ayurveda is the oldest system of healing. The name derives from two root words in Sanskrit (the ancient Indian language): *ayus*, which means life, and *veda*, which means knowledge or science; therefore in English, Ayurveda is "life knowledge" or "life science."

At the heart of Ayurveda is our intimate connection to the elements in nature, and how they can help us to achieve a physical and spiritual balance in all aspects of our lives. For the sake of our health and well-being, this balance can be accomplished through a number of means, including diet and exercise. The ancient sages of India, who lived in the mountains practicing meditation and yoga, believed that all material forms, including our bodies, are made up of five essential elements—ether, air, fire, water, and earth—in varying degrees, so maintaining a balance among these five elements is key to our physical, mental, and spiritual health.

Historically, the ideas and philosophies of Ayurveda were transmitted orally through the Vedas (ancient songs). The oldest song known is the "Rig Veda" ("in praise of knowledge"), which is almost as old as Ayurveda itself, and describes healing herbs and how they can be used. Later, by about 500 BCE, Ayurvedic knowledge began to be written down by the writers Charaka, Sushruta, and Vagbhata, which hastened its popularity. Two hundred years later, Ayurveda thrived with the advent of Buddhism, which was established in India under the rule of Ashoka the Great, and spread to China and Japan. But the Muslim invasion of India in the twelfth century CE led to Ayurveda being widely replaced by the Muslim system of healing, then further suppressed centuries later by the British, who feared the powers of the Ayurvedic doctors who were able to heal (or kill, if need be) in minutes by pressing specific *marma* (acupressure) points. With the return of Indian independence and the leadership of Mahatma Gandhi in the twentieth century, Ayurvedic schools and medical practices finally rose once again.

Today, this ancient and holistic healing science is arguably more popular than ever, and is a source of influences for many medical practitioners both east and west. Ayurvedic schools throughout India teach herbal medicine, massage, surgery, psychiatry, obstetrics, gynecology, astronomy, the use of mantra, meditation, and yoga among many other healing practices—to improve every aspect of life, balancing body, mind, and spirit. And most importantly, because Ayurveda considers food an integral part of its healing system, it originated some of the oldest and most time-tested principles of nutrition. Indian women cooking in their homes know a lot about Ayurveda and regularly use its principles in their meal preparation both to maintain health and to cure a variety of illnesses, from the common cold to more serious ailments, with appropriate foods that balance the doshas. Currently, these ancient remedies are now being proven scientifically and practiced around the world, most notably by Dr Deepak Chopra, the medical doctor and well-known scholar of Ayurveda.

Vata = Air   Pitta = Fire   Kapha = Earth

What are Doshas?

We are all born with three doshas that make up our body constitution. Most of us have a stronger primary dosha, a secondary dosha, and a third less prominent dosha; a few people are naturally balanced in all three. It is through Ayurveda that we try to bring all three doshas into balance. For example, a woman who is a Vata (meaning her primary dosha is Vata) would look to eat foods and engage in activities that are considered to have Kapha and Pitta qualities to bring herself into balance. Since our doshas reflect the elements of air, fire, and earth, it is not surprising that our food and environs affect each of these elements differently. For example, some people enjoy spicy food, while others cannot handle it; similarly, some may thrive in cool weather, and others may detest it. On page 16 is the Dosha Questionnaire, which will help you to determine your primary and secondary dosha; you will then learn how to prepare meals appropriate for your body type by incorporating foods or ingredients that reduce (−) your primary dosha and increase (+) the other two doshas, thus bringing you into balance. In general, if you feel out of balance, look for recipes that decrease (−) your primary dosha. For example, if you are a Pitta, look for recipes that have "− ". It is important to familiarize yourself with all three doshas so you can be more attuned to your body. Don't be afraid to experiment to find out what's right for you!

Our doshas and our lifestyles

In our modern world, where we are always on the go and cell phones, laptops, and cars seem to be constant companions, it is easy for us to get a Vata imbalance. In general, if our Vata is over-stimulated, we need to calm it by eating warmer, heavier, moist foods with some "good oils" (p. 26), which include the salty, sour, and sweet tastes. Meditation and rest also helps Vata to cool down and unwind. Every time Vata goes into overdrive and we start to feel stressed, it is important to take a silent five-minute break and do nothing.

If our Pitta is aggravated, we feel fiery, aggressive, and confrontational. At these times, it is important to eat cooling foods like cucumbers (cool as a cucumber!), drink cool (but not cold) drinks, and include lots of raw fruits and vegetables in our meals. Avoid sour, fatty, and spicy foods as well as artificial stimulants. Eat meals in an atmosphere of serenity and order, go for walks in parks or on beaches as much as possible, and avoid strenuous physical exertion or overheating.

When Kapha is out of balance, we feel dull and lifeless, and can't get off the couch. It is important for us to get moving. Regular and varied exercise is extremely important when we have excess Kapha. We also need to reduce butter, oil, and sugar in our diet, increase consumption of foods with the pungent, bitter, and astringent tastes, incorporate stimulating, hot, and spicy ingredients, and avoid cold drinks. To balance Kapha, we should eat light, warm meals, avoid eating to pacify the emotions, and go for brisk walks after eating.

Vata
Element: Air

People born with Vata as their primary dosha are energetic, creative, and natural risk-takers who often initiate projects; however, when Vata is out of balance, they experience nervousness, anxiety, fear, fatigue, and depression. Other physical signs of Vata imbalance include constipation, dryness, flatulence, weight fluctuations, poor circulation, decreased sweating, and feeling easily exhausted.

Those with excess Vata or who have Vata as their primary dosha should concentrate on calming their anxiety and turning their fear into joy and fatigue into energy by following the Ayurvedic principles for reducing Vata.

Pitta
Element: Fire

People born with Pitta as their primary dosha are natural leaders and administrators, capable of taking precise, decisive, and focused action; however, when Pitta is out of balance, they experience mood fluctuations, irritability, increased body temperature, restlessness, and impatience. Other physical signs of Pitta imbalance include broken capillaries, weight fluctuation, sweatiness, sleeplessness, and an over-active mind.

Those with excess Pitta or who have Pitta as their primary dosha should focus on turning irritability into directed, positive action, and balancing body temperature and moods, by following the Ayurvedic principles for reducing Pitta.

Kapha
Element: Earth

People born with Kapha as their primary dosha are the pillars of their communities. They have the ability to "follow through," seeing projects to completion, and are affectionate and good-natured, experiencing the least mood fluctuations of the three doshas; however, when Kapha is out of balance, they experience sluggishness, feelings of being "stuck in a rut," strong attachments, addictions, possessiveness, over-sensitivity, and laziness. Other physical symptoms of Kapha imbalance include excess weight, cellulite, lack of motivation, and puffiness.

Those with excess Kapha or who have Kapha as a primary dosha should turn stagnant energy into activity, find freedom from attachments and addictions, and be creators of their own positive choices by following the Ayurvedic principles for reducing Kapha.

Dosha Questionnaire

This test will help you determine your primary and secondary doshas. Take no more than fifteen minutes to answer all the questions, as your first response that comes to mind is usually the best one. Circle the number that best pertains to you, and don't worry about being perfect. Once you have answered all questions, add up your Vata, Pitta, Kapha scores separately. The highest number is your primary dosha, the second highest will be your secondary dosha. Sometimes people have an equal score in all three doshas, although this is quite rare. Once you know your primary dosha, you will be able to choose foods and activities that keep you in balance and harmony; remember that we each possess a combination of all three doshas to varying degrees, and need to keep them all in balance.

It is a good idea to complete this questionnaire twice, the first time informed by your current lifestyle and environment (*vikruti*) and the second by your experiences as a young child (*prakruti*). In Ayurveda, knowing the difference between your prakruti and vikruti can give you new insight into your body, and how to restore it to optimal health. An important means of doing this is through diet, but remember that our health is also influenced by our lifestyle choices, environment, emotional state, the amount of exercise we do, and the people around us. (It is also beneficial to do this questionnaire every few years as our body constitution naturally changes over time.)

Vata		DOES NOT APPLY		SOMETIMES APPLIES		OFTEN APPLIES	
I perform activities very fast		1	2	3	4	(5)	6
I learn quickly and forget easily		1	2	3	4	(5)	6
I am enthusiastic and lively		1	2	3	(4)	5	6
I have a thin physique and don't gain weight easily		(1)	2	3	4	5	6
I am light and fast on my feet		1	2	(3)	4	5	6
I can be indecisive		1	2	3	4	(5)	6
I get bloated or constipated easily		(1)	2	3	4	5	6
My hands and feet tend to be cold		(1)	2	3	4	5	6
I worry and am anxious a lot		1	2	3	4	(5)	6
I don't like cold weather, food, or drinks		1	2	3	(4)	5	6
I speak quickly and my friends consider me a chatterbox		1	2	3	4	5	(6)
I am moody and emotional		1	2	3	4	5	6
I have difficulty falling asleep or I am a light sleeper		1	(2)	3	4	5	6
I have dry skin		1	2	3	(4)	5	6
I have an active imagination and my mind is often restless		1	2	3	4	5	(6)
My energy levels fluctuate		1	2	3	4	5	(6)
I get excited easily		1	2	3	(4)	5	6

64

Pitta	DOES NOT APPLY		SOMETIMES APPLIES		OFTEN APPLIES	
I am efficient	1	2	3	4	5	6
I am precise and orderly	1	2	3	4	5	6
I have a well-balanced body shape and a medium build	1	2	3	4	5	6
I am strong-willed, maybe forceful and am not easily influenced by others	1	2	3	4	5	6
I get tired easily and feel uncomfortable in hot weather	1	2	3	4	5	6
I perspire easily	1	2	3	4	5	6
I am impatient and quick to anger, though I may conceal it	1	2	3	4	5	6
I have a hard time skipping meals	1	2	3	4	5	6
I have a good appetite and can eat large amounts if I want to	1	2	3	4	5	6
I am determined, stubborn, and can be critical	1	2	3	4	5	6
I rarely get constipated	1	2	3	4	5	6
I can be a perfectionist	1	2	3	4	5	6
I prefer cool temperatures to hot	1	2	3	4	5	6
I enjoy cool foods and drinks	1	2	3	4	5	6
Overly spicy foods don't agree with me	1	2	3	4	5	6
I have difficulty with people disagreeing with me	1	2	3	4	5	6
I love good challenges and am focused in my efforts to achieve my goals	1	2	3	4	5	6

Kapha	DOES NOT APPLY		SOMETIMES APPLIES		OFTEN APPLIES	
My actions are slow and deliberate	1	(2)	3	4	5	6
I gain weight easily and lose it slowly	1	2	3	4	(5)	6
I am patient and even-tempered	1	2	(3)	4	5	6
I am not bothered if I skip a meal	1	2	(3)	4	5	6
I get congested easily and may have sinus problems	1	2	(3)	4	5	6
I sleep very deeply	1	2	(3)	4	5	6
I prefer eight or more hours sleep	1	2	3	4	5	6
I am a slow learner but have an excellent long-term memory	1	2	3	4	(5)	6
I don't get sick often	1	2	3	4	(5)	6
I don't like humidity or damp weather	1	2	3	4	(5)	6
I have smooth, soft skin	1	(2)	3	4	5	6
I have a large, solid body build	1	2	(3)	4	5	6
I have a slow metabolism	1	2	(3)	4	5	6
My energy levels are strong and I have good stamina and endurance	1	2	(3)	4	5	6
I am affectionate, caring, and sweet natured	1	(2)	3	4	5	6
I eat slowly	(1)	2	3	4	5	(6)
I make my decisions methodically	(1)	2	3	4	5	6

Once we become familiar with the various Ayurvedic body types, we can use this knowledge to understand the personalities around us. People's strengths and weaknesses, and when their doshas are in and out of balance, become more predictable, and we can now set up harmonious groups with a balance of Vatas, Pittas, and Kaphas. The Vatas would initiate the projects and ideas, the Pittas would organize, focus, and lead them, and the Kaphas would see them through to completion. Now, of course, we all have a combination of the three doshas (or we couldn't get out of bed in the mornings, organize ourselves to get to work, and carry out the projects of the day!), but in most people, one dosha tends to predominate. If a dosha is out of balance—Pitta is getting irritated and frustrated, Kapha is feeling dopey and sedated, and Vata is running around fractured and anxious—one would avoid the foods that increase the dosha if it is in excess or add more of the foods that increase the dosha if it is depleted. Once you have learned the principles of Ayurvedic cooking, you will know how to balance your unique constitution with food. For example, you will learn how to use spices to either increase your element of fire (Pitta) or decrease it; how to "ground" your element of air (Vata) by using good oils or fats and sweet tastes (which are not necessarily "sugary"; foods such as bread, rice, and cilantro are considered sweet in Ayurveda); and how to activate a lethargic state (Kapha) through increased movement and the consumption of more raw foods. Throughout this book, I explain the basics of Indian cooking and how to get started if you have never tried it before. As a result, you will increase your repertoire of tasty, nutritious vegetarian cooking and notice an increase in your sense of balance, well-being, and energy.

Some of the ingredients used in these recipes may sound exotic, but most can be found at your local grocery store. I suggest that you be a little adventurous in your shopping and explore ethnic neighborhoods wherever possible—like your city's Little India, Japantown, Chinatown, and Little Italy—for ingredients. Stores in these areas usually carry fresh produce, herbs and spices, whole grains, and a wide variety of beans, lentils, and vegetable protein often not found in conventional supermarkets.

There is an extensive Appendix at the back of the book to introduce you to eating differently for each season, as these too have Vata, Pitta, or Kapha qualities. Various menu plans emphasize the six tastes, and you'll find a *panchakarma* (a simple cleanse) that includes meditation and massage to help clear the body and mind of toxins. I also include yoga postures for your doshas as well as alternative therapies (*vashtu*) that will help you maintain a balanced sense of well-being in your home or office surroundings.

I wish you well on your new or continued adventures in the world of Ayurveda.

The Tastes of Ayurveda

Ayurveda divides food into six tastes that influence the three doshas and thereby influence our overall sense of satiation and well-being. The six tastes are sweet, sour, salty, bitter, pungent, and astringent; each one affects our doshas differently. (Many foods have a combination of two or three tastes, such as oranges, which are considered both sweet and sour.) Ayurveda recommends that all six tastes be included in each meal; when they are, we will be left feeling harmonious, peaceful, and calm, as each dosha has been nourished. Note that only a little of each taste is necessary for it to satisfy and balance us; more is not necessarily better, and in fact, in certain situations it can be detrimental or toxic.

The guidelines offered here will teach you how to harmonize your doshas, and bring yourself back into balance when necessary. Although it is important to have the six tastes at every meal, don't become overly concerned with this, as it should be a goal, not a rule. As you learn to listen to your body, you will start to be attuned to how the various tastes affect you. Remember that as you get to know which tastes are good for your dosha, you may not be eating foods you typically would, but it is those familiar foods that may have been sending your dosha out of balance. Give your body the time it needs to get used to new tastes, and the subsequent feeling of balance that comes from changing your ingrained eating habits.

Here are the tastes that decrease, or pacify, each dosha:
Vata is pacified by sweet, sour, and salty tastes.
Pitta is pacified by sweet, bitter, and astringent tastes.
Kapha is pacified by pungent, bitter, and astringent tastes.

Sweet: Rice, bread, honey, milk, ghee, oils, all meats, and most "sweets" are considered sweet in Ayurveda. Most legumes, lentils, and beans are considered sweet as well as astringent, which increases Vata. An exception is urad dal (split black lentils), which are considered sweet and not astringent, so they calm Vata. Grains and vegetables, which contain carbohydrates, are considered sweet, and increase Kapha while decreasing Pitta and Vata. Foods with the sweet taste are considered heavy and therefore grounding.

Sour: Lemon, vinegar, yogurt, cheese, tomatoes, grapes, plums, and other sour fruits increase Pitta and Kapha and decrease Vata. These foods should be consumed in small amounts and not at all by those with excess Pitta or Kapha. Sour foods promote digestion, are good for the heart, and warm the body. But an excess of these foods can cause irritation, dizziness, or loss of vitality.

Salty: Salt, kombu (and all other seaweeds), soy sauce, pickles, chutneys, bouillon, and salty condiments increase Kapha and Pitta and decrease Vata. Having at least a little salt in our diets is essential for our health; it also aids digestion. But consumed in excess, salty foods can cause bloating and water retention, or lead to inflammatory conditions. Too little may result in illness, thyroid problems, or leg cramps.

Pungent: Ginger, cumin, black pepper, cinnamon, cayenne, chilies, radishes, onions, and garlic decrease Kapha and increase Pitta and Vata (but a little of these foods are good for Vata due to their warming effect). Pungent tastes heat the body, stimulate digestion, and eliminate excessive fluids, thereby relieving colds and bronchitis. They also help to get our metabolism moving if we are feeling sluggish. Consumed in excess, they can cause anger and aggression, as well as burning sensations, dizziness, dryness, and increased thirst.

Bitter: Green leafy vegetables (e.g., kale, spinach), bitter gourd, turmeric, fenugreek, lemon and orange rind, dark chocolate, and olives increase Vata and decrease Pitta and Kapha. They cool Pitta when out of balance and too fiery, and lighten Kapha when too heavy. Consumed in excess, bitter can produce envy, jealousy, and yes, bitterness.

Astringent: Beans, lentils, apples, pears, cabbage, broccoli, cauliflower, and potatoes increase Vata and decrease Pitta and Kapha. Consumed in excess, they produce flatulence, constipation, and a dryness of the body.

Taste

Taste (*rasa*) in Ayurveda is the basis of understanding how we can use food to balance the doshas and is made up of three parts:

1. **Rasa**: is the first flavor we have when we eat something; it affects our mental and emotional state.

2. **Virya** is the effect each food has on our digestion.

3. **Vipak** is the long-term effect of eating something.

Some foods will lighten the body and others will have a more grounding effect. Heavier foods take more energy (*agni*) to digest. Light foods are easy to digest and integrate. Moist tastes will lubricate the body, whereas dry tastes will use up fluids (cause an astringent affect).

Because Ayurveda was developed in India, many Indian meals are well balanced in the six tastes; however, other cultures have also developed rich cuisines that are naturally balancing. Ayurvedic principles, once understood, can be used for any style of cooking. In these days of global interrelationships, an exciting array of ingredients are available to create a meal that can balance the doshas. Once you develop your senses and get to know each taste and its effect on your constitution (doshas), you can use this knowledge to maintain your optimum state of health.

Sweet taste (rasa) = earth and water
This has a cooling virya and its vipak is moist and grounding. A little promotes feelings of love, amiability, and friendship.

Sour taste (rasa) = earth and fire
This has a heating virya and its vipak is heavy and moist. A little of this promotes clear practical thinking.

Salty taste (rasa) = fire and water
This has a warming virya; however, its vipak becomes sweeter, moist and grounding if eaten in moderation.

Pungent taste (rasa) = air and fire
This has a light and dry virya and a heating affect. Its vipak is one of enlivening passionate movement if eaten in moderation.

Bitter taste (rasa) = air and ether
This has a cold, light, and dry virya and initially has a cooling effect. Its vipak has a lightening and drying effect over time. A little aids clear thinking.

Astringent taste (rasa) = air and earth
This has a cool, light, and dry virya. Its vipak becomes slightly warmer over time. It instills a straightforward, practical approach to life.

The six tastes each have a singular effect on the doshas, and when combined create another effect, so as you experiment in the kitchen, you can choose the combinations that suit you.

Getting Started

Basic herbs and spices for Ayurvedic cooking

Herbs and spices are essential in Ayurveda; they stimulate the appetite and increase our ability to digest what we eat, increasing our overall health and well-being. Here is a list of basics herbs and spices you should keep on hand in your cabinet or refrigerator. See the Food Guidelines Chart in the Appendix (p. 390) for information on what herbs and spices are appropriate for each dosha.

Dry: Bay leaves; black pepper; cardamom, ground and whole (pods); cayenne pepper; chilies, red; cinnamon sticks and cinnamon bark; cloves, whole; coriander, ground; cumin, ground and whole; curry leaves; fennel seeds; fenugreek; garam masala; mustard seeds, black; mustard seeds, crushed and whole; turmeric

Slicing chilies releases their flavor and heat. Use a sharp knife and slice in half lengthwise, keeping the end intact so it appears whole and can easily be removed by the stem before serving.

Fresh: Cilantro; chilies, green; garlic; ginger

Fresh is always best

Just as freshly ground coffee has more aroma and flavor, the fresher the spices, the more flavorful your food will be. I recommend keeping a coffee grinder on hand just for your spices. Whole dried spices can keep in the freezer for up to a year; grind them as you need them just as you would with coffee. Ground spices will keep for 4–6 months in a spice rack. To clean the coffee grinder, grind ½ slice of bread into breadcrumbs, then discard.

Garam masala

Garam masala (which means "hot spices") is an Indian blend of dried spices that can be used in the same way as black pepper or other seasonings. It is a warming food which also stimulates digestion and circulation. For seasoning, only a little is needed, e.g., ¼–½ tsp.

Preheat oven to 200°F (95°C).

To break cinnamon sticks, place between a folded dishcloth and crush with a hammer or a rolling pin.

5 cinnamon sticks, broken (see note)
¼ cup (60 mL) black peppercorns
¼ cup (60 mL) whole cardamom pods
⅛ cup (30 mL) whole cloves

Sprinkle ingredients evenly on a baking sheet. Roast for 20–30 minutes, stirring from time to time to ensure they do not brown. Remove from oven and allow the mixture to cool. Break open each cardamom pod by squeezing between thumb and forefinger. Place cardamom seeds in mixture and discard pods. In a coffee grinder (not one usually used for coffee), grind ingredients until they become a fine powder. Store in an airtight container.

Good oils and fats

Oils are the main source of good, healthy fats in our diets. In general, choose oils that are expeller-pressed, which are those that have been extracted from seeds or nuts through a chemical-free mechanical process; or cold-pressed oils, which are expeller-pressed in a heat-controlled environment of less than 120°F (49°C). Unrefined oils—oils left in their virgin state after pressing—are very rich in nutrients, but when used for cooking, they have a lower smoke point (the temperature at which oil begins to decompose and give off fumes). Always store all types of oils in the refrigerator after they have been opened to extend their shelf life and maintain their nutritional value. Olive oil is the exception; it can be stored at room temperature.

Buy a spray bottle that works on a vacuum principle and fill with olive oil. These bottles make it easy to spray veggies lightly with oil so you don't over-saturate them.

Here are the good oils I recommend; use organic versions wherever possible:

- **Coconut oil** has a nice flavor and is full of nutrients that are retained at high temperatures.

- **Flax seed oil**, like hemp oil, is full of essential omega-3 fatty acids. Use unheated, and add it to shakes, salad dressings, cereals, or toast. Refrigerate after opening and use within six weeks.

- **Ghee** (p. 27) is butter that is free of impurities and cholesterol. Use sparingly if you are trying to lose weight. It is very calming to the nervous system. For great flavor and to calm Vata, use a little ghee mixed with a good oil when sautéing. Ghee can be stored at room temperature.

- **Grapeseed oil** maintains its healthy properties at high temperatures. Use sparingly if you are trying to lose weight.

- **Hemp oil**, like flax seed oil, is full of the essential omega-3 fatty acids and should be used unheated, such as in shakes and salad dressings. Refrigerate after opening and use within six weeks.

- **Olive oil** is an all-purpose oil as it is readily available, affordable, and cooks well at high heat without losing its nutritional value. Also use in salads, soups, and sauces.

- **Sesame oil** is another healthy oil. I recommend using only high quality versions that can be purchased at health-food stores. Sesame oil is more expensive, but you only need to use a little for wonderful flavor.

Good fats, an essential part of our diet, can be found in olives, avocados, almonds, walnuts, pistachios, pecans, and other nuts and seeds (including nut and seed butters). The key to health is to consume these good fats and oils in moderation. A diet too low in fat can lead to attention deficit disorder, heart disease, cancer, autoimmune disorders, skin and joint problems, premenstrual problems, and depression and other mood disorders. On the flipside, a diet too high in fat (particularly "bad" fats) can lead to obesity, cancer, and heart disease.

Trans fats are the worst of the "bad fats"; they clog up arteries and impair blood flow, which increases the risk of heart attacks and strokes. Trans fats are most often found in junk food, so it is best to avoid virtually almost all fast, fried, and processed foods, including packaged cookies, candy, crackers, non-dairy creamers, and instant and frozen foods. If you don't have enough time to cook, go to a health-food store or local market and pick up something quick and healthy. Always read the package label so you know what you are putting in your body. Avoid trans fats as much as possible; this includes products that have hydrogenated or partially hydrogenated fats such as monoglycerides and diglycerides.

Ghee

Clarified butter, also known as ghee, is butter with the milk solids removed. Ghee is a digestive aid that improves the absorption of nutrients from food it's used with. It also is known to improve memory, lubricate the connective tissues, and act as a catalytic agent to carry the medicinal properties of herbs to the body. Ghee calms both Pitta and Vata, but should be used sparingly by Kapha and those who have high cholesterol or suffer from obesity. Ghee doesn't need to be refrigerated as the impurities have been removed.

To make ghee: In a pot on medium heat, melt 1 lb (500 g) unsalted butter completely (watch carefully to ensure it doesn't burn). Bring to a boil. Skim off foam with a slotted spoon and discard. Reduce heat to low. Stir occasionally for 15–20 minutes. When the whitish curds turn light brown, it is ready. Skim off additional foam, then pour through a sieve or cheesecloth into a glass container with a tight lid to store. Discard the curds at the bottom of the pan.

Paneer

Paneer is homemade cheese, similar in taste to Ricotta and cottage cheese, but better for you, as its souring process makes it easier to digest. Paneer is used in various Indian vegetable entrées such as Spicy Paneer & Zucchini Kebabs (p. 84) and West Bay Biriani (p. 208). You can also sauté paneer before adding to vegetable dishes—an easy way to add protein. Paneer is similar to tofu in texture as well as its ability to absorb flavors. In fact, you may substitute tofu in all the recipes that call for paneer, although it is worth trying paneer for its wonderful subtle flavor. If you are pressed for time, paneer is usually available packaged in Indian grocery stores, sold in cubes or large blocks.

To make paneer:
8 cups (2 L) whole milk
6 tbsp plain yogurt
¼ cup lemon juice, strained through a fine sieve

In the Ayurvedic tradition, bringing milk to a boil then cooling it makes it easier to digest. Often those who have a low tolerance for dairy find that they can enjoy it again when they follow this practice. Heating the milk also sterilizes it without destroying its nutritional properties.

In a large heavy pot on high heat, bring milk to just before a boil (watch closely to ensure it does not burn). As soon as foam begins to rise, remove pot from heat. Ideally, the milk should be taken off the heat as soon as it start frothing, so that important nutrients are not destroyed and the milk is not denatured. This sterilizes the milk without destroying B vitamins.

Add yogurt and lemon juice to milk and mix well. The curds will start to solidify and separate from the liquid whey. Over a bowl, strain the mixture through a piece of cheesecloth, reserving the curds (paneer) in the cheesecloth. Wrap the cloth tightly around the curds, squeezing out the excess liquid.

Place the paneer, still wrapped in the cheesecloth, on a cutting board, and lay another board or baking sheet on top of it. Weight it down with about 15 lb (7 kg) of heavy jars or cans and let sit at room temperature for 6–8 hours, until cheese is firm (consistency of firm tofu). Unwrap and cut into ¾-in (2-cm) cubes. Cover and refrigerate until ready to use. The cheese can be frozen and used as needed. It will keep for up to 3 months in the freezer.

Makes 6–8 servings.

Good salt

"Good" salts are those in their original form and contain many essential minerals and trace elements that, in small amounts, help maintain the healthy functioning of our bodies. These include potassium, magnesium, calcium, manganese, iron, and zinc. Sea salts also contain natural iodine. All good salts are so much more flavorful than table salt!

Some of my favorite salts are:

Sea salts are created by evaporating sea water. Their gray color comes from the clay and minerals found at the bottom of salt pools.

Himalayan crystal salt contains 84 essential trace minerals. It is considered one of the purest salts on the planet, uncontaminated by toxins and pollution, as it comes from an ancient layer beneath the Himalayas, 250 million years old. Himalayan salt contains less iodine than sea salt, so I add seaweed to my meals or iodine drops to my shakes to make up for this.

Hawaiian red clay sea salt has a wonderful pinkish tinge that comes from traces of iron found in the volcanic clay.

Celtic sea salt is carefully harvested with wooden rakes to maintain its composition, nutrients, and flavor.

Fleur de sel, the *crème de la crème* of sea salts, is mined only at a certain time of the year when the best salts with their mineral deposits rise to the surface of the salt pools and are then raked in.

The commonly found iodized table salt is "bad" salt. It has been denatured by being heated to over 1,200°F to make it look pure white. (It is sometimes compared to refined white sugar.) This process removes most of the salt's essential minerals and elements. The heating process reduces it to sodium chloride, which can create toxic residues in our bodies that contribute to gallstones, kidney stones, arthritic conditions, and cellulite. Our bodies are unable to absorb this salt as effectively as "good" natural salts, resulting in less than optimum well-being.

Why organics?

Organic foods are more nutrient-dense than those found in many grocery stores today, although more grocery stores now have special organic sections in response to increasing customer demand. Organic foods contain higher levels of vitamins, polyphenols, antioxidants, flavonoids, essential fatty acids (good oils), and essential minerals. Organic foods are grown in soil that is rich and full of minerals and without the use of chemical fertilizers and pesticides, so they don't contaminate our bodies. This growing practice also supports the environment, as we are not damaging it with pesticides or nitrate fertilizers or leaving the soil barren.

Organically certified milk and dairy products come from animals that are not given drugs or growth hormones. Raw dairy products are the purest.

Sprouting beans and lentils

Sprouting beans and lentils increases their digestibility and significantly increases their nutritional value. This process breaks proteins and carbs down into easily digestible amino acids, starches, and sugars. Sprouted beans are a rich source of protein, vitamins, and minerals, making them known as a super food. The yogis were said to have existed almost entirely on sprouted beans when they lived in the Himalayas. Here is a basic way to sprout beans and lentils to create a very nourishing and gentle food.

In a large bowl or pot of water, soak 2 cups (500 mL) beans or lentils overnight. In the morning, drain and rinse in a colander. Set colander over bowl or pot to aerate and cover with a clean damp dishcloth. Leave in indirect light. In the evening, rinse again thoroughly. Once again, drain over bowl or pot and cover with damp dishcloth. Repeat the next morning and evening. By then, they will start to sprout little tails. When tails are about ¼-in (½-cm) long, store in an airtight container and refrigerate for up to 4 days or use immediately.

Soaking nuts and seeds

Soaking nuts and seeds overnight in water (2 parts water to 1 part nuts and/or seeds) increases their digestibility (agni), an important focus of Ayurveda. Soaking breaks down enzyme inhibitors that protect the seeds until they are planted and allows the seeds to become "live" food. Adding a little salt to the soaking water also helps to reactivate the enzymes, increasing the nut or seed's high nutritional value, and further aids digestion.

After Soaking

Rinse nuts before eating or using them in a recipe. Store in the refrigerator and rinse daily. Use within 2–3 days. If can't use your nuts up in 2–3 days, you can turn them into nut milk (p. 323) or nut butter by adding a little purified water and blending. Use within 2–3 days. If you want to keep the nut butter longer, use a little oil instead of purified water.

Make sure the nuts you buy are fresh, not rancid; this eradicates the nourishment. To test for rancidity, smell and taste the nuts before using them. When the oils in nuts are rancid, they taste bitter and acrid, and have become toxic, or *ama*, in Ayurveda.

Nuts are rich in natural good oils or essential fatty acids. They are great for enhancing brain health and the neurotransmitters that create the mind-body-spirit connection, energetically (or electrically) "turning the lights on." They are also great for softening the skin and are known to help create "the glow" that so many natural foodists talk about.

SOAKING NUTS AND SEEDS	
NUT OR SEED	SOAKING TIME
Almonds	8–12 hours maximum
Buckwheat seeds	up to 12 hours maximum
Cashews	1–8 hours maximum
Chia seeds	11 hours*
Pumpkin seeds	4–9 hours maximum
Sesame seeds	4–8 hours maximum
Sunflower seeds	4–9 hours maximum
Walnuts	1–8 hours maximum

Note: Soak 1 part nuts in 2 parts water. Add a pinch of good salt to the soaking water.

*Soak chia seeds to full expansion. They will become sticky. If you don't soak them before using them in a recipe, drink lots of water or the chia seeds you ingest will absorb the liquids in your body. Once chia seeds are soaked, they will keep for about a week in the refrigerator and can be used in desserts, shakes, dressings, or porridge.

Soaking for longer than the maximum times may cause the nuts to rot.

These nuts and seeds don't need soaking:
• Flax seeds (grind them)   • Pine nuts
• Hemp seeds   • Pistachios

Roasting and deydrating
If nuts are roasted or dehydrated until completely dry (preferably at no higher than 150°F [66°C] to preserves all the enzymes that make them a live food), they will keep in an airtight container for a few months. The longer you soak them, the longer it takes to dry them.

Blanching
You can blanch almonds after soaking them. Drain, then cover in hot water. When the water becomes cool enough to touch, the skins will pop off easily. Discard the skins.

What the Symbols Mean

Each recipe includes the three dosha symbols:

 = Vata  = Pitta = Kapha

as well as information on how the specific recipe affects each dosha:

[+]   means that the recipe increases the qualities of the dosha and may aggravate you.

[slightly +]   means that the recipe slightly increases the qualities of the dosha and may aggravate you if you have this in excess.

[Ø]   means that the recipe has a neutral effect on the dosha.

[-]   means that the recipe balances or decreases the qualities of the dosha.

Recipes may also include ingredient modifications to help calm specific doshas; e.g., a recipe such as Upma (page 48) slightly increases Pitta unless you omit the green chili. (For more ideas on modifying recipes to suit your dosha, see the Food Guidelines Chart on page 390.)

    Some recipes have a tridoshic symbol, meaning they are appropriate and calming for all three doshas.

    Finally, some recipes have a vegan symbol (i.e. contain no animal products).

Remember, don't let the recipes intimidate you! Be open to experimenting, listen to your body, and discover how good you'll feel by cooking the Ayurvedic way.

Chia Seeds

Breakfast

We know that our bodies and brains are at their optimum when fueled. Numerous studies show that children who eat breakfast do well in school. Just as vehicles break down if running on empty reserves, our balance is thrown off and our bodies are put into extreme stress modes when we don't give them the nutrients they need. In this section, I have included a variety of breakfasts filled with nourishing ingredients to satisfy you depending on your mood, appetite, and dosha levels.

If your dosha is predominantly Vata, you may want to start your day with grounding comforting foods such as Quick Oats the Old-Fashioned Way (p. 41). If Kapha is your primary dosha, you may want something lighter and more uplifting, such as Michelle's Quick and Yummy Egg on Quinoa Breakfast (p. 62). If Pitta is your primary dosha, you may sometimes wake up so focused on the day's goals that you forget about breakfast, then crash later in the day. Instead, make yourself a shake—like the Brain Power Blueberry and Almond Shake (p. 36)—to nourish and center yourself with before embarking on your day or to take with you.

So eat your breakfast and power up your day! Mood swings will even out, and you will pass your great energy (*prana*) on to whomever you meet and into whatever you do.

Brain Power Blueberry & Almond Shake

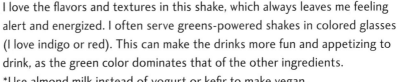

I love the flavors and textures in this shake, which always leaves me feeling alert and energized. I often serve greens-powered shakes in colored glasses (I love indigo or red). This can make the drinks more fun and appetizing to drink, as the green color dominates that of the other ingredients. *Use almond milk instead of yogurt or kefir to make vegan.

Iodine is essential for good thyroid function, our metabolism, and brain health. If you are low in iodine (many of us are), an easy way to get it is in liquid form. It is available in health-food stores.

⅓ cup (80 mL) blueberries
¼ cup (60 mL) kefir or yogurt (omit for vegan)
2 tbsp flax seed oil
1 tbsp hemp seeds
1 cup (250 mL) unsweetened cranberry juice
½ cup (125 mL) almond milk (p. 320)

5 lemon balm leaves
1 drop iodine (optional, if low in iodine)
1 drop liquid vitamin D (optional, in winter, or if not getting enough sunlight)
2 tsp greens (or according to instructions on your brand)

In a blender or Magic Bullet, combine all ingredients and blend until smooth.

Makes about 2–2¼ cups.

Vitamin D is important for optimum brain health, bone density, and the immune system. It is naturally produced by the body when it is exposed to sunlight. In the winter season, or if wearing sunblock in the summer, it can be difficult to get this essential vitamin. An easy way to supplement with vitamin D is in liquid form, available at health-food stores. Remember that the quality of your supplements is important, so check out your sources carefully.

Greens powder is a super food, rich in chlorophyll, that promotes a healthy immune system and a good alkaline/acid balance to help prevent disease. You can find it easily at organic grocers or health-food stores

Warming Mango
 Raspberry Shake

I make this shake when I spot nice mangos while grocery shopping. They always take me back to my hometown, Mombasa, Kenya, where I grew up, which was abundant with mango trees. *Note:* Soak almonds overnight (p. 30).
*To make vegan, omit kefir.

Mangoes are considered warming in Ayurveda, and they have lots of vitamins A and C as well as fiber.

⅓ cup (80 mL) chopped mango
⅓ cup (80 mL) raspberries
2 tbsp kefir (optional)
2 tsp greens (or according to instructions on your brand)
2 tbsp flax seed oil

1 tsp agave nectar or to taste (optional)
1 cup (250 mL) purified water or cranberry juice
5 almonds, soaked overnight and blanched

In a blender or a Magic Bullet, blend all ingredients, serve in colorful glasses, and drink!

Makes 1 serving.

Kefir is rich in lactobacilli and tastes similar to yogurt, with a slightly more tart flavor. It is excellent for restoring the digestive system and is a natural antibiotic. Take a tablespoon of kefir before traveling to help protect against infection.

To blanch almonds: *Place in a bowl or mug. Cover with enough boiling water to cover. Let sit until lukewarm, but no longer or they'll lose their crunch. Rub the skins off using your fingers.*

+

-

-  # Cleansing Shake

The lemon juice adds a cleansing effect and great flavor contrasted with the sweetness of the pear.

*
*To make vegan, omit kefir.

1 sliced and cored pear
½ cup (125 mL) hemp seeds
1 tbsp greens (or according to
   instructions on your brand)
1 cup (250 mL) chopped Swiss chard

2 tbsp flax seed oil
2 cups (500 mL) almond milk
2 tbsp fresh lemon juice
2 tbsp kefir
1 tbsp agave nectar (optional)

In a blender or Magic Bullet, combine all ingredients and blend until smooth.

Makes 2 servings.

Patrick's Strawberry, Coconut & Cacao Morning Shake

 You will not believe this is good for you—it tastes sinfully delicious, but it's packed with nutrients, electrolytes, and antioxidants. Organics are always recommended; in this recipe it is essential that the cream cheese is organic. See benefits of raw cocoa on p. 288.

Coconut water, available at Indian grocery and health-food stores, is full of electrolytes that the body craves. Drink coconut water after a workout and feel the replenishment.

1 cup (250 mL) strawberries
• *To reduce Pitta: use raspberries*
¼ cup (60 mL) rice protein powder
2 tbsp raw chocolate (cocoa)

1 ¼ cups (310 mL) coconut water
1 tbsp organic cream cheese
2 tbsp flax seed oil

In a blender or Magic Bullet, combine all ingredients and blend until smooth.

Makes 1 large or 2 small servings.

Patrick's Vital Flax & Cream Cheese Spread

slightly +

My friend Patrick looks 10–20 years younger than his biological age. Of course, I wanted to know what he was eating for breakfast! He says the molecular structure of this mixture creates oxygen without stress on our systems and helps maintain a healthy pH balance in our bodies. (As with Patrick's recipe on p. 39, the cream cheese must be organic.) It is delicious on toast, celery, or crackers. Patrick also adds it to his breakfast shakes to high-power his mornings. I attest to Patrick's claim that this brings vitality and energy to the day.

Process flax seeds in a coffee grinder that you don't use for coffee. Process them as you need them, as the beneficial oils in the seeds quickly become rancid when exposed to air.

⅔ cup (160 mL) organic cream cheese
⅓ cup (80 mL) ground flax seeds
2 tbsp flax seed oil

In a small bowl, mix all ingredients together with a fork.

Makes 1 cup (250 mL).

-

 -

 +

Quick Oats the Old-Fashioned Way

What makes this recipe so great is that soaking the oats not only makes them much quicker to cook, it also makes them much easier to digest and more beneficial, as the rich nutrients are being more fully absorbed. I fully recommend doing this rather than buying "quick oats," which have been denatured and have lost some valuable nourishment.

Oats are known in many cultures to enhance intuition, endurance, and energy. They are rich in B vitamins, calcium, iron, magnesium, phosphorus, and potassium. They are low in gluten.

Note: Soak oats and raisins overnight (p. 30).

Phytates in oats may slow the absorption of some minerals. Phytates can have a beneficial chelating or detoxifying effect; however, when ingested frequently, they may slow the absorption of some minerals and irritate the digestive tract. Soaking grains overnight in acidulated water (p. 30) reduces phytates and not only makes grains much quicker to cook but more beneficial to eat and easier to digest.

⅓ cup (80 mL) oats
⅔ cup (160 mL) water for soaking oats
2 tsp lemon juice (or vinegar, yogurt, or kefir)
8 raisins

2 tbsp water for soaking raisins
½ – ¾ cup (125–185 mL) water for cooking
⅛ tsp good salt (p. 29)
agave nectar, to taste (optional)

In a medium bowl, add oats and soaking water. Stir in lemon juice, cover, and leave to soak overnight. In a small bowl, add raisins and soaking water, cover and leave to soak overnight. Then add both oats and raisins to a small saucepan with additional cooking water and salt. Bring to a boil. Reduce heat to low and simmer until done. Stay close to the stove, as this will be done in about 5 minutes! Serve with agave nectar if desired.

Makes 1 serving; multiply quantities for as many people as you have present at breakfast.

 -
slightly
 +
 +
slightly

Variation: Add 5 soaked blanched almonds, chopped just before serving.

+

+

-

Quinoa Breakfast Porridge

I love how I feel after eating this porridge; satisfied without feeling heavy. Cozy on a cool morning eaten warm, also great cooled on a summer morn.

Quinoa is an ancient grain packed with protein, fiber, and essential amino acids. It is a source of vitamins B and E as well as iron, calcium, and phosphorus.

1 cup (250 mL) quinoa
1 cup (250 mL) diced apples
2 cups (500 mL) water
¼ cup (60 mL) dried cranberries
¼ tsp ground cinnamon
½ cup milk of your choice (I like almond milk)

In a medium pot on high, combine all ingredients except milk and bring to a boil. Reduce heat to low and let simmer, cover with a tightly fitting lid, and cook until done, about 15 minutes. Serve with a dash of milk of your choice.

Makes 2 large or 4 small servings.

Start Your Morning Seeds Fruit Porridge

You'll love the textures of this porridge, and how the slow carbs keep you fueled all morning. *Note:* Soak cereal and seeds overnight (see p. 30 and chart on p. 31).

*To make raw, use sliced banana or berries instead of 9-grain porridge.

 - +

Unsulfured currants are high in iron, calcium, vitamin C, and fiber—a great way to sweeten your cereal with a bounty of nutrients.

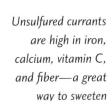

⅔ cup (160 mL) 9-grain porridge cereal
2 cups soaking water
1 tbsp + 2 tsp lemon juice (may use vinegar, yogurt, or kefir instead)
2 tbsp black currants

2 tsp soaked chia seeds
2 tbsp soaked pumpkin seeds
1 grated apple
1⅓ cup (315 mL) water (for cooking)
¼ tsp ground cinnamon

In a medium bowl, combine 9-grain cereal with soaking water and lemon juice and mix with a fork. Cover and leave in a warm place overnight (such as the oven, turned off but with the light on).

In the morning, combine all ingredients, except cinnamon, in a small pot, and bring to a boil. Reduce heat to low and simmer for 5–7 minutes. Sprinkle with cinnamon and serve with milk and/or maple syrup if desired.

Please note: you may add chia seeds, pumpkin seeds, and a pinch of cinnamon just before serving to keep them raw.

Makes 1 serving; multiply quantities for as many people as you have present at breakfast.

 - +
slightly

Variation 1: Use steel-cut oats instead of 9-grain cereal and cook for 10–15 minutes.

 - +
slightly

Variation 2: Add chia seeds and pumpkin seeds with the cinnamon and do not cook; instead, toss in a bowl and serve.

 - -

To make this raw, use sliced banana or berries instead of 9-grain porridge.

-
-
slightly + # Chia Seed, Fruit & Nut Porridge

 This is a highly nutritious breakfast that will energize you all morning and delight you with each bite. *Note:* Soak chia seeds and walnuts before preparing this recipe (see pp. 30 and 31).

½ cup (125 mL) soaked chia seeds
2 tbsp soaked walnut pieces
  • *To reduce Pitta and Kapha: use less or omit*
2 tbsp water
2 tbsp shredded coconut
  • *To reduce Kapha: use less or omit*

4 tbsp diced dried figs (about 4)
2 tbsp pistachios
  • *To reduce Pitta and Kapha: use less or omit*
almond milk, to taste (optional)
agave nectar, to taste (optional)

Drain soaked walnuts and chia seeds and combine with all remaining ingredients.

Makes 2 servings.

Nut-n-Seed Granola

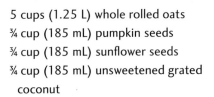

Invest the time to make this tasty nourishing recipe. It creates an easy breakfast when topped with fresh or dried fruit and yogurt or milk of your choice. (I like hemp seed milk, a vegan alternative.) *Note:* Soak the almonds (p. 30).

5 cups (1.25 L) whole rolled oats
¾ cup (185 mL) pumpkin seeds
¾ cup (185 mL) sunflower seeds
¾ cup (185 mL) unsweetened grated
  coconut

¾ cup (185 mL) soaked slivered
  almonds,
¼ cup (60 mL) flax seeds
½ cup (125 mL) coconut oil
½ cup (125 mL) maple syrup

Preheat oven to 300°F (180°C).

In a large bowl, combine rolled oats, pumpkin seeds, sunflower seeds, grated coconut, slivered almonds, and flax seeds and set aside.

In a small pot on low heat, melt coconut oil. Remove from heat. Add oil and maple syrup to dry ingredients and stir to mix well. Spread onto 2 baking sheets and bake for 10 minutes. Remove from oven, toss mixture and bake for another 10 minutes. Allow mixture to cool and become crispy. Store in an airtight container for up to 1 month.

Makes 8 cups (2 L).

Teresa's Berry Good Breakfast

Teresa invited me for breakfast one morning and introduced me to her favorite way to start the day. She says she gets excited just thinking about getting out of bed to eat this. I can see why: it's crunchy, colorful, nutritious, and delicious. *To make vegan, use nut milk and Cashew Cream, p. 298) in place of milk and yogurt. *Note:* Soak seeds and grains overnight (p. 30).

Concord grape juice is filled with flavonoids and powerful antioxidants.

2 cups (500 mL) mixed blackberries, raspberries, and blueberries
¼ cup (60 mL) soaked pumpkin seeds (p. 31)
2 tbsp soaked chia seeds (p. 31)
2 tsp soaked raw buckwheat seeds (p. 31)

2 tsp hulled hemp seeds
⅛ tsp Celtic sea salt
¼ cup (60 mL) granola (p. 45)
¼ cup (60 mL) Concord grape juice
½ cup (125 mL) milk
½ cup (125 mL) yogurt or Cashew Cream (p. 298)

Divide ingredients evenly into two cereal bowls, layering artfully in order of the ingredients list.

Makes 2 servings.

The seed mixture is filled with fiber, iron, manganese, and other important trace minerals. You can buy this premixed. If making your own mixture, combine 1 tbsp chia seeds and 2 tsp buckwheat seeds. You may also choose to use only 1 or 2 kinds of seeds and add 2 tsp hemp seeds later as these do not need to be soaked.

Chia and buckwheat seeds can also be sprouted. Chia seeds take 3 days and buckwheat 2 days. Follow chart on p. 31. However, we do not recommend sprouting them for this breakfast.

slightly –

+

+ # Stenya's Raw Energizing Breakfast

Stenya moved to Bowen Island one summer so she could work with us at my eco-clothing store, Movementglobal. She often invited me to share her wonderful breakfasts in the garden and recently shared this recipe with me. This sustained us even while doing physically demanding work. *Note:* Soak nuts and seeds overnight (p. 30).

Goji berries are full of antioxidants and fiber—they have even more than blueberries and kale.

½ cup raw almonds
¼ cup (60 mL) raw pumpkin seeds
⅛ tsp Himalayan salt
2 cups (500 mL) soaking water
¼ cup (60 mL) goji berries

In a bowl, combine almonds, seeds, and salt and soaking water. Cover with a plate or cloth and let sit overnight. In another bowl, soak berries in ½ cup (125 mL) water, cover with a plate or cloth, and let sit overnight. In the morning, drain and rinse nuts and seeds. In a blender, combine nuts and seeds, goji berries, and berries' soaking water and blend to a smooth consistency. If needed, add extra water 1 tbsp at a time. Scrape the nutty goodness into a bowl and enjoy every mouthful slowly.

Makes 1–2 servings or 1 serving and enough for a snack later.

–
–
+  Upma

* Upma is a delicious hot cereal breakfast, traditional in South India. It is made with grains, vegetables, and flavorful spices. Sometimes the onions are omitted and nuts may be added. I love the savory flavors in this simple dish. To reduce Kapha, add a minced garlic clove in the last 2 minutes of sautéing the onions and add more green chilies.

*To make vegan, replace ghee with good oil (p. 26).

Roasting grains removes allergens from wheat and makes them lighter to digest.

1 cup (250 mL) cream of wheat cereal (farina)
1 tbsp good oil (p. 26)
1 tsp ghee (or butter)
1 tsp black mustard seeds
½ tsp ground turmeric
1 tsp minced green chili
  • To decrease Pitta: omit

½ cup (125 mL) chopped red onions
⅓ cup (80 mL) chopped cilantro leaves
½ tsp good salt (p. 29), or to taste
3 cups (750 mL) water
1 tsp lemon juice
½ cup (125 mL) grated coconut
4 lemon wedges
¼ cup (60 mL) chopped cilantro

In a frying pan on medium, dry-roast cream of wheat until it begins to turn brown, stirring constantly for 3–4 minutes. Pour into bowl and set aside. In a medium saucepan on medium, heat oil and ghee. Test to see if single mustard seed pops; when it does, oil is hot enough to add rest of mustard seeds. Cover with a lid. Seeds will pop in about 20 seconds. Remove lid and immediately add turmeric, green chilies, onions, and cilantro. Sauté for 6 minutes, until onions turn golden brown. Add salt and water and bring mixture to a boil. Add cream of wheat and whisk to prevent lumps while boiling for 2 minutes. Reduce heat to low, cover, and cook for another 4–5 minutes. Stir in lemon juice. Garnish with coconut, lemon wedges, and chopped cilantro.

Makes 4 servings.

slightly +

+

- # Dosas (South Indian Crêpes)

This South Indian recipe is one of my favorite savory breakfasts. If I can't get to a local dosa restaurant, I make these at home. They take some practice to make, so don't give up! I've given you two recipes to choose from; one with homemade flour, which is more nutritious, and one with store-bought flour.

In India, dosas can be eaten plain or with savory fillings such as Masala Potato Dosa Filling (p. 52). They are also traditionally served with a watery dal (also called sambar). Serve dosas with dal in a small bowl on the side. Also serve with your favorite chutneys, like Green Cilantro Garlic Chutney (p. 278), and a small bowl of plain yogurt. Use small bowls for individual condiment servings. The best way to eat dosas is with your fingers. Tear a piece off, dip and moisten the dosa in dal, then dip it into a chutney and enjoy! *Note:* The dosa batter needs to soak for 12–36 hours.

Continued on next page

Masala Dosa with Homemade Flour

This homemade batter makes the dosas highly nutritious as the flour is leavened by fermentation, protecting us from disease and increasing the digestive enzymes. They are really delicious and worth the time it takes to make them.

1 cup (250 mL) urad dal
3 cups (750 mL) water
6 tbsp water
2 cups (500 mL) rice flour
¼ cup (125 mL) cup diced onions
  (optional)
½ tsp ground coriander (optional)

1 tsp minced ginger or Green Chutney
  (p. 276) (optional)
½ tsp diced fresh green chili (optional)
½ tsp good salt (p. 29)
3 tbsp cold water
6–8 tsp ghee (or butter)

Soak urad dal in water for about 3 hours or overnight. Drain the dal and add to a blender or a food processor with 6 tbsp water and blend until the lentils are ground to a thick paste or batter. Add to 2 cups rice flour. Stir well and place in a bowl, covered with a slightly damp tea towel, at warm room temperature for at least 12–36 hours (overnight is easy). Use this batter to make dosas. Stir in chopped onions, ground coriander, ginger, green chili, salt, and cold water.

Heat 1 tsp ghee in a frying pan and melt. Pour in 6 tbsp batter and spread evenly. Fry for 2–3 minutes until bubbles begin to form on top. Then flip and cook the other side until brown, about 2 minutes. Set aside covered while you cook the rest.

Makes 6–8 servings.

slightly +

Masala Dosa with Urad Dal Flour

This recipe is a slightly quicker way to make dosas if you do not have the time to soak the flour and make your own. For this you will have to buy your urad dal flour from an Indian grocery shop.

Urad dal flour is available at Indian grocery stores and is sometimes called black mung, black lentil, or black gram flour. Urad dal are ¼-in (6-mm) long beans with a black husk; the kernel is pale yellow. It is available dried, whole, split, and hulled. Warm and heavy, it is one of the dals that is very beneficial and nourishing for Vata in small amounts.

1½ cups (375 mL) rice flour
1 cup urad dal flour (see note)
½ tsp good salt (p. 29)
¼ tsp fenugreek
2 cups water
6 tsp coconut oil (or other good oil,
   see p. 26)

In a medium bowl, combine all ingredients except the oil. You may need to add an additional ¼ cup (60 mL) water to make a semi-thin paste (crêpe batter consistency). Refrigerate for at least 12–36 hours. (The longer it soaks, the more tart it becomes.)

In a large frying pan on medium-high heat, melt ½ tsp coconut oil evenly over surface. Add ¼ cup (60 mL) batter and tilt pan so that it spreads evenly. Spread another ½ tsp oil at the edges and on top of dosa. When bottom is golden brown, flip and brown other side. Repeat with remaining oil and batter.

Makes 6 servings.

+

slightly +

- # Masala Potato Dosa Filling

* You can use this filling with either of the previous dosa recipes. This is my favorite filling to order when I am in a dosa restaurant. The recipe is quite easy to make and great either in a dosa or a spelt pan-crêpe (p. 64).
*To make vegan, replace ghee with good oil (p. 26).

1 tbsp good oil (p. 26)
1 tbsp ghee (or butter)
1½ tsp black mustard seeds
10 curry leaves
½ tsp ground turmeric
1½ tsp grated ginger
1 tbsp green minced chili

1½ cups (375 mL) chopped onions
3 cups (750 mL) potatoes, cubed ¾ in (2 cm)
good salt (p. 29), to taste
1 tbsp + 2 tsp lemon juice
¼ cup (60 mL) chopped cilantro

In a large frying pan on medium-high, heat oil and ghee. Add mustard seeds, cover, and once popped (about 20 seconds), add curry leaves, turmeric, ginger, chili, and onions, and cook until onions are soft, about 4 minutes. Add potatoes and stir to coat with seasonings. Add 1 cup (250 mL) water and bring to a boil. Reduce heat to low, cover, and let simmer until potatoes are soft and almost breaking up, about 15–20 minutes. If you need more water, add 1 tbsp at a time. Season with salt, to taste. Add lemon juice and cilantro. Stir to mix well and serve rolled in a masala dosa (p. 50) or spelt pan-crêpes (p. 64). These are crispy and so are not folded over at the ends. Serve seam-side down on a plate.

Makes 6 servings.

-

slightly +

- ❀ # Parsi Scrambled Eggs

I love the delicate flavor and color of the saffron and the warming spices in these eggs.

Serve with toast or chapatis.

1 tbsp milk
3 strands saffron
3 eggs
  • *To reduce Pitta: use 3 egg whites and 1 egg*
1 tbsp ghee (or butter)
  • *To reduce Kapha: use 1 tsp*
½ medium red onion, chopped
1 garlic clove, crushed or finely minced
  • *To reduce Pitta: omit*

½ tsp minced ginger
1 tsp minced green chili
  • *To reduce Pitta: omit*
½ tsp garam masala
⅛ tsp cayenne
  • *To reduce Pitta: omit*
¼ tsp good salt (p. 29)
¼ cup (60 mL) chopped cilantro

In a small saucepan, heat milk just until it starts to froth (do not boil) and remove from heat. Stir in saffron and set aside to melt. In a mug or bowl, beat eggs and set aside. In a medium saucepan, heat ghee on medium high, add onions and sauté for 2 minutes. Add garlic, ginger, green chili, garam masala, and cayenne and sauté for 1 minute. Stir saffron milk mixture into egg mixture, then add to onions. Reduce heat to low and cook for no longer than 2 minutes, stirring eggs to ensure even cooking. Remove from heat, season with salt, and garnish with cilantro.

Makes 2 servings.

Flying to Hawaii Frittata

 Before going to Hawaii, I cleaned out my refrigerator and used the ingredients to invent this tasty recipe. It kept me energized and grounded while lots of Vata (wind) movement was going on! Serve this on its own or with a salad to make it brunch or lunch.

1 tsp good oil (p. 26)
1 tsp ghee (or butter)
2 tbsp minced onions
¼ cup (60 mL) diced leeks
2 tbsp sliced green onions
½ cup (125 mL) diced potatoes
½ cup (125 mL) thinly sliced small zucchini
½ cup (125 mL) finely diced yellow bell pepper

1 minced garlic clove
• *To reduce Pitta: omit*
2 eggs
1 tsp vegetable bouillon powder
¼ tsp good salt (p. 29)
¼ tsp ground black pepper
1 tbsp pesto
½ cup (125 mL) grated old hard cheese (I like Asiago, Parmesan, or cheddar)

In an ovenproof frying pan on medium high, heat oil and ghee. Add onions and sauté for 1 minute. Add all vegetables and garlic, and sauté on medium heat until onions caramelize and zucchini and yellow peppers begin to brown. Meanwhile, break eggs into a small bowl and beat. Add vegetable bouillon powder, salt, and pepper to eggs and stir to mix well. Pour eggs evenly over vegetable mixture and turn heat to low. Once egg settles a bit (about 1 minute), spread pesto evenly over egg mixture, then sprinkle grated cheese evenly over top and place frying pan under a broiler with door open. Watch carefully and when cheese starts to melt and bubble (about 1 minute) and turn slightly golden brown, serve.

Makes 2 servings.

slightly +

 # Swiss Cheese & Mushroom Frittata

This is not only a delicious breakfast, it also makes a tasty snack later in the day.

I like the combination of ghee and olive oil as it can cook at a higher temperature for longer without burning while retaining a nice flavor. This is a good way to calm Vata, Pitta, and Kapha nerves without increasing Kapha too much.

1 tsp good oil (p. 26)
1 tsp ghee (or butter)
⅓ cup (80 mL) finely diced onions
½ tsp minced garlic
¾ cup (185 mL) sliced mushrooms
  (oyster, shiitake, portobello)
¼ cup (60 mL) diced red bell pepper

3 eggs
⅓ cup (80 mL) milk
1 cup (250 mL) baby spinach leaves
½ cup (125 mL) grated Swiss or
  Gruyère cheese
¼ cup (60 mL) chopped parsley

In an ovenproof frying pan on medium, heat oil and ghee. Add onions and sauté for 3 minutes, then add garlic and sauté for another 3 minutes. Add mushrooms and red peppers and cook until vegetables soften, about 5 minutes. Meanwhile, in a small bowl, beat eggs and milk. Pour over cooked vegetables and stir in spinach. Continue to cook for another 2–3 minutes, watching carefully as eggs start to set. Sprinkle grated cheese evenly over eggs and vegetable mixture. Place under broiler for 2–3 minutes and remove when the egg has set and cheese begins to bubble. Garnish with parsley.

Makes 2 servings.

-

 +

 ø

Fresh from the Garden Omelette

It was a gorgeous sunny summer day, and the tomatoes had just ripened on the vine on my back deck. The Swiss chard was waiting to be picked. Inspired, I created this fresh omelette. As the tomatoes and chard contribute their own liquids, this recipe does not require additional water or milk.

Using Swiss chard with red and yellow stems (sometimes called "rainbow chard") makes this recipe colorful.

2 eggs
1 tbsp good oil (p. 26)
1¾ cups (415 mL) chopped tomatoes
 (save liquid)
2 cups (500 mL) chopped Swiss chard

¼ tsp good salt (p. 29), or to taste
freshly ground pepper, to taste
2 tbsp finely grated Parmesan or other
 aged hard cheese

In a mug or small bowl, beat eggs and set aside. In a medium frying pan on medium high, heat oil. Add tomatoes and sauté until they soften, about 6 minutes. Add Swiss chard to pan and sauté for another 3–4 minutes, until chard softens slightly. Pour beaten eggs into pan. Season with salt and pepper. Shake pan slightly so egg settles evenly. Cook for 2 minutes, then sprinkle cheese over eggs. Cover with a lid, letting eggs cook in their own steam. Uncover and place under broiler for 2 minutes, or until cheese begins to brown.

Makes 2 servings.

- _{slightly} + ø Variation: Add ½ tsp whole cumin seeds. When oil is hot, drop 1 cumin seed into the oil to test; if it sizzles and turns white, add rest of seeds and let sizzle for 30 seconds before adding tomatoes.

Sona's Fresh Cilantro, Mushroom & Chili Flake Omelette

Sona, my sister-in-law, ate this omelette as a child in Mumbai. She now lives in Europe and can't always find the same green chili she grew up with, so uses Italian dry red chili flakes.

7 eggs
1 tbsp good oil (p. 26)
2 tsp ghee (or butter)
1 cup (250 mL) chopped onions
½ cup (125 mL) chopped mushrooms

1 cup (250 mL) chopped tomatoes
½ cup (125 mL) chopped fresh cilantro
½ tsp Italian dried red chili flakes
½ tsp good salt (p. 29)
½ tsp ground black pepper

In a medium bowl, beat eggs and set aside. In a large frying pan on medium high, heat oil and ghee. Add onions and reduce heat to medium. Cook until onions soften, about 3 minutes. Add mushrooms and tomatoes. Sauté for 1 minute. Pour in eggs. Sprinkle with cilantro, chili flakes, and salt and pepper. Cover pan, reduce heat to low, and cook for 3 minutes, or until eggs have just set.

Makes 8 servings.

−
 +
 −

Sunday Brunch Quinoa Egg Bake

This recipe is wonderful, as the quinoa cooks while it bakes, so you can get other things prepared for your guests for Sunday brunch.

Many baking recipes require cooked quinoa, but this does not.

1 tsp good oil (p. 26) or ghee (or butter)
½ cup (125 mL) red quinoa
8 eggs
1¼ cups (310 mL) milk
1 tbsp chopped garlic
• *To reduce Pitta: use less or omit*

1 tsp fresh thyme
½ tsp Himalayan salt
½ tsp ground black pepper
2 cups (500 mL) packed baby spinach
1 cup (250 mL) grated Asiago or old cheddar cheese

Preheat oven to 350°F (180°C). Grease a 9 x 9-in (23 x 23-cm) baking dish with oil or ghee and set aside. Rinse quinoa in a sieve and drain. In a large bowl, combine eggs, milk, garlic, thyme, salt, and pepper and whisk until frothy. Stir in quinoa and spinach until well mixed. Pour into baking dish, cover tightly with lid or foil, and gently shake from side to side so quinoa settles evenly on bottom. Bake for 45 minutes or until eggs have just set. Remove lid or foil and sprinkle evenly with cheese. Return to oven and bake for 10 minutes. Remove from oven and set aside to cool for 5 minutes. Slice into squares and serve.

Makes 6 servings.

− + − Variation: Replace garlic with 1 tbsp sliced green onions; replace thyme with 1 tsp minced serrano chili.

slightly +

+

- Quinoa & Scrambled Eggs

I love using this nourishing ancient grain instead of toast with my eggs. This can be eaten in a bowl with a spoon, which makes it easy to serve and clean up.

1 tbsp good oil (p. 26)
  • *To decrease Vata: add 1 tsp ghee (or butter)*
½ cup (125 mL) chopped onions
3 garlic cloves, minced
  • *To reduce Pitta omit*

2 tbsp chopped fresh parsley
½ cup (125 mL) cooked red quinoa
4 eggs
¼ tsp good salt (p. 29)
¼ tsp ground black pepper
2 tbsp grated Parmesan (optional)

In a medium frying pan on medium, heat oil. Add onions and sauté for 5 minutes. Stir in garlic and parsley and sauté for 2 minutes. Stir in cooked quinoa and cook for another 2 minutes. Add eggs, season with salt and pepper, and scramble. Cook until eggs are no longer runny but still soft, about 3 minutes. Sprinkle with Parmesan cheese.

Makes 2 servings.

- + - Variations: Use cilantro and ½ tsp minced serrano chilies instead of parsley.

Michelle's Yummy Egg on Quinoa Breakfast

Michelle Harrison always glows. She's an in-demand actress and a hands-on mum of a lively 4-year-old son, Ethan. She shared with me one of her breakfast recipes; it's simple, nutritious, and easy to take with her on the ferry from Bowen Island to Vancouver if she is going to an acting job.

Tip: I often lay the eggs in their shells on top of the quinoa to steam after the quinoa has cooked for 10 minutes, and re-cover the pot. This allows me to use only one pot to make the dish if I have not already boiled my eggs.

Seaweed (kelp) is a source of iron, vitamin C, and iodine, which is good for the thyroid and helps to balance hormones. Keep kelp flakes handy in a jar or powdered kelp in a salt shaker to add flavor and nutrition to your meals.

½ cup (125 mL) quinoa
1 cup (250 mL) water
1 tsp ghee (or butter)
 • To reduce Kapha: use less or omit

2 hard-boiled eggs, diced
1 tbsp Bragg sauce or shoyu, to taste
2 tbsp kelp flakes, to taste

In a small pot, bring quinoa and water to a boil. Reduce heat to low, cover, and simmer until cooked, about 15–20 minutes. Stir in ghee. Top quinoa with diced eggs, season with Braggs or shoyu, and sprinkle with kelp flakes.

Makes 2 servings.

slightly

Variations: Add 1 tbsp chopped chives and pinch of cayenne as a garnish.

-
slightly +

Sprouted Pan-Crêpes with Easy Berry Compote

I love serving these for friends with fresh berry compote and agave nectar as a breakfast treat. *Note:* Soak flour in buttermilk overnight (see why on p. 66). If you don't have time to soak these they will still turn out (see photo p. 65).

Ancient cultures knew that sprouted flour is easily digestible, maintains minerals and nutrients, and has a great flavor and texture. It is becoming more and more readily available in health-food stores today.

Crêpes:
1 cup sprouted spelt flour
1 cup (250 mL) buttermilk
1 egg

¼ tsp good salt (p. 29)
½ tsp baking soda
1 tbsp good oil (p. 26)
1 tsp good oil (p. 26) or spray

In a medium bowl, combine flour and buttermilk and mix lightly. Set in a warm place overnight (such as the oven, turned off but with the light on). In a small bowl or mug, lightly beat egg and add to flour mixture. Stir in salt, baking soda, ½ cup (125 mL) water, and 1 tbsp oil until well mixed. In a frying pan on medium-high, heat oil. Add ¼ cup (60 mL) of mixture per each pan-crêpe. Shake pan from side to side to create a thin crêpe. Lower heat as pan heats up. When bottom side is light brown (about 1 minute), flip and cook other side for 1 minute. Remove from heat. Spread with ¼ tsp ghee and stack on a plate. Repeat until batter is used up.

Makes about 8 crêpes.

- - -
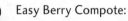
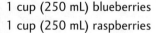

Easy Berry Compote:
1 cup (250 mL) blueberries
1 cup (250 mL) raspberries

In a small saucepan on medium-high, heat berries and 2 tbsp water for 2 minutes. Reduce heat to low and cook for 3 minutes. If the mixture looks dry, add extra water 1 tbsp at a time.

Makes about 2 cups (500 mL).

- ⚫
slightly + 🔥
- ❀ # The Most Delicious Spelt Pancakes

Soaking the batter overnight gives these delicious pancakes a slight sourdough flavor, helps the pancakes rise more easily, and makes them easily digestible to fuel us for the day. (*Note:* If you don't soak the batter they will still turn out.) Serve with maple syrup - 🔥 agave nectar or honey - ❀ or any of the sweeteners - ⚫ I also like to serve these with berries and 1 tbsp of kefir or yogurt.

I made a batch of these with Stenya who showed me the secret to perfectly round pancakes: continuously pour the batter from one spot in the center of your frying pan without moving your pouring hand around in circles. The batter will naturally flow into a perfect circle.

1 cup (250 mL) spelt flour
1 cup (250 mL) buttermilk or yogurt
1 egg
½ tsp good salt (p. 29)

½ tsp baking powder
1 tbsp good oil (p. 26)
1–2 tsp good oil (p. 26) or spray

In a medium bowl, lightly mix flour and buttermilk with a fork. Set in a warm place overnight. (I like the inside of the oven, turned off but with the light on. Some people use the top of a refrigerator or a spot near a heater.) In the morning, in a small bowl or mug, lightly beat egg and stir into flour mixture. Add salt, baking powder, and oil, and stir until well mixed. Spray or lightly oil a frying pan with oil and add ¼ cup (60 mL) of pancake mixture. Cook for 1–2 minutes, until bottom of pancake starts to turn brown. Flip to other side and cook for another 1–2 minutes. Repeat for remaining pancake batter.

Makes 2–4 servings.

Soaking flour in buttermilk or yogurt adds lactobacilli, which break down complex starches and phytic acid and activates digestive enzymes. Soaking also softens the whole grain flour without destroying valuable nutrients. Many people who have grain allergies can often eat soaked grains.

Pauline's Travel Scones

My friend Pauline offered me this delicious and simple recipe for scones. Everyone who tries them loves them. They are easy to take with you when traveling and food isn't readily available or you don't want to resort to fast food. These scones can easily be popped into the toaster to reheat, but they also taste great cold, served with jam. Thank you, Pauline! xo

1 cup (250 mL) rolled oats
  (not instant)
½ cup (125 mL) yogurt
1 cup (250 mL) spelt flour
1 tbsp panela or granulated gur
¾ tsp baking powder

¼ tsp baking soda
½ tsp ground anise
2 tbsp chilled butter
  • *To further reduce Vata: use an
  additional 1–2 tbsp butter*
1 egg (at room temperature)

Preheat oven to 375°F (180°C). Lightly grease a baking sheet. In a large bowl, combine oats and yogurt. Mix well and set aside for 15 minutes. In a medium bowl, combine spelt flour, panela, baking powder, baking soda, and anise. Add butter and, using a pastry cutter (or two knives), cut and blend into pea-sized pieces. In a small bowl, beat egg lightly with a fork, then add to oatmeal mixture and blend well. Add spelt flour mixture to wet oatmeal mixture and mix with a wooden spoon, then with your hands. Lightly flour a clean surface and knead dough 3 or 4 times. As good as this feels, don't overdo it; overhandling will make the scones tough. If this mixture is too dry (the consistency should be quite firm), add 1 tbsp of yogurt. Form dough into a ball, then pat into a flat circle about ¾ in (2 cm) thick and 6½ in (16.5 cm) in diameter. Slice into 8 evenly shaped triangles. Place on lightly greased baking sheet and bake for 15 minutes. Check after 12 minutes by inserting a toothpick into the center of a scone; if this comes out clean, they are ready. They should just start to turn golden; do not brown them.

Makes 8 scones.

slightly +

-

- # Karen's Potato Pancakes

Karen came over one morning to help me test recipes and spontaneously made potato pancakes as an accompaniment with the applesauce we had just made with apples from Jeto's tree. These pancakes are very simple, crispy, and delicious. Serve them with Applesauce (p. 303).

1 packed cup (250 mL) peeled and coarsely grated potatoes
1 egg
3 tbsp milk

4 tbsp spelt flour
⅛ tsp good salt (p. 29)
1–1½ tsp ghee (or butter)

In a medium bowl, add grated potatoes. Break egg over potatoes and mix well. Add milk, flour, and salt and stir to mix well. In a frying pan (cast iron works well) on medium, heat ghee. When hot, add ½ cup (125 mL) of pancake mixture and spread evenly into a circle. When bottom of pancake is browned and crisp, about 3–4 minutes, cook other side for 3–4 minutes. Make sure center is well cooked. Do not use high heat, as potatoes need time to cook through. Repeat until batter is used up. (Alternately, you can cook all the batter at once and cut the big pancake into pizza-like wedges to serve.)

Makes 2 servings.

+ - -   Variation: Add 1 tbsp chives to the potato mixture.
slightly

slightly +

Amrita's Potato Pancakes

I've always loved the flavor of potato pancakes. Once Karen showed me how easy they are to make, I came up with my own spicier version. I love eating this with natural yogurt served on the side.

To test the heat of a serrano or jalapeño chili, smell it; the stronger the scent, the hotter the chili. Or, cut a tiny bit off the end and bite it. Have a spoonful of yogurt standing by to cool you off. This will let you know how much to add. Some green chilies are much hotter than others and ¼ of the chili will do. Wash your hands well before touching your face or eyes.

1 packed cup (250 mL) peeled and
   coarsely grated potatoes
1 egg
3 tbsp milk
4 tbsp spelt flour

⅛ tsp good salt (p. 29)
¼ cup (60 mL) chopped cilantro
½ green chili minced, to taste
1 tsp ghee (or butter)
½ tsp black mustard seeds

In a medium bowl, add grated potatoes. Break egg over potatoes and mix well. Add milk, flour, salt, cilantro, and green chili and mix well again. In a large frying pan (cast iron works well) on medium, heat ghee. When hot, add mustard seeds and make sure they don't pop out of the pan. Then immediately add all of the pancake mixture into the center of the pan. Spread evenly into a large circle. Watch carefully as the pancake sizzles and crisps up. (Do not use high heat, as potatoes need time to cook through.) When bottom side is just browned, about 3–4 minutes, cook other side for 3–4 minutes. Cut potato pancake into pizza-like wedges to serve.

Makes 2 servings.

Sabzi (p. 74)

Appetizers & Snacks

Appetizers served before the main course are a good way to gently kindle our digestive fire (agni), preparing our bodies to digest the main meal. In this section, I have put together a variety of nourishing dishes, including some appetizer platters that have the six essential tastes Ayurveda recommends to calm all our doshas at each meal.

Ayurveda encourages eating balanced meals and generally does not encourage snacking.

Healthy snacks, however, can help avoid blood-sugar highs and lows, which can tamper with our metabolisms and make us feel tired and cranky. The delectable snack recipes here offer nourishing alternatives to reaching for junk food in an energy slump. I have also included trail mixes, like Go Anywhere Trail Mix (p. 88), and savory snacks, such as Inspired Pakoras (p. 90) or Kale Chips (p. 86), that are easily portable.

+

-

- # Six Tastes Bean Dip & Veg Platter

* (raw)

* (vegan) This platter is always fun to eat, colorful, and nourishing. I love making it ahead so it frees me up later to spend time with my friends or on a creative project. I often get comments about how easy it is to digest as it seems my guests can tell that I cook the beans from scratch (p. 76).

*To make vegan, omit yogurt. *To make raw, omit rice crackers.

3 cups (750 mL) bean dip (p. 76)
2 cups (500 mL) broccoli florets
2 cups (500 mL) cauliflower florets
2 cups (500 mL) celery sticks
2 cups (500 mL) zucchini sticks

2 cups (500 mL) cherry tomatoes
1 cup (250 mL) plain yogurt
½ cup (125 mL) black olives
2 packages brown rice crackers

Put bean dip in a bowl and place in the center of a large platter. Arrange vegetables, yogurt, olives, and crackers artfully around it.

Makes 6 servings.

Six Tastes Cheese & Crudité Platters

This flavorful array is a great way to combine the six tastes of Ayurveda and entertain your guests. Enjoy perusing the cheese section of your favorite grocery store to see what is tantalizing, or make an outing of going to a specialty cheese shop and tasting the suggestions of the trained staff.

3 cheeses (1 soft, 2 hard, your choice)
1 apple, cored and sliced
1 pear, cored and sliced
4 tbsp lemon juice
1 bunch grapes
½ cup (125 mL) olives
1 bunch (at least 6) radishes, topped
  and tailed

2 cups celery sticks
2 baguettes
1 package brown rice crackers
1 package rye crackers
½ cup (125 mL) extra virgin olive oil
¼ cup (60 mL) balsamic vinegar

Arrange cheeses on a cheese board or plate. Place apple and pear slices in a bowl and toss with lemon juice. Surround cheese artfully with apple and pear slices and grapes. Place olives and radishes on a plate with celery sticks. Place baguettes on a breadboard and crackers in a basket. Pour olive oil into a shallow bowl then balsamic vinegar into center to use for dipping bread.

Makes 6–8 servings.

-
-
slightly + # Sabzi

Sabzi means "green" in Persian. Ameeta, my yogini artist cousin from Los Angeles, made this fresh appetizer for family and friends one day when she was on a visit to Vancouver. It was so memorable that I had to call her up to ask her for the list of ingredients. In Iran, they eat sabzi in the summer as an appetizer with friends so the group can enjoy each other's company and get their digestive juices going before the main meal. I really enjoyed the feeling of community that developed that day as we broke bread together. Sabzi also can be served as an entrée.

I like shopping for these ingredients in Persian markets, as I find they have the freshest herbs and breads, as well as high-quality cheeses.

6 Persian cucumbers (Japanese cukes make a good substitute)

1 bunch (at least 6) radishes

1 block (6 x 6 in/15 x 15 cm) feta cheese (French or Bulgarian preferably)

1 large bunch fresh basil leaves

1 large bunch fresh tarragon

1 large bunch fresh mint

6 large squares of Persian flat or sangak bread

Note: Sangak bread is as flat as a roti and can easily be rolled up around a filling. Each large square comes with perforated marks so that it can easily be torn into smaller rectangles. These are used to make the small roll-ups.

Arrange ingredients artfully on a platter or a variety of artistic plates and cups. Guests slice their own cucumbers, radishes, and feta to put in their rectangles of bread with sprigs of basil, tarragon, and mint to make roll-ups.

Makes 6 servings.

Nancy's Marinated Madagascar Peppercorn & Goat Cheese Spread

Nancy, who is always very cheerful and helpful, works at the Bowen Island General Store. She shared with me the recipe for this simple and tasty appetizer. Serve with a fresh baguette or brown rice crackers. It is great for winding down with friends in the evenings or on weekends.

1 lb (500 g) soft goat cheese (about 3 small logs)
2 tbsp chopped parsley
2 tbsp chopped fresh thyme
1 tsp chili flakes
1 tsp Madagascar peppercorns

½ cup (125 mL) chopped sundried tomatoes packed in oil
½ cup (125 mL) chopped black olives
2 garlic cloves, minced
¾ cup (185 mL) extra virgin olive oil

Slice goat cheese into ¼-in (6-mm) pieces with a hot knife, then in half again. Arrange on a serving dish. Sprinkle with herbs, spices, tomatoes, olives, and garlic. Drizzle evenly with olive oil. Cover and let sit at room temperature for 4 hours.

Makes 6–8 servings.

+

- # Warm Yellow Bell Pepper &
- # Bean Dip

I love all the flavors in this bean dip! I eat it with vegetables, baked taco chips, or brown rice crackers.

Kidney beans are rich in fiber and zinc, which boosts collagen and helps maintain the elasticity of our skin.

2 tbsp good oil (p. 26)
• *To reduce Kapha: use less*
2 cups (500 mL) chopped onions
1 cup (250 mL) diced yellow bell peppers
½ tsp ground cumin
2 cloves garlic
• *To reduce Pitta: use less or omit*

½–1 serrano or jalapeño chili
• *To reduce Pitta: omit*
2 cups (500 mL) cooked kidney or pinto beans (p. 182)
good salt (p. 29), to taste
pepper, to taste
fresh coriander sprigs, for garnish

In a large frying pan on medium-high, heat oil. Stir in onions, yellow bell peppers, and cumin. Reduce heat to medium and sauté for about 6 minutes. In a food processor, add garlic and chili (if using) and mince. Add to onions and peppers mixture and continue sautéing for 3–4 minutes until onions turn golden and peppers soften. Without cleaning food processor, add beans and purée. Then add beans to mixture in frying pan. Add salt and pepper to taste and mix well. Continue to cook until beans are warmed through. Garnish with coriander sprigs just before serving.

Makes about 4 cups (1 L).

+

-

- # Egyptian Fava Bean Hummus

Nagar, an Egyptian friend who is a fabulous cook, told me about this recipe that is popular in her native land. Easy to make and delicious served with pita bread, rice crackers, or vegetables, it's also wonderful used as a spread for sandwiches or wraps.

Fava beans (also known as broad beans) have been around for thousands of years. They are filled with nutrients including iron, magnesium, and potassium, and vitamins A and K. Containing essential amino acids that are great neuro-transmitters, making them a healthy food for the brain, fava beans are also low in fat.

2 peeled garlic cloves
2 cups (500 mL) cooked fava beans
2 tbsp tahini
2 tbsp extra virgin olive oil
2 tbsp lime or lemon juice

½ tsp Himalayan salt
¼ tsp ground cumin
¼ tsp cayenne
• *To reduce Pitta: omit*

In a food processor, mince garlic. Add all other ingredients and purée until smooth.

Makes about 2 cups (500 mL).

-
-
- # Mango Salsa

This is simple to make and always popular. Serve with taco chips or brown rice crackers.

1 cup (250 mL) diced ripe mangoes
1 red bell pepper, diced
¾ packed cup (185 mL) chopped
  cilantro leaves
½ tsp good salt (p. 29)
1 tbsp lemon juice

In a medium bowl, mix all ingredients. Cover and set aside to marinate for at least 10 minutes before serving.

Makes about 2 cups (500 mL).

-
+
- # Spicy Tomato Salsa

Freshly made salsa is tasty, packs a punch, and is very easy to make. When handling chilies, remember not to rub your eyes before thoroughly washing your hands.

Tomatoes are high in antioxidants and rich in vitamins A and C and potassium.

1 cup (250 mL) finely chopped celery
1 cup (250 mL) chopped cilantro
2 serrano, or jalapeño chilies, minced
 • *To reduce Pitta: use less or omit*
½ cup (125 mL) chopped onions

2 cups (500 mL) diced tomatoes
3 tbsp lime juice
1 tbsp extra virgin olive oil
1 tsp good salt (p. 29)
fresh cilantro sprig, for garnish

In a medium-sized decorative bowl, combine all ingredients and garnish with cilantro just before serving.

Makes about 4 cups (1 L).

-

-

+ # Zucchini Hummus

I had been looking forward to making this since Philippa, one of my yoga clients, told me this hummus became a staple for her when she switched to a raw diet. This is my version. I pick the parsley from my veggie garden. It is a delicious and light way to make hummus. Serve with raw veggies or baked chips.

Hemp seeds are filled with the perfect ratio of essential fatty acids, making them great brain food. They're wonderful for lubricating and calming the nervous system, among other benefits.

2 garlic cloves
  • *To reduce Pitta: use 1 or omit*
2½ cups (625 mL) chopped zucchini (about 2 medium zucchinis)
2 tbsp parsley
½ cup (125 mL) raw tahini
⅓ cup (80 mL) hemp seeds

¼ cup (60 mL) extra virgin olive oil
¼ cup (60 mL) lemon juice (about 1½ lemons)
½ tsp Himalayan salt
⅛ tsp cayenne, or to taste
  • *To reduce Pitta: omit*

In a food processor, pulse garlic until finely minced. Add all remaining ingredients and pulse until smooth. Adjust for seasoning.

Makes about 3 cups (750 mL).

-
slightly + # Baby Bocconcini, Basil & Tomato
slightly + Skewers

These colorful mini kebabs allow the cook time to enjoy the party and are always a winner. They are also nice to take for lunches and picnics. I love making these in the summertime when my balcony-grown grape tomatoes and basil are ready. They look gorgeous served side-by-side on a rectangular plate.

Bocconcini means "small mouthfuls" in Italian. This is an unripened mild cheese that originated in Naples and was made from the milk of the water buffalo; now it is mostly made from cow's milk. Like any cheese, it's a good source of calcium and protein. It has a nice spongy texture and absorbs other flavors well.

20 6-in (15-cm) wooden skewers
20 baby bocconcini cheese balls
20 basil leaves
20 grape tomatoes
20 pitted black olives

Thread each skewer consecutively with 1 baby bocconcini, 1 basil leaf, 1 grape tomato, and ending at tip with one olive. To easily ensure olive is close to the tip of the skewer, place bocconcini about half-way up.

Makes 4–6 servings.

-
-
slightly + # Spicy Paneer & Zucchini Kebabs

These are tasty and fun to eat at a party with friends or to take to work for a snack.

Paneer is a home-made cheese that has a delicate, mild flavor that absorbs other flavors well. It is produced by a souring process that makes it easy to digest (see recipe, p. 28). If you don't have time to prepare your own paneer, you can find it in Indian grocery stores, sold in cubes or large blocks.

1 pkg toothpicks
1 tbsp good oil (p. 26)
1 tbsp ghee (or butter)
1 tsp whole cumin seeds
1 cup (250 mL) 1-in (2.5-cm) cubes paneer (p. 28)
¼ tsp ground turmeric
¼ tsp good salt (p. 29), to taste

¼ tsp cayenne, to taste
• *To reduce Pitta: omit or use less*
⅓ cup (80 mL) chopped fresh cilantro
¼ cup (60 mL) lemon juice
1 cup (250 mL) thinly sliced small zucchinis
⅓ cup (80 mL) fresh cilantro, for garnish
6–8 lemon wedges, for garnish

In a large frying pan on medium high, heat oil and ghee. Drop 1 cumin seed into the oil to test; if it sizzles and turns white, add rest of cumin seeds and let sizzle for 30 seconds. Stir in paneer cubes, turmeric, salt, and cayenne. Sauté for 3–4 minutes, until paneer starts to brown. Remove from heat and place in a medium bowl. Add chopped cilantro and lemon juice and toss to mix and marinate. Add zucchini slices to same pan with remaining spices and oil and sauté on medium-high heat for 2 minutes on each side—watching carefully so as not to burn. Toss to mix with paneer in bowl. Let sit for 5 minutes so flavors are absorbed by the paneer. Thread 1 paneer cube then 1 zucchini slice on end of each toothpick and place standing on a decorative plate. Garnish with cilantro and lemon wedges.

Makes 4–6 servings.

+

-

slightly +

Himalayan Salt & Lime-Flavored Edamame

When I was seventeen, I traveled to Japan on an exchange program, where I tasted salty edamame for the first time as a bar snack. They were fun to eat and as addictive and tasty as any greasy trans-fat loaded potato chip, without the unwanted side effects—in fact, they are very nutritious. Now these are friends with benefits! To eat, scrape the beans out of the pods gently with your teeth savoring the salty lime flavor and discard the pods into empty bowls.

Edamame (soybeans) are high in fiber and essential minerals. They are also a good source of protein, calcium, and iron, and are low on the glycemic index.

3 cups (750 mL) water
3 cups (750 mL) edamame in pods
1 tsp good salt (p. 29), for cooking
1 tsp Himalayan salt (or other high-quality salt)
4 tbsp lime juice
¼ tsp ground cumin (optional)

In a large pot, bring water to a boil. Add edamame and salt and bring to a boil again. Cook for about 4 minutes. Take care not overcook. Drain edamame in a colander and rinse with cold water (to stop the cooking process and maintain bright-green color). In a decorative serving bowl, toss edamame with Himalayan salt, lime juice, and cumin.

Makes 4–6 servings.

+ - +
slightly

Variation: Sprinkle with coarsely ground pepper instead of cumin.

slightly + # Kale Chips

vegan

This snack is often considered raw as it is cooked at such a low temperature. My friend Patrick shared these chips with me. They were such a delicious crispy snack that I pleaded with him to give me the recipe! They are baked at very low heat in order to preserve the enzymes. You can use a dehydrator (available at some health-food stores) or use a very low heat in your oven. *Note:* Soak cashews overnight (p. 31).

Kale is a member of the cabbage family. It is a good source of vitamins A, C, and K, and is full of fiber and antioxidants. A blood cleanser due to its high chlorophyll content, it is also alkalizing, which helps maintain our bodies optimal pH balance. It also contains important trace minerals.

1 cup (250 mL) raw soaked cashews (p. 31)
1 tsp Himalayan salt, to taste
1 tsp apple cider vinegar
2 tbsp good oil (p. 26)

⅓ cup (80 mL) water
5 cups (1.25 L) kale leaves, spines removed and torn into bite-sized pieces

Preheat oven to 170°F (77°C) or 150°F (66°C) if your oven allows it. (If so, cook for slightly longer.)

In a food processor, mix cashews and salt with apple cider vinegar (Patrick does this in a coffee grinder in batches). Scrape into a large bowl, then add oil and water and mix. It should have a cake batter-like consistency. Toss kale to coat leaves with mixture. Place kale on lightly oiled cookie sheets and bake in oven for 4–6 hours or in dehydrator overnight. Store in an airtight container.

Makes 4 servings.

-
-  Goji Berry & Roasted Almond
+  Trail Mix

 Keep these with you when you need a powerful energy boost. If you don't think you can eat it all within one day, toast or dehydrate the almonds before adding them to the mix. This preserves them and also make them crispier. *Note:* Soak almonds overnight (p. 31).

1 cup (250 mL) dried goji berries
1 cup (250 mL) soaked and blanched
  almonds (p. 31)

In a bowl, mix berries with nuts.

Makes 2 cups (500 mL), about 4 servings.

The wonderful flavor and high nutritional content of goji berries keep us satiated. They are filled with antioxidants, vitamins, minerals, and fiber, and are anti-carcinogenic. Rich in vitamin C, gogi berries also contain essential amino acids, beta-carotene, iron, and B vitamins.

Go Anywhere Trail Mix

This mix offers tasty instant sustenance wherever you are.
Note: Soak all ingredients overnight (p. 31).

¼ cup (60 mL) raisins
½ cup (125 mL) water
¼ cup (60 mL) raw pumpkin seeds
¼ cup (60 mL) raw sunflower seeds
¼ cup (60 mL) raw cashews
1 tsp good salt (p. 29)
2 cups (500 mL) water

In addition to their fabulous color and flavor, cranberries contain plenty of antioxidants and can prevent or alleviate urinary tract infections.

In a small bowl, soak raisins in ½ cup (125 mL) water. In a medium bowl, soak remaining ingredients, including salt, in water. Set both aside for 6–8 hours. Drain, combine, and take as your energizing snack for the day.

Makes 1 cup (250 mL), about 2–4 servings.

   Variation: Use dried cranberries instead of raisins.

Spicy Pumpkin Seeds

Ancient tribes including the Aztecs knew that pepitas (the word for pumpkin seeds in Spanish) soaked in salt water and then dried are easier to digest, making their nutrients more available to us. These are a delicious portable snack.
Note: Soak seeds overnight (p. 31).

1 cup (250 mL) raw hulled pumpkin
  seeds
3 cups (750 mL) water
1 tsp good salt (p. 29)

¼ tsp cayenne
  • *To reduce Pitta: omit*
¼ tsp garam masala
  • *To reduce Pitta: omit*
¼ tsp ground cumin

Preheat oven to 170°F (77°C). In a medium bowl, soak pumpkin seeds in water and 1 tsp salt overnight (at least 7 hours but not longer than 8 hours). Drain. Add spices to a medium bowl and mix well. Add pumpkin seeds and toss to coat with spices. Spread evenly on a baking tray in a single layer. Bake until dry and crisp, about 6 hours. Store in an airtight container. *Note:* This can also be done in a dehydrator or baked at 150°F (66°C) if your oven allows.

Makes 1 cup (250 mL).

slightly +

slightly +

- # Inspired Pakoras

Pakoras are tasty vegetable bites coated in a gram (chickpea) flour batter. Traditionally they are deep-fried, but this is a baked version. They can be served as a tea-time snack or appetizer. I made this recipe up one day when I was craving a healthy, spicy Indian snack. These taste great served alone or with Green Chutney (p. 276) and/or Tamarind Chutney (p. 279).

Filling:
2 tsp good oil (p. 26)
1 tsp black mustard seeds
½ cup (125 mL) chopped onions
1½ tsp minced ginger
1½ tsp minced garlic

½ cup (125 mL) diced Roma or other tomatoes
1½ cups mixed vegetables (cauliflower, carrots, broccoli, peas)
¼ cup (60 mL) lemon juice
¼ cup (60 mL) chopped fresh cilantro

Batter:
2 cups (500 mL) gram (chickpea) flour
1½ cups (375 mL) yogurt
1 tsp cayenne

¾ tsp ground cumin
1 tsp good salt (p. 29)
¾ tsp baking powder

Preheat oven to 350°F (180°C). In a frying pan on medium, heat oil. Add mustard seeds, cover, and when popped (about 20 seconds), uncover and add onions and ginger. Sauté for 4 minutes, then add garlic, tomatoes, and mixed vegetables Sauté for 5 minutes, then add lemon juice and cilantro. If the vegetables start sticking, add up to an additional ¼ cup (60 mL) of water.

In a bowl, combine gram flour, yogurt, cayenne, cumin, salt, and baking powder and stir to mix well. Add lightly cooked vegetables from frying pan and stir to ensure vegetables are well coated. Pour into a lightly oiled 9 x 5-in (2 L) loaf pan and bake for 60–70 minutes. When a toothpick inserted into the center of the loaf comes out clean, it is done. Slice and serve.

Makes 6–8 servings.

slightly +

-

- # Green Chutney Mushroom Caps

A spicy spin on traditional stuffed mushroom caps.

20 large button mushrooms
1 tsp good oil (p. 26)
2 tsp ghee (or butter)
1 cup (250 mL) crumbled feta cheese
¼ cup (60 mL) Green Chutney (p. 276)

Preheat oven to 350°F (180°C). Remove stems from mushrooms. Finely dice stems and set aside. In a frying pan on medium, heat oil and ghee. Add mushroom stems and sauté for 4 minutes. In a bowl, combine cheese, chutney, and sauteed mushrooms. Spoon mixture into mushroom caps and place them on a lightly greased baking sheet. Bake for 10–12 minutes.

Makes 4 servings.

Barley Salad with Apples and Walnuts (p. 94)

Salads & Salad Dressings

In keeping with Ayurvedic principles, to keep our bodies in balance, it is important to eat some raw food at every meal, as the enzymes and fiber aid digestion. However, eating completely raw meals is not generally recommended by Ayurveda, as they can be difficult to digest, especially for Vata.

The best time to eat more raw foods for all doshas is during the summer, a hot Pitta season (see Eating for the Seasons, p. 361). We have done this naturally throughout the ages in order to cool down. (To read more on raw food and the doshas, see p. 358.)

In addition to raw salads, this chapter includes salads with cooked ancient grains like quinoa, barley, and wild rice to please the palate and appeal to different constitutions. Some of the salads can be used as refreshing side dishes and others as delicious balanced meals that include the six tastes of Ayurveda.

At the end of this chapter are a number of salad dressings filled with the good oils that are essential for our bodies; they keep us glowing and boost our brain power. Vatas can use the oily dressings liberally while Pittas and Kaphas are balanced by them in smaller amounts. I also recommend using these dressings on steamed vegetables as well as on your own creations.

slightly +

-  Barley Salad with Apples
- & Walnuts

This is a gorgeous, nourishing salad that I love having for lunch as it keeps me going throughout the day. *Note:* Soak barley and walnuts overnight (see p. 30 and p. 31). If you forget to soak the barley, cook it for 35–40 minutes.

Barley is an ancient grain that was prized by the Egyptians for providing strength and clarity. It is also known to tone the liver. Soaking barley makes it easy to digest and shortens the cooking time.

½ cup (125 mL) barley
1½ cups (375 mL) water for soaking
 + 1¼ cups (310 mL) water for cooking
½ tsp Celtic sea salt
6 cups (1.5 L) loosely packed
 arugula leaves
¾ cup (185 mL) sliced celery
1 red apple, cored and cut into
 small cubes (leave skin on)

¼ cup (60 mL) chopped parsley
½ tsp Celtic salt, to taste
⅛ tsp cayenne
 • To reduce Pitta: omit
¼ cup (60 mL) soaked walnuts
⅓ cup (80 mL) Olive Oil, Lemon Juice,
 and Honey Dressing (p. 146)

In a bowl, soak barley in 1½ cups (375 mL) water overnight or for 7 hours. Drain and rinse barley and add to a medium saucepan with 1¼ cups (310 mL) water, and salt. Bring to a boil, then reduce heat to low, cover, and simmer until barley is tender, about 15 minutes. Drain and cool. In a salad bowl, combine barley with remaining ingredients. Toss with dressing and serve.

Makes 4 servings.

slightly +

- # Roots & Sprouts Salad

I came up with this tasty simple salad after one of our long evening swims in King Edward Bay off the south coast of Bowen Island. My friend Jlonka gave me fresh beets and carrots from her garden, and I combined them with mixed lettuce and baby spinach from mine. The chia seeds in the dressing and prana (life)-filled ingredients replenished us. *Note:* Soak almonds overnight (p. 31).

1 cup (250 mL) grated carrot
1 cup (250 mL) grated beet
2 loosely packed cups (500 mL)
  sunflower sprouts
3 cups (750 mL) mixed greens
½ cup (125 mL) soaked and slivered
  almonds
½ cup (125 mL) Chia Seed & Lemon
  Dressing (p. 132)

In a bowl, combine salad ingredients and toss with dressing just before serving.

Makes 4–6 servings.

 - +
slightly

Variation: Omit the slivered almonds and substitute ¼ cup (60 mL) unsulfured currants. Toss with Creamy Cashew Dressing (p. 133).

-
-

slightly + # Black Rice Salad

Here is another great recipe that Ameeta, my yogini cousin from Los Angeles, shared with me. I like preparing this salad ahead of time and eating it after I come back from teaching a yoga class; this gives it time to fully absorb the flavors. *Note:* Soak rice 4–7 hours before preparing recipe (p. 30).

Black rice has high nutritional value and was prized in the imperial courts of China as well as among other ancient cultures. It is high in iron and fiber because the bran is left on the rice, and has a rich, nutty flavor.

2 cups (500 mL) black wild rice
4 cups (1 L) water for soaking + 4 cups (1 L) water for cooking
½ tsp Himalayan salt
1 tbsp extra virgin olive oil
½ bunch parsley, chopped (about 2 cups [500 mL])

2 cups (500 mL) chopped mint
½ cup (125 mL) very finely chopped green onions
⅓ cup (80 mL) of Ameeta's Hot Dijon Dressing (p. 143)
• To reduce Pitta: omit mustard

In a bowl, soak rice in 4 cups (1 L) water for 4–7 hours. Drain and place in a medium pot with 4 cups (1 L) water and ½ tsp salt. Bring to a boil. Reduce heat to low, cover with a tightly fitting lid, and simmer for 30 minutes. Drain rice. In a salad bowl, combine rice with remaining ingredients. Toss with dressing, then let marinate for at least 10 minutes before serving.

Makes 6 servings.

+

-

-  # Egyptian Fava Bean Wrap Salad

 My friend Nagar is from Egypt, where fava beans have been popular literally for "ages." She shared this recipe with me. It has a wonderful variety of textures and flavors.

2 cups (500 mL) cooked fava beans
1 cup (250 mL) diced cucumber
1 cup (250 mL) diced tomato
½ cup (125 mL) chopped fresh mint
½ cup (125 mL) chopped parsley
¾ cup finely chopped red onions
¼ cup (60 mL) tahini (p. 274)
1 tbsp water

¼ cup (60 mL) fresh lemon juice
2 tsp minced garlic cloves
⅛ tsp cayenne
  • *To reduce Pitta: use paprika instead*
¾ tsp good salt (p. 29), to taste
½ tsp ground black pepper, to taste
1 head red lettuce leaves, washed and dried

In a large decorative bowl, toss all ingredients except lettuce leaves. Place lettuce leaves in another large bowl or platter. These can be used to roll up bean salad like a wrap or burrito.

Makes 4–6 servings.

-
-
slightly +

Snug's "Fortifying" Salad

The Snug Café on Bowen Island is famous for this energizing salad! *Note:* Soak nuts and seeds overnight (p. 30) and cook rice and lentils before preparing. (This recipe will still work without pre-soaking the seeds, if you so choose.)

2 cups (500 mL) cooked wild rice
1 cup (250 mL) chopped carrots
1 cup (250 mL) chopped celery
1 cup (250 mL) cooked brown masoor
   lentils
½ cup (125 mL) dried cranberries
1 cup (250 mL) diced yellow bell
   peppers

1 cup (250 mL) chopped parsley or
   cilantro
½ cup (125 mL) soaked almonds
½ cup (125 mL) soaked pumpkin seeds
⅓–½ cup (80–125 mL) Simple
   Cleansing Lime Dressing (p. 147)

In a large salad bowl, combine all salad ingredients and toss with dressing.

Makes 6–8 servings.

+

-

- # Broccoli & Cauliflower Floret Salad

I love picking greens fresh from the mixed-lettuce container in my backyard garden. Serve with rye crackers (or your favorite crackers) and Egyptian Fava Bean Hummus (p. 78) for an easy, light meal. Chew this salad well in order to digest the full omega-3 goodness in the whole flax seeds, or grind the seeds just before adding.

2 cups (500 mL) mixed greens (e.g., arugula, rocket, red, and butter lettuce)
½ cup (125 mL) broccoli florets
½ cup (125 mL) cauliflower florets
½ cup (125 mL) sliced new carrots
¼ cup (60 mL) raisins
1 tsp whole flax seeds
⅓ cup (80 mL) Simple Cleansing Lime Dressing (p. 147)

In a salad bowl, combine all salad ingredients and toss with dressing.

Makes 2–4 servings.

Tamarind & Chickpea Salad

I love swimming in the ocean from May to October with a group of Bowen Island swimmers. When I took this to the beach to share with my friends Jlonka and Marcelle for a taste test, they gave it rave reviews. They savored the sweet and sour tastes of the tamarind chutney combined with the chickpeas and fresh vegetables. *Note:* Cook the black chickpeas before preparing this recipe. Conventional chickpeas will also work as a substitute if you cannot find the black ones.

Kala channa (black chickpeas) are available at Indian grocery stores. Some people find them easier to digest than the larger conventional chickpeas.

1 cup (250 mL) cooked kala channa (black chickpeas) (p. 182)
½ cup (125 mL) sliced and quartered cucumbers
1 cup (250 mL) chopped red bell peppers
6 pear-shaped yellow tomatoes (or other variety), quartered

1 tbsp chopped chives
¼ cup (60 mL) chopped parsley
½ cup (125 mL) Tamarind Chutney (p. 279)
good salt (p. 29), to taste
¼ tsp garam masala
¼ tsp ground cumin

In a large bowl, combine all ingredients. Let marinate for at least 15 minutes before serving.

Makes 2–4 servings.

slightly +

-

- # Hawaiian Chickpea Salad

 At Christmas recently, I discovered the "Big Island" of Hawaii for the first time. I felt as though I hit an oasis when I came across a great health-food store just outside of Kona. It became one of my favorite haunts. This recipe was inspired by one of the salads I enjoyed there. It fueled me to wander around the Volcanoes National Park and the black sand beaches. *Note:* Cook the chickpeas before preparing this recipe.

6 cups (1.5 L) mixed greens
2 cups (500 mL) pea sprouts
1 cup (250 mL) diced red bell peppers
  • *To reduce Vata: use grated carrots or beets*
¼ cup (60 mL) sliced green onions
1 cup (250 mL) diced celery

1 cup (250 mL) diced cucumbers
1 cup (250 mL) cooked chickpeas
  • *To reduce Vata: use kala channa (black chickpeas), available at Indian grocery stores*
½ cup (125 mL) Big Island Dressing (p. 138)

In a bowl, combine all salad ingredients. Toss with dressing and serve.
Makes 6–8 servings.

+

-

- # Curried Chickpea & Quinoa Salad

This is wonderful served warm or cold. The spices combined with the sweetness of the onions add great flavor to this dish, and the turmeric gives it a warm yellow color. *Note:* Cook the quinoa before preparing this recipe.

2 tbsp extra virgin olive oil
¾ cup sliced onions
1 tsp ground cumin
½ tsp ground turmeric
¼ tsp cayenne
  • To reduce Pitta: use ½ tsp paprika instead
1 tsp minced garlic

1¾ cups (415 mL) cooked chickpeas
  • To reduce Vata: use black chickpeas
2 cups (500 mL) sliced zucchini
2 tbsp lemon juice
good salt (p. 29), to taste
ground black pepper, to taste
¼ tsp garam masala (optional)
2 cups (500 mL) cooked red quinoa

In a large frying pan on medium, heat oil. Add onions and sauté for 6 minutes. Add cumin, turmeric, cayenne, and garlic and sauté for 2 more minutes. Add chickpeas and zucchini. Sauté until zucchini is soft, about 5 minutes. Add all remaining ingredients. Mix well and remove from heat.

Makes 4–6 servings.

- - - Variation: Use red azuki beans instead of chickpeas.

Turmeric, long a staple in Ayurvedic medicine, has anti-inflammatory and anti-oxidant properties, is a natural antibiotic, and strengthens digestion. It is used to ward off sore throats and colds and can be used to cauterize wounds and stop bleeding, among other health benefits. Keep it handy in the kitchen; if you cut yourself badly immediately sprinkle some over the wound before bandaging it. Protect your clothing, as turmeric stains.

slightly + # Brown Rice Mediterranean Salad

* This is great for a take-to-work lunch or as a side dish. *Note:* Cook the rice and chickpeas before preparing this recipe.

*To make vegan, omit cheese.

2 cups (500 mL) cooked brown short grain rice

1½ cups (375 mL) cooked chickpeas
• *To reduce Vata: use black chickpeas*

1 cup (250 mL) halved grape tomatoes, with juices
• *To reduce Pitta: use diced red bell peppers*

1½ cups diced cucumber

1 cup (250 mL) crumbled feta cheese

¾ cup (185 mL) pitted black olives

⅓ cup (80 mL) sliced green onions

2 cups (500 mL) chopped parsley

¼ cup (60 mL) chopped walnuts

¼ cup (60 mL) chopped fresh mint or dill

½ cup (125 mL) fresh lemon juice

¼ cup (60 mL) extra virgin olive oil

2 tsp minced garlic
• *To reduce Pitta: use less or omit*

good salt (p. 29), to taste

freshly ground black pepper, to taste

In a large bowl, toss all ingredients together and serve.

Makes 6–8 servings as a main dish and 8–10 as a side.

+ − + Variation 1: Use cooked bulgur wheat instead of rice.
slightly

+ + −   Variation 2: Use cooked quinoa instead of rice.
slightly

slightly +

–

– # Mexican Corn & Bean Salad

 This colorful salad is fast and easy to put together and has great dosha-calming tastes. *Note:* Cook the black beans before preparing this recipe.

Avocadoes are full of B vitamins and folic acid that helps rid our body of ama (toxins) in Ayurveda. Full of the essential oils that our bodies and brains need avocadoes are cholesterol-free and really calm Vata. Pitta should eat them in moderation. To reduce Kapha, avoid or eat in very small amounts.

2 cups (500 mL) corn kernels
¾ cup (185 mL) cubed avocados
  • *To reduce Kapha: use less or omit*
¾ cup (185 mL) finely chopped red onions
  • *To reduce Pitta: omit*
1 loosely packed cup (250 mL) chopped fresh cilantro
1½ cup cooked black beans
1½ cup diced fresh tomatoes
  • *To reduce Pitta: omit*

1 jalapeño pepper, minced
  • *To reduce Pitta: omit*
¼ cup (60 mL) fresh lime juice
2 tbsp sweet paprika
1 tsp ground cumin
2 tsp minced garlic
  • *To reduce Pitta: omit*
1 tsp dried oregano or 2 tsp fresh
½ cup (125 mL) Spicy Garlic Cumin Dressing (p. 140)
  • *To reduce Pitta: omit or decrease garlic*

In a salad bowl, combine all ingredients and let marinate for at least 10 minutes. Toss just before serving.

Makes 6 servings.

+

slightly +

-

Kale & Quinoa Salad

This salad makes a great picnic lunch or side dish. *Note:* Soak pumpkin seeds overnight (p. 31) (this recipe will still work if you do not pre-soak them) and cook the quinoa before preparing.

Kale is rich in nutrients, full of vitamins A, C, and K and iron, plus it's a good source of fiber and has a grounding, earthy flavor.

3 cups (750 mL) cooked quinoa
1 carrot, diced
2 cups (500 mL) finely chopped kale
   (remove the tough spine first)
¼ cup (60 mL) unsulfured currants
¼ cup (60 mL) sliced green onions
¼ cup (60 mL) soaked pumpkin seeds
½ cup Spicy Garlic Cumin Dressing
   (p. 140)

In a salad bowl, combine all ingredients. Let sit for at least 10 minutes before serving.

Makes 4–5 servings.

slightly +

–

– # Lemon Quinoa Salad

 This salad has each of the six tastes of Ayurveda that will keep your tastebuds fulfilled and your doshas happy. The protein and good carbs in the grain will satisfy you without making you feel too full. *Note:* Cook the quinoa before preparing this recipe.

4 cups (1 L) cooked quinoa
2 cups (500 mL) diced red bell peppers
1 cup (250 mL) unsulfured black currants
¾ cup (185 mL) sliced green onions (only white or light-green)

⅓ cup (80 mL) lemon juice
1 cup (250 mL) chopped fresh cilantro
½ tsp ground coriander
½ tsp ground cumin
1 tsp paprika
½ tsp good salt (p. 29), to taste

In a salad bowl, combine all ingredients together and let marinate for at least 15 minutes so flavors can marry.

Makes 6–8 servings.

+

-

- # Edamame & Bell Pepper Salad

 I enjoy the taste of edamame beans any time, especially in this crunchy salad. This colorful dish is packed with vitamins, minerals, protein, and fiber.

3 cups (750 mL) cooked edamame
1 cup (250 mL) diced red bell pepper
1 cup (250 mL) diced yellow bell
  pepper
1 cup (250 mL) diced cabbage

¼ cup (60 mL) toasted sesame seeds
¼ cup (60 mL) chopped flat leaf parsley
½ cup (125 mL) Miso Sesame Dressing
  (p. 135)

In a salad bowl, combine all ingredients and toss with dressing.

Makes 4–6 servings.

slightly +

- # Fresh Wheat Berry & Navy Bean
- Salad

 This is a satisfying, hearty salad. Note: Soak the wheat berries overnight (p. 30) and cook the beans before preparing this recipe.

A wheat berry is a whole unprocessed kernel of wheat that's been stripped only of its inedible outer hull, leaving all the vitamins (A, B, E) and minerals (magnesium, phosphorous, selenium, zinc, and iron) intact. Wheat berries are considered sweet and cool in Ayurveda and balance all three doshas.

1 cup (250 mL) wheat berries
2 cups (500 mL) cooked white navy beans (p. 182)
1 English cucumber, diced
1 large red bell pepper, diced
4 green onions, sliced
1 large tomato, diced
  • *To reduce Pitta: omit*

2 garlic cloves, minced
  • *To reduce Pitta: use less or omit*
1 cup (250 mL) chopped fresh parsley
good salt (p. 29), to taste
ground black pepper, to taste
¼ cup (60 mL) extra virgin olive oil
¼ cup (60 mL) rice wine vinegar

In a medium bowl, soak wheat berries overnight in 4 cups (1 L) water. Drain and place in a medium pot. Add enough water to cover berries with 2 in (5 cm) water. Bring to a boil, then reduce heat to low and simmer, partially covered, for about 1 hour. Drain and cool. In a salad bowl, combine wheat berries with remaining ingredients and serve.

Makes 6–8 servings.

-
-
- # Summer Beach Salad

My friend Pauline gave me garlic scapes from her garden, and I used them to flavor this salad that I made for our beach potluck dinner. We spent the evening listening to the surf, watching the sunset, and enjoying our freshly cooked meal.

Garlic scapes are the curly green shoots that look and taste a bit like green onions with a mild garlic flavor.

4 cups (1 L) mixed greens (butter and red leaf lettuce, arugula, etc.)
½ cup (125 mL) cauliflower florets
1 cup (250 mL) chopped asparagus (2-in/5-cm pieces)
½ cup (125 mL) chopped garlic scapes
¾ cup (185 mL) diced red bell peppers
2 cups (500 mL) roughly torn pea sprouts

In a salad bowl, combine mixed greens and set aside. In a medium saucepan fitted with a steam basket, add cauliflower, asparagus, and garlic scapes. Cover saucepan, bring water to a boil, and steam for 5 minutes. Place vegetables in a colander and run under cold water to stop the cooking process. Drain vegetables well. Add steamed vegetables and remaining ingredients to mixed greens and toss with dressing of your choice.

Makes 4 servings.

slightly +

-

- # Karen's Greek Salad

 My friend Karen is a great hostess and loves to serve fabulous salads. Here is one of our favorites.

* *To make vegan, omit cheese.

1 head romaine lettuce, torn into
  bite-sized pieces
½ cup (125 mL) pitted Kalamata olives
  • *To reduce Pitta and Kapha: use less or
  omit*
4 green onions, chopped

1 cup (250 mL) chopped cucumbers
5 tomatoes, chopped
½ red bell pepper, chopped
¼ cup (60 mL) cubed feta cheese
⅓–½ cup (80–125 mL) Greek Dressing
  (p. 141)

In a salad bowl, combine all ingredients and toss with dressing.

Makes 4–6 servings.

+

-

- # Crunchy Rainbow Salad

 Enjoy this delicious salad for its synergy of goodness and flavors.

1½ cups (375 mL) arugula
1 cup (250 mL) red leaf lettuce
½ cup (125 mL) chopped carrots
½ cup (125 mL) diced red cabbage
⅓ cup (80 mL) grated beets
¼ cup (60 mL) chopped celery

¼ cup (60 mL) chopped red bell
  pepper
¼ cup (60 mL) chopped parsley
¼ cup (60 mL) chopped pea shoots
⅓ cup (80 mL) Lime, Honey & Cilantro
  Dressing (p. 140)

In a large bowl, combine all ingredients and toss with dressing.

Makes 4 servings.

A rainbow diet of colorful vegetables is not only delicious, but also contains phytonutrients that keep us healthy.

slightly +

 # EAT's Salad

* (raw)

* (vegan)

My friends Faith and Niall created one of the best "fast"-food chains in London. They always serve nourishing food with fresh wholesome ingredients at the cutting edge. If you are at Heathrow airport or near a trendy subway station in London, look for EAT to get your wheatgrass and acacia berry smoothie or a superfood lunch salad. This salad was inspired by a memory of what I ate the last time I was there. Serve it in a Bento box (Japanese lunch box) or other compartmentalized platter so you can pick and choose how much of each ingredient you wish to savor.

*To make raw and vegan, use grated raw beets and omit cheese.

2 cups (500 mL) mixed sprouted greens
1 cup (250 mL) mixed and chopped roasted yellow and red beets
1 cup (250 mL) grated carrots

½ cup (125 mL) crumbled goat cheese
¼ cup (60 mL) soaked pumpkin seeds
2 tbsp hemp seeds
⅓ cup (80 mL) Chia Seed & Lemon Dressing (p. 132)

Arrange ingredients separately in the compartments of a Bento box or on a platter. Serve with dressing on the side.

Makes 2 servings.

-
+
slightly +

Beet & Goat Cheese Salad

Kate Koffey made this tasty dish with beets she grew in her backyard. Members of the hiking club enjoyed it at the veggie potluck she hosted after we all hiked to the top of Bowen Island's Mount Gardner and back. *Note:* Cook the beets before preparing this recipe.

4 cups (1 L) cooked and cubed beets
  (1-in/2.5-cm chunks)
¾ cup (185 mL) crumbled soft goat
  cheese
2 tsbp apple cider vinegar
2 tbsp lime juice
1 tbsp Dijon mustard
½ cup (125 mL) walnut oil
¼ tsp good salt (p. 29)
¼ tsp ground black pepper

In a salad bowl, combine beets and goat cheese. In a small bowl, whisk together remaining ingredients and toss with beets and cheese.

Makes 4 servings.

–

 slightly +

 +

Mixed Greens & Crushed Pistachio Salad

This is a light, delicate green salad. The pistachios add a fresh, nutty flavor.

5 cups (1.25 L) mixed greens
½ cup (125 mL) finely chopped
  pistachios
¼ cup (60 mL) extra virgin olive oil
¼ cup (60 mL) lemon juice

In a salad bowl, combine all ingredients, toss, and serve.

Makes 4 servings.

slightly +

-

- # Refreshing Fennel Salad

When the mandarin oranges and fennel are combined with the spinach and arugula, we can more easily absorb the rich nutrients of the greens while enjoying the delicious medley of flavors.

Fennel is an immune booster, full of vitamin C and fiber.

5 cups (1.25 L) baby spinach leaves
2 cups (500 mL) arugula, torn into
  bite-sized pieces
1 fennel bulb, thinly sliced
2 cups (500 mL) peeled and
  segmented mandarin oranges
½ cup (125 mL) sliced red onions
½ cup (125 mL) Orange & Balsamic
  Dressing (p. 142)
¼ cup (60 mL) chopped mint leaves

In a large shallow bowl, arrange a bed of spinach and arugula. Layer sliced fennel, mandarin orange segments, and red onions. Pour dressing over and garnish with mint.

Makes 6 servings.

slightly +

 # Spinach & Berry Salad

Spinach is loaded with goodness that the strawberries help us to absorb. This energizing salad also has gorgeous colors and tastes.

*To make vegan, omit cheese.

6 cups (1.5 L) baby spinach leaves
2 cups (500 mL) strawberries
1 cup (250 mL) blueberries
½ cup (125 mL) crumbled soft
  goat cheese
  • *To reduce Kapha: use less or omit*
½ cup (125 mL) pecans
  • *To reduce Kapha: use less or omit*
½ cup (125 mL) Chia Seed & Lemon
  Dressing (p. 132)

In a salad bowl, combine all ingredients and toss with dressing.

Makes 4 servings.

slightly +

-

- # In a Jiffy Crunchy Salad

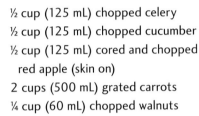

One day, the Movementglobal team was multi-tasking and needed to recharge. I came up with this salad; walnuts and olive oil to fuel the brain and calm all our nerves tossed with fresh live (prana-rich) ingredients. We were instantly replenished.

½ cup (125 mL) chopped celery
½ cup (125 mL) chopped cucumber
½ cup (125 mL) cored and chopped
  red apple (skin on)
2 cups (500 mL) grated carrots
¼ cup (60 mL) chopped walnuts

⅓ cup (80 mL) blueberries
½ cup (125 mL) chopped parsley
3 tbsp rice wine vinegar
3 tbsp extra virgin olive oil
good salt (p. 29), to taste
ground black pepper, to taste

In a large salad bowl, combine all ingredients and toss to mix well.

Makes 3–4 servings.

+

slightly +

- # Alkalizing Cabbage Salad

I started making raw cabbage salads for my lunches and noticed how good they left me feeling. Now I understand why: cabbage is alkalizing, which helps the body absorb minerals and nutrients and thereby increases energy.

2 cups (500 mL) sliced red cabbage
2 cups (500 mL) sliced green cabbage
2 cups (500 mL) julienned carrots
1 cup (250 mL) chopped flat leaf
   parsley
¼ cup (60 mL) unsulfured currants
½–¾ cup (125–185 mL) Creamy
   Cashew Dressing (p. 133)

In a salad bowl, combine all salad ingredients and toss with dressing.

Makes 6 servings.

+

 -

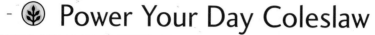 - # Power Your Day Coleslaw

One morning I wanted to take a quick-to-make lunch to work and threw this salad together in minutes. You can do the same if you always have soaked almonds and raisins on hand as I do. I noticed that I had continuous energy, even though I was short-staffed at my store. Then I realized I had been nibbling on this salad throughout the day and knew there was something extra-special about it. I shared the recipe with my friends who began taking it for lunch too. They also love the tastes and energy it gives them and keeps passing it on! *Note:* Soak nuts and raisins overnight (p. 31).

2 cups (500 mL) sliced red cabbage
2 cups (500 mL) sliced green cabbage
¼ cup (60 mL) soaked blanched
  almonds
  • *To reduce Kapha: use pumpkin seeds*
1 cup (250 mL) cored and diced red
  apple (skin on)

1 cup (250 mL) chopped parsley
¼ cup (60 mL) soaked raisins
¼ cup (60 mL) fresh lemon juice
¼ cup (60 mL) extra virgin olive oil
good salt (p. 29), to taste
ground black pepper, to taste

In a large salad bowl, combine all ingredients and toss to mix well.

Makes 4–6 servings.

 + + - Variation 1: Add 2 cups (500 mL) cooked quinoa.
slightly

 - - - Variation 2: Add 2 cups (500 mL) cooked barley.

-

+

+ # Singapore Coleslaw Stack

* (raw)

(vegan)

I discovered this salad at a restaurant while in Toronto, to attend a film festival where the award-winning films of my friend Peg's students were being shown. This salad was artfully presented, and the flavors and textures were delicious. It nourished me as I worked with yoga studios and store buyers for my company, Movementglobal.

*To make raw, omit noodles.

2 cups (500 mL) finely sliced bok choy
1 cup (250 mL) crispy salad noodles
1 cup (250 mL) grated carrots
1 cup (250 mL) bean sprouts
½ cup (125 mL) crushed peanuts
¼ cup (60 mL) sesame seeds
½ cup (125 mL) Singapore Dressing
  (p. 136)

Layer salad ingredients on 4 plates, then drizzle each with dressing and serve.

Makes 4 servings.

-
-
slightly + # Tropical Chutney Salad

* Sylvia Adams, a fellow islander, shared the recipe for this scrumptious salad with my friend Karen, who shared it with me, and now I'm sharing it with you. Pass it along!

* To make raw and vegan, omit chili sauce.

1 large mango, peeled, seeded and diced
1 small papaya, peeled, seeded and diced
2 tomatoes, diced
1 avocado, peeled, seeded, and diced

½ cup (125 mL) chopped cilantro
¼ cup (60 mL) sliced green onions
¼ cup (60 mL) shredded unsweetened coconut
dash Thai sweet red chili sauce

In a bowl, combine all ingredients and toss to mix well. Refrigerate to chill before serving.

Makes 4–6 servings.

slightly +

\+

- # Garlic for Life Salad

I thoroughly enjoy this salad that my friends Don and Lisa make on our regular poetry reading and writing evenings. The ingredients will surprise you and the flavors will delight you. To top it all off, it is a serious immune booster! Don and Lisa say, "Enjoy it daily with a glass of red wine on a small boat with a kitten purring on the table."

Garlic is a pungent, spicy herb. It is antibacterial and antiseptic and can be used as a treatment for intestinal worms. Garlic is also helpful in preventing heart disease, lowering cholesterol and blood pressure, regulating blood-sugar levels, preventing diabetes-related conditions, treating allergies, reducing arthritis, counteracting bone loss, and treating ailments related to cancer.

2 apples, peeled, cored, and chopped

2 tomatoes, chopped

1 nectarine, chopped (leave skin on)

1 banana, sliced

2 cups (500 mL) blueberries

8 garlic cloves, minced

6 large strawberries, sliced

1 tbsp extra virgin olive oil

In a large salad bowl, combine all salad ingredients, then toss with olive oil just before serving.

Makes 4 servings.

-

 -

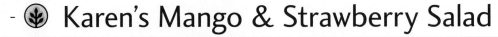 - # Karen's Mango & Strawberry Salad

As my friend Karen does, you can make this recipe a little differently each time; feel free to adjust the amounts of each ingredient to suit your mood. Karen often makes this salad for friends and it is always popular.

1 head romaine lettuce, torn into
   pieces
3 green onions, sliced
1 large or 2 small mangoes, peeled,
   seeded, and chopped
1 cup (250 mL) quartered strawberries
½ cup (125 mL) Karen's Strawberry
   Dressing (p. 131)

In a salad bowl, combine all salad ingredients, then toss with dressing and mix well.

Makes 4 servings.

slightly +

-

-  # Oriental Zippy Bean Tofu Salad

 I order this often at Artisan Eats restaurant on Bowen Island while I enjoy the spectacular views of ocean and mountains on my lunch breaks. This is my own at-home version. I love using the string beans from my garden.

3 cups (750 mL) sliced string beans
¾ cup (185 mL) chopped tofu
  • *Vata: lightly sauté medium-hard tofu*
  • *Kapha: use soft tofu*
2 tbsp toasted sesame seeds
2 tbsp sesame oil

2 tbsp Bragg sauce
1 tsp chili flakes
  • *To reduce Pitta: use less or omit*
  • *To reduce Kapha: use more*
1 tbsp fresh grated ginger
3 tbsp orange juice

In a pot, lightly steam green beans for 4–5 minutes. Drain and rinse. In a bowl, combine all ingredients. Toss to mix well. Cover and let marinate for 1 hour.

Makes 4 servings.

+ - - Variation: Add 1 cup (250 mL) diced red bell peppers.

slightly +

-

- # Açai Salad Dressing

The fruity flavor of this dressing is refreshing and you'll know you are adding a powerful punch to your salad.

½ cup (125 mL) açai juice
2 tbsp extra virgin olive oil
3 tbsp rice wine vinegar
¼ cup (60 mL) blueberries
1–2 tbsp agave nectar, to taste

In a blender or Magic Bullet, purée all ingredients.

Makes about 1 cup (250 mL).

Açai berries are grown in Brazil and Peru. They are a good source of antioxidants and vitamins and are one of the most powerful superfoods on the planet.

slightly –

\+

–

Karen's Strawberry Dressing

This is a delicious salad dressing and ideal for festive occasions like Valentine's Day, given its lovely strawberry color. Used as an everyday salad dressing, it offers a wonderful alternative to the common lemon and olive oil dressing, and adds a nice variety, especially if on a cleanse. Because strawberries already contain acids, this dressing does not need much lemon juice.

⅔ cup (160 mL) strawberries
2½ tbsp lemon juice
¼ cup (60 mL) extra virgin olive oil
good salt (p. 29), to taste
ground black pepper, to taste

In a blender or Magic Bullet, purée all ingredients until smooth.

Makes about ¾ cup (185 mL).

Strawberries contain five different acids: citric acid, ascorbic acid, malic acid, ellagic acid, and pantothenic acid. The total amount of each acid varies based on the variety of strawberry, how it is stored, and for how long.

-

slightly +

slightly + # Chia Seed & Lemon Dressing

This dressing has wonderful texture and flavor and is a great way to use chia seeds, which are full of protein and essential oils and help keep our digestive systems clean and flowing.

2 tbsp soaked chia seeds
3 tbsp lemon juice
4 tbsp extra virgin olive oil
  • To *reduce Kapha: use 2 tbsp*

1 tbsp agave nectar (optional)
¼ tsp good salt (p. 29)
¼ tsp ground black pepper

In a small jug, stir all ingredients to mix well.

Makes just over ½ cup (125 mL).

Chia seeds are an inexpensive and easy way to get your omega-3s, calcium, and protein. Chia seeds should be soaked (2 parts water to 1 part seeds) for 11 hours so they expand completely before being eaten (p. 31). These seeds were cultivated and highly valued by the ancient cultures of the Aztecs and Mayans.

slightly −

+ # Creamy Cashew Dressing

raw

vegan

Cashews give this dressing a delicious nutty flavor and creamy texture.
Note: Soak the cashews for 1–8 hours (p. 31).

1 cup (250 mL) soaked raw cashews
¼ cup (60 mL) +3 tbsp water
3 tbsp lemon juice, or to taste
2 tbsp apple cider vinegar
¼ tsp good salt (p. 29), or to taste

Drain and rinse soaked cashews. In a blender purée all ingredients until smooth.
If mixture is too thick, add additional water 1 tbsp at a time.

Makes about 1 cup (250 mL).

Cashews are filled with good oils that the body needs, and they're lower in fat than many other nuts. Also a good source of protein, they calm the nervous system. They can be soaked for as little as 1 hour and this recipe will still work.

-
-
slightly +

Cashew Cream & Miso Dressing

Cashews add a delicious flavor and creamy texture to this salad dressing, providing protein and calming the nervous system. I love the blend of miso and lemon tastes. *Note:* Soak the cashews overnight (p. 31).

1½ cups (375 mL) soaked raw cashews	1 tbsp miso paste
½–⅔ cup (125–160 mL) water	1 tbsp lemon juice

Drain soaked cashews. In a food processor or blender, pulse cashews to crumble. Add ½ cup (125 mL) water, miso, and lemon juice and blend until completely smooth. If too thick, add more water 1 tbsp at a time.

Makes about 1½ cups (375 mL).

−

+

slightly +

Miso Sesame Dressing

raw

vegan

A simple but very flavorful robust dressing.

¼ cup (60 mL) fresh lemon juice
¼ cup (60 mL) sesame oil
¼ cup (60 mL) tahini

2 tbsp miso paste
⅓ cup (80 mL) water

In a blender or Magic Bullet, purée all ingredients until smooth. If too thick, add more water 1 tbsp at a time.

Makes just over 1 cup (250 mL).

–

slightly +

+ # Singapore Dressing

This dressing has delicious sweet-and-sour Asian tastes. The cilantro not only packs in even more flavor, it also calms all the doshas.

¼ cup (60 mL) lime juice
1 tsp red chili sauce (I like Vietnamese)
• *To reduce Pitta: omit*
½ cup (125 mL) chopped fresh cilantro

2 tbsp tamari
2 tbsp rice wine vinegar
2 tbsp orange juice
¼ cup (60 mL) toasted sesame oil

In a large jar with tightly fitting lid, combine all ingredients and shake vigorously to mix. Let sit for 10 minutes, then shake again before using.

Makes about ¾ cup (185 mL).

-
+
+

Tahini & Lemon Dressing

The creamy texture and nutty flavor of this dressing comes from the tahini (p. 274), which is made from ground sesame seeds, a good source of calcium. This can be used as a salad dressing or a delicious sauce over falafel (ground chickpea patties).

½ cup (125 mL) tahini
½ cup (125 mL) lemon juice

¼ cup (60 mL) water
¼ tsp good salt (p. 29), to taste

In a blender, purée all ingredients until smooth. If too thick, add more water 1 tbsp at a time.

Makes about 1¼ cups (310 mL).

Big Island Dressing

I first created this dressing in Hawaii and love the flavor of the rich manuka honey and the Hawaiian salt (which is full of essential minerals) mixed with the other ingredients. I also like the balanced way I feel after eating a salad with this dressing. Salt calms Vata and increases Pitta if used in excess. It also increases Kapha as it retains water, but a little is essential to balance all three doshas.

½ cup (125 mL) extra virgin olive or hemp seed oil

¼ cup (125 mL) balsamic vinegar (to make this raw, use lemon juice)

2 garlic cloves, minced
  • *To reduce Pitta: use less or omit*

1 tbsp Dijon mustard
  • *To reduce Pitta: use less or omit*

2 tbsp manuka honey

¾ tsp Hawaiian red clay sea salt

½ tsp ground black pepper, to taste

In a jar or a blender, combine all ingredients and whisk or blend until smooth.

Makes about 1 cup (250 mL).

Manuka honey is made by bees that feed on the manuka or tea tree plant and is highly prized in traditional medicine for its antibacterial properties. Some of the best manuka honey comes from New Zealand. Manuka is the Maori name for tea tree. This honey has a delicious, distinctive flavor and is a boost to the immune system. When applied topically, it can speed up the healing of cuts, burns, acne, and cracked skin. It also alleviates digestive ailments, sore throats, colds, and eye infections.

slightly –

Ameeta's Lemon Flax Asian Dressing

This dressing has delicious flavors. Sesame and flax seed oils calm the nerves and improve brain health, and ume plum vinegar stimulates digestion. The ume plum, called umeboshi in Japan, is prized for its organic acids and health benefits, including alleviating cramps.

3 tbsp toasted sesame seed oil
4 tbsp lemon juice
2 tbsp rice wine vinegar
1 level tsp Dijon mustard
  • *To reduce Pitta: omit*

1 tbsp flax seed oil
1 tbsp ume plum vinegar (available at Asian food markets) (if you can't find it, use red wine vinegar)

In a large jar with a tightly fitting lid, combine all ingredients and shake vigorously to mix well.

Makes about ⅔ cup (160 mL).

+ -

Spicy Garlic Cumin Dressing

This dressing adds a healthy flavorful zip to any salad. The cumin calms all the doshas and aids digestion.

1 garlic clove, minced
½ tsp ground cumin
¼ tsp cayenne
• *To reduce Pitta: use less or omit*

½ cup rice wine vinegar
2 tbsp lime juice
good salt (p. 29), to taste

In a large jar with a tightly fitting lid, combine all ingredients and shake vigorously to mix well.

Makes just over ½ cup (125 mL).

 - +

Lime, Honey & Cilantro Dressing

*

Cilantro calms all the doshas and adds superb flavor, while extra virgin olive oil calms the nervous system (especially for Vata) and grounds the light quality of leafy green salads.
*To make vegan, use agave nectar or maple syrup instead of honey.

¼ cup (60 mL) extra virgin olive oil
¼ cup (60 mL) lime juice
1 tbsp honey
• *To reduce Pitta: use maple syrup or agave nectar*
1 heaping tbsp chopped cilantro

In a bowl, whisk all ingredients together and use immediately (within ½ hour).

Makes just over ½ cup (125 mL).

-
+
+

Greek Dressing

Lemon, olive oil, and oregano are the base for most Greek salad dressings. In this one, I really enjoy the flavor of fresh basil leaves.

¼ cup (60 mL) finely chopped fresh
  basil leaves
¼ cup (60 mL) lemon juice
1 cup (250 mL) extra virgin olive oil
good salt (p. 29), to taste
ground black pepper, to taste

In a large jar with a tightly fitting lid, combine all ingredients and shake vigorously to mix well. Let sit for at least 15 minutes before serving.

Makes about 1⅛ cup (315 mL).

- - +
slightly

Variation: Use 1 tbsp fresh or 2 tsp dried oregano instead of basil.

Basil is considered a holy plant in India and is revered in Ayurvedic herbalism. It is antibacterial, an antiseptic, and a diuretic; it also calms the nerves and clears the aura. Basil is considered pungent and heating and therefore good for calming Vata and Kapha, but not to be used if there is excessive Pitta.

-

-

slightly +

Orange Juice & Balsamic Dressing

This is a delicious light dressing with fresh sweet-and-sour flavors.

¼ cup (60 mL) freshly squeezed orange juice
2 tbsp balsamic vinegar

1 tbsp extra virgin olive oil
• *To decrease Vata: use 2 tbsp*
¼ tsp good salt (p. 29)

In a large jar with a tightly fitting lid, combine all ingredients and shake vigorously to mix well.

Makes just under ½ cup (125 mL). (Vata version with extra tbsp olive oil makes ½ cup [125 mL.])

−

 +

 +

Ameeta's Hot Dijon Dressing

 vegan

Apple cider vinegar is delicious and full of health benefits. It is naturally fermented, increases the enzymes that aid digestion, and contains malic acid, which also helps with digestion. Mustard has the pungent taste in Ayurveda that warms the body, helps to stimulate digestion, and eliminates excess fluid. It has also been known to alleviate migraines.

4 tbsp extra virgin olive oil
2 tbsp apple cider vinegar
1 tbsp hot Dijon mustard
½ tsp fleur de sel (p. 29)
2 tbsp lemon juice

In a large jar or small jug, whisk all ingredients until smooth.

Makes ½ cup (125 mL).

Yogurt & Mint Dressing

The cooling mint and yogurt provide a refreshing contrast with the garlic's wonderful pungent flavor.

2 garlic cloves
   • *To reduce Pitta: omit*
1 cup (250 mL) yogurt
2 tbsp water

¼ cup (60 mL) fresh mint
1 tbsp lemon juice
¼ tsp good salt (p. 29), to taste
¼ tsp ground cumin

In a blender or Magic Bullet, mince garlic. Add all other ingredients and purée until smooth.

Makes 1¼ cups (310 mL).

-
-
- # Sweet & Sour Dressing

 This dressing is light yet very flavorful.

 2 tsp rice wine vinegar
2 tbsp lime juice
1 tbsp agave nectar

In a small jar with a tightly fitting lid, combine all ingredients and shake vigorously to mix well.

Makes 2–3 servings.

- + - Variation: Add ¼ tsp Italian dried red chili flakes.

slightly + # Olive Oil, Lemon & Honey Dressing

This dressing is so tasty, people are always asking for the ingredients. Then they exclaim at how easy it is; equal parts of 3 ingredients! You can make as much or as little as you want!

*To make vegan, use maple syrup or agave nectar instead of honey.

¼ cup (60 mL) extra virgin olive oil
¼ cup (60 mL) tbsp lemon juice
¼ cup (60 mL) honey

In a large jar with a tightly fitting lid, combine all ingredients and shake vigorously to mix well.

Makes ¾ cup (185 mL).

-

slightly +

+ # Simple Cleansing Lime Dressing

This simple dressing brings out the true flavor of salad ingredients and is great to use over bountiful salads when on a cleanse. (See p. 369 and *The Modern Ayurvedic Cookbook*, p. 299.)

¼ cup (60 mL) fresh lime juice
¼ cup (60 mL) extra virgin olive oil

In a small jar with a tightly fitting lid, combine ingredients and shake vigorously to mix well.

Makes ½ cup (125 mL).

-
-
+ # Calming Avocado Dressing

Avocadoes give us the good fats that are calming to our nervous systems and make us glow. This is a great dressing if you are eating a completely raw meal, especially for Vata.

¾ cup (185 mL) roughly chopped avocado
2 tbsp extra virgin olive oil

½ tsp good salt (p. 29)
4 tbsp lime juice
4 tbsp cup water

In a blender or Magic Bullet, blend all ingredients until smooth.

Makes about 1¼ cups (310 mL).

–

 +

slightly +

raw

vegan

Yogurt & Avocado Dressing

If you like creamy dressings and avoid them because many of them seem too heavy, here is a deliciously healthy one for you! Japanese pepper is made from a dried red chili that is not as hot or pungent as cayenne, yet is packed with flavor.

¾ cup (185 mL) roughly chopped
  avocado
¾ cup (185 mL) yogurt
2 tsp fresh or ¾ tsp dried dill

2 tbsp lime juice
¼ tsp good salt (p. 29)
¼ tsp Japanese red pepper (or a pinch
  of cayenne)

In a blender, combine all ingredients and purée until smooth.

Makes about 1½ cups (375 mL).

Sprouted Mung & Shiitake Ramen Soup (p. 152)

Soups

Soups are nourishing as appetizers, snacks, and complete meals. As an appetizer, soup gets the digestive juices warmed up and ready for the main course; as a snack, soup provides a great energy boost; and as a main course, a soup with the six essential tastes balances all the doshas. Soups are replenishing and healing when our agni (digestive fire) is low, or in the winter when our bodies are using extra energy to keep us warm. They can be especially useful during the changing of the seasons as our bodies acclimatize.

In this chapter, I have included some delicious soups both light and hearty as well as a few raw recipes to offer a variety for all seasons.

slightly +

Sprouted Mung & Shiitake Ramen Soup

Each year in mid-August during "Bowfeast" weekend, we residents of Bowen Island celebrate local produce and feast together. This soup was the first course at a communal dinner I hosted and was heartily received. It included string beans and Swiss chard grown in my balcony container garden and carrots and mushrooms from the farmers' market. Sesame oil calms the nervous system, especially for Vata. Shiitake mushrooms enhance the immune system and are beneficial to all doshas.

Buckwheat, though often thought of as a grain, is actually a seed. Rich in iron, antioxidants, and magnesium, it is also high in fiber and known to regulate blood-sugar levels. It contains all 8 essential amino acids (the building blocks of protein), is gluten-free, and has a rich earthy flavor. "Soba" is the Japanese word for buckwheat.

1 tbsp good oil (p. 26)
1 tbsp sesame oil
1 tbsp minced ginger
3 tsp minced garlic
  • *To reduce Pitta: omit*
1 green chili, minced
  • *To reduce Pitta: use less or omit*
2 cups (500 mL) grated carrots
1 cup (250 mL) sliced fresh shiitake mushrooms
8 cups (2 L) vegetable stock

1 cup (250 mL) chopped string beans (1-in/2.5-cm pieces)
2 cups (500 mL) mung bean sprouts
⅓ cup (80 mL) tamari
3 cups (750 mL) chopped Swiss chard
5 oz (150 g) soba (buckwheat) noodles (1 bunch; these are often sold in separate bunches)
4 tbsp miso paste
  • *To reduce Pitta and Kapha: use 2 tbsp*
4 tbsp lemon juice

In a large pot on medium-high, heat oils. Add ginger, garlic, and green chili and sauté for 1 minute. Add carrots and mushrooms and sauté until they begin to soften, stirring to prevent them from burning, 3–4 minutes. Add vegetable stock and string beans and cook for about 10 minutes. Add sprouts, tamari, Swiss chard, and noodles and continue to cook for about 5 minutes. Remove from heat, stir in miso paste until it dissolves, and add lemon juice. Taste for seasoning and add more tamari if needed. If the soup is too thick, add water as needed and adjust seasoning.

Makes 8 servings.

 + -
slightly

Variation: Substitute unsprouted split yellow mung lentils for sprouted mung beans.

Five-Minute Sprouted Urad Dal Soup

This simple, nourishing dal is grounding and easy to digest because it is sprouted. Sprouting also increases vitamins A, B, and C and iron, among other nutrients. I like to keep some dal sprouting continuously so that I always have it to add to salads, soups, or wraps. The cumin and hing (asafetida) aid digestion.

Urad dal are black-skinned, cream-colored seeds with an earthy flavor. Whole urad dal are known as black lentils; split urad dal as white lentils. They are slightly heavy and therefore grounding and restorative for Vata.

4 cups (1 L) sprouted whole urad dal (black lentils) (p. 30)
6 cups (1.5 L) vegetable stock
3 slices ginger (about 1-in/2.5-cm round and 1/4-in/6-mm thick)
¼ tsp ground turmeric
⅛ tsp hing (asafetida)
½ tsp ground cumin

1 green chili, sliced in half lengthwise, leaving end intact (so it appears whole and can easily be removed by the stem before serving)
• *To reduce Pitta: omit*
good salt (p. 29), to taste
cayenne, to taste
¾ cup (185 mL) chopped fresh cilantro

In a large saucepan, bring all ingredients to a boil. Reduce heat to low and simmer until dal is softened, about 5 minutes.

Makes 4 servings.

Hing (asafetida) is used in tiny amounts (just a pinch or about tsp) in lentil dishes and some vegetarian dishes. It reduces flatulence, aids digestion, and balances Vata. Hing, available in Indian grocery stores, has a strong, distinct, pungent smell which becomes mild—with a flavor similar to onions and garlic—once cooked. Like garlic, hing is considered an antiviral.

Slicing chilies releases their flavor and heat. Use a sharp knife, and keep the end intact. Chilies are always optional. If you have excess Pitta, use very little or omit.

Wild Mushroom & Leek Soup

This is an easy starter soup before a meal to get your digestive juices going.
*To make vegan, replace ghee with good oil (p. 29) and omit yogurt.

Wild mushrooms are an excellent source of minerals such as iron, potassium, phosphorous, copper, and selenium and are a good source of B vitamins. Mushrooms are balancing for all doshas when added to warm, moist soups or sauces.

1 tbsp ghee (or butter)
¼ cup (60 mL) minced shallots
1 leek, sliced, white and light green
    parts only
3 cups (750 mL) sliced mixed oyster,
    shiitake, and chanterelle mushrooms

6 cups (1.5 L) vegetable stock
2 tbsp fresh thyme
1 tsp fresh oregano
½ cup (125 mL) yogurt
good salt (p. 29), to taste
ground black pepper, to taste

In a large saucepan on medium, heat ghee. Add shallots and leeks and sauté for 5 minutes, then add mushrooms and sauté for 7 minutes. Add stock, thyme, and oregano and bring to a boil, then reduce heat to low and simmer for 15 minutes. Remove from heat and let cool slightly before stirring in yogurt. Season with salt and pepper.

Makes 6 servings.

slightly +

- # Lentil Porcini Chili

Helen, who is renowned for the delicious and nourishing soups that she makes at Village Baker on Bowen Island, shared this wonderful recipe with me. She says that she loves it on a cold day after shoveling snow. Helen also says that the chili works well with whatever vegetables you may have (especially useful to know if you are snowbound!). The chili can be made the consistency of thick soup or into a more substantial dal by reducing the amount of stock and increasing the amount of lentils. I have adjusted this recipe in keeping with Ayurvedic principles.

Dried porcini mushrooms add a wonderful, deep, woodsy flavor to dishes. They are generally soaked in hot water before using. These tasty delicacies offer many nutritional benefits including vitamins (A, B, and C), minerals (iron, calcium, potassium), and some protein.

2 tbsp good oil (p. 29)
2 onions, finely chopped
2 garlic cloves, crushed
  • *To reduce Pitta: use 1*
2 green chilies, chopped
  • *To reduce Pitta: use less or omit*
2 red bell peppers, diced
2 green bell peppers, diced
2 grated carrots
2 tsp ground cumin
2 bay leaves
1 cup (500 mL) green lentils
2 cups (500 mL) sliced mushrooms
  (button or your favorite)
1 cup (250 mL) dried porcini
  mushrooms

1 tbsp ground dried porcini mushroom
  (grind in coffee grinder)
6 cups (1.5 L) vegetable stock
2 cups (250 mL) water
5 cups (1.25 L) chopped tomatoes,
  with juices
1 tbsp tomato paste
1 tsp Dutch fine cocoa powder or raw
  cacao powder
1–1½ cups (1 bunch) finely chopped
  cilantro
4 tbsp lime juice
good salt (p. 29), to taste
ground black pepper, to taste

In a large pot on medium-high, heat oil. Add onions, garlic, chilies, bell peppers, and carrots and sauté for 4 minutes. Add cumin and sauté for 2 minutes, and then add bay leaves, lentils, fresh mushrooms, dried mushrooms, mushroom powder, vegetable stock, water, tomatoes, tomato paste, and cocoa powder. Stock should cover vegetables; if more liquid is needed, add more stock or water. Bring to a boil, then reduce heat to low and simmer for 30 minutes, until porcini mushrooms and lentils are soft and tender. Add cilantro and lime juice. Season with salt and pepper.

Makes 6 servings.

-
+
-

Poets' Split Pea Soup

I made this on a wet day in April to inspire our poetry writing and reading evening; the poets approved wholeheartedly. I like the way the lemon juice and cilantro really bring out the flavors of the vegetables and split peas. This soup will leave you feeling satisfied but not overly full. (Remember to remove the bay and sage leaves before serving, or warn your guests not to bite into these.)

Cilantro is not only delicious, it acts as a chelator, helping to clean toxins, fungus, and yeast from our bodies. This fresh herb is antibacterial and a good source of fiber, vitamins A, thiamine, B6, C, E, and K as well as zinc and other great minerals, so add it liberally to your meals.

1 tbsp good oil (p. 26)
1½ cups chopped onions
2 tsp minced garlic
2 tsp minced ginger
2 tbsp minced jalapeño pepper
 • *To reduce Pitta: use less or omit*
1½ cups chopped carrots
¾ cup (185 mL) chopped celery
1 cup (250 mL) chopped parsnip

6 cups (1.5 L) vegetable stock
1 cup (250 mL) dried split peas
2 bay leaves
2 sage leaves
4–6 tbsp lemon juice, to taste
2 tbsp tamari
good salt (p. 29), to taste
¼ cup (60 mL) chopped fresh cilantro, for garnish

In a medium pot on medium-high, heat oil. Sauté onions for 2 minutes, then add garlic, ginger, jalapeño, carrots, and celery and sauté for another 4 minutes. Add parsnip, vegetable stock, split peas, and bay and sage leaves. Bring to a boil, then reduce heat to low, cover, and simmer until split peas are soft, about 40–45 minutes. Add lemon juice, tamari, and salt. Garnish with cilantro.

Makes 2 large or 4 small servings.

Raw Creamy Tomato & Pine Nut Soup

slightly –

This is a refreshing soup, especially in the summer when the tomatoes have just ripened on the vine and the basil is thriving.

4 medium tomatoes
¼ cup (60 mL) fresh basil
¼ cup (60 mL) pine nuts
1 tbsp extra virgin olive oil
2 garlic cloves
½ tsp ground black pepper

½ tsp Himalayan salt
2 tbsp chopped fresh basil
2 tbsp toasted pine nuts
12 celery sticks for dipping, about 4-in (10-cm) long

Tomatoes are rich in vitamins A and C, potassium, and antioxidants known to help prevent cancer and lower blood pressure.

In a food processor, blend tomatoes, basil, pine nuts, oil, garlic, pepper, and salt until smooth. Garnish with chopped basil leaves and pine nuts and serve with celery sticks for dipping into soup.

Makes 2 servings.

 + +

Variation: In a medium pot on medium-low, heat soup until warm. Remove from heat before it boils. Sprinkle with 2 tbsp Asiago cheese and garnish with basil and pine nuts.

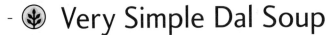

Very Simple Dal Soup

The flavor of this soup is simple and nourishing. (Remember to remove the peppercorns and cloves before serving or warn your guests not to bite into these.)

1½ cups red lentils
6 cups (1.5 L) vegetable stock
24 whole black peppercorns
10 whole cloves
• *To reduce Pitta: use less or omit*

½ tsp ground turmeric
½ tsp good salt (p. 29)
1 tbsp lemon juice, to taste
¼ cup (60 mL) chopped fresh cilantro

In a large pot on medium-high, bring lentils and stock to a boil. Reduce heat to low, skim off foam with a slotted spoon, and discard. Then add peppercorns, cloves, turmeric, and salt and let simmer until done, about 20 minutes. Stir in lemon juice and sprinkle with cilantro just before serving.

Makes 4 servings.

 – – Variation: Use 1½ cups split yellow mung dal instead of red lentils.

+

+

-

Beat the Cold Spicy Soup

* Having a cold usually means we have a Kapha imbalance. To rebalance, we should include more pungent, bitter, and astringent tastes in our meals—all of which are in this soup. Turmeric is a natural antibiotic, as is garlic. If you cannot eat hot food, omit the serrano chilies. If you do not have a cold and find this too spicy, you can cool it down with yogurt as a condiment or serve it over rice. Dairy is not recommended if you do have a cold, as this increases Kapha.

*To make vegan, replace ghee with good oil (p. 26).

Bouquet garni:
8 whole peppercorns
1-in (2.5-cm) long stick cinnamon
2 whole cloves
1 bay leaf
1 loose-leaf teabag

Soup:
1 tbsp ghee (or butter)
1 tbsp good oil (p. 26)
½ cup (125 mL) chopped red onions
2 serrano chilies, minced
• *To reduce Pitta: use less or omit*
¼ tsp cayenne
1 tsp ground turmeric
2 tsp garam masala
1 tbsp ground cumin
1 tbsp minced ginger
1 tbsp minced garlic
½ cup (125 mL) sliced celery

½ cup (125 mL) sliced carrots
1¾ cups chopped tomatoes, with their juices
2 tbsp tomato paste
½ cup (125 mL) sliced red cabbage
½ cup (125 mL) diced apple
1½ cups diced potatoes
4 cups (1 L) water
4 tbsp vegetable bouillon powder
¾ cup (185 mL) red lentils
3 packed cups (750 mL) baby spinach leaves

Place all bouquet garni ingredients into loose-leaf teabag and set aside. In a large pot on medium, heat ghee and oil. Add onions, chilies, cayenne, turmeric, garam masala, and cumin and sauté for 2 minutes. Add ginger, garlic, celery, and carrots and sauté for another 2 minutes. Stir in tomatoes, tomato paste, cabbage, apple, potatoes, water, bouillon, and lentils. Add bouquet garni teabag. Bring all ingredients to a boil, then reduce heat to low and simmer for 20 minutes. Add spinach and cook for another 2 minutes. Remove teabag before serving.

Makes 6 servings.

My easy new way to create a bouquet garni is to use empty loose-leaf teabags, generally available in Asian markets or specialty tea shops. These bags are much easier to use than cheesecloth and string. You can also choose to leave your herbs loose as long as your guests know they are for flavor and not to be eaten. This is common in Indian cuisine.

+
−
−

Weekend Minestrone Soup

The tasty beans in this soup have lots of fiber, iron, and calcium and create a complete protein when mixed with a whole grain like the brown rice macaroni. After my friend Pauline tried this, she wrote: "That was the best minestrone I have ever had. I'm intrigued by your method of preparing the beans because they were so easily digested." So this is for you, Pauline! This is a two-step recipe: Soaked beans are cooked in herbs and spices first to flavor them and make them easily digestible, then they are added to the soup. *Note:* Soak beans overnight (p. 31).

Flavorful beans:

1 cup (250 mL) soaked kidney beans

2 cups (500 mL) soaked small white beans

3 garlic cloves, peeled

1 tsp herbes de Provence

2 bay leaves

8 black peppercorns

3 slices fresh ginger (1-in/2.5 cm rounds, about ¼-in/6-mm thick)

¼ tsp ground turmeric

1–2 tsp good salt (p. 29)

1 tsp vegetable stock

¼ cup (125 mL) diced celery, including leaves

Drain soaked beans. In a large saucepan with 5 cups (1.25 L) water, bring beans to a boil. Skim off foam with a slotted spoon and discard. Add remaining ingredients and reduce heat to low. Simmer for 1–1½ hours.

2 tsp good oil (p. 26)
1 cup (250 mL) diced onions
½ stalk diced celery
½ cup (125 mL) diced carrot
1 cup (125 mL) chopped zucchini
½ cup (125 mL) diced green beans
4 garlic cloves, minced
5 cups cooked (1.25 L) flavorful beans
  (if you have extra, you can use them
  in a salad)

4 cups (1 L) vegetable stock
1 14-oz (398-mL) can tomatoes,
  chopped
2 tbsp chopped fresh parsley
1 tsp dried oregano
½ tsp ground black pepper
1 tsp fresh or ¼ tsp dried thyme
½ cup (125 mL) small brown rice pasta
  shells
4 cups (1 L) chopped Swiss chard

In a large saucepan on medium-high, heat oil. Add onions and sauté for 2 minutes, then add celery and carrots and sauté for 2 more minutes before adding zucchini, green beans, and garlic. Sauté for 3 minutes, then add all remaining ingredients (including cooked flavorful beans), except Swiss chard. Bring to a boil, reduce heat to low, and simmer for 10 minutes. Add Swiss chard and cook for another 4 minutes.

Makes 6–8 servings.

Hearty White Bean & Barley Stew

Barley is a great source of magnesium, helps lower cholesterol, and is beneficial for healthy arteries and heart. It is a good source of fiber and is used as a preventative for type 2 diabetes as well as gallstones. *Note:* Cook the white beans before preparing this recipe (p. 180).

1 tbsp good oil (p. 26)
1 cup (250 mL) chopped onions
 (1-in/2.5 cm chunks)
1 cup (250 mL) sliced celery
1 cup (250 mL) chopped turnip
 • *To reduce Pitta: use potato*
1½ cups (375 mL) chopped carrots
 (1-in/2.5 cm chunks)
2 garlic cloves, minced
 • *To reduce Pitta: use 1 or omit*
2 cups (500 mL) chopped tomatoes
1 cup (250 mL) chopped green bell
 peppers (1-in/2.5 cm chunks)

• *To reduce Vata: use green beans or okra*
2 cups (500 mL) vegetable stock
2 cups cannellini (white kidney) beans,
 cooked al dente
 • *To reduce Vata: use 2 cups cooked azuki beans, or 1 cup uncooked red lentils*
¼ cup (60 mL) barley
1 tsp fresh or ½ tsp dried thyme
good salt, to taste (p. 29)
½ cup (125 mL) chopped fresh parsley,
 for garnish

In a large pot on medium, heat oil. Add onions, celery, turnip, and carrots and sauté for 3–4 minutes. Add garlic, tomatoes, and bell peppers and sauté for 3 minutes. Add stock, beans, barley, and thyme and simmer for 40 minutes. Season and serve garnished with parsley.

Makes 6 servings.

Refreshing Vegetable & Yu Choy Miso Soup

I had just bought Bowen Island-grown carrots from the local farmers' market and had on hand freshly plucked Asian greens from Julia's garden, so I was inspired to create this recipe. The greens, easily found in Asian markets, are similar to spinach. They are part of the mustard family, which is prized in Ayurveda for its healing properties. I like to serve this soup with extra wedges of lemon to squeeze into it. *Note:* Soak barley overnight.

1 tsp good oil (p. 26)
1 tsp toasted sesame oil
½ cup (125 mL) chopped onions
1 cup (250 mL) chopped carrots
½ cup (125 mL) chopped celery
1 tsp finely minced garlic
  • *To reduce Pitta: omit*
¼ cup (125 mL) white wine or cooking wine (optional; you can use vegetable stock or water instead)
¼ cup (60 mL) chopped green beans

1 cup (250 mL) sliced fresh shiitake mushrooms
1 cup (250 mL) small cauliflower florets
6 cups (1.5 L) vegetable stock
½ cup (125 mL) soaked barley
1 cup (250 mL) chopped yu choy, with stems and flowers
2 tbsp miso
¼ cup (60 mL) chopped parsley

In a large pot on medium-high, heat oils. Add onions and sauté for 1 minute, then add carrots, celery, and garlic and sauté for another 30 seconds before adding wine, green beans, and mushrooms. Sauté for another 3–4 minutes, then add cauliflower, vegetable stock, and barley. Bring to a boil, then reduce heat to low and simmer for about 15 minutes or until barley is cooked al dente. Add yu choy and cook for 4–5 minutes. Stir in miso and parsley. Remove from heat and serve immediately.

Makes 6 servings.

Asparagus, Mushroom & Barley Soup

This is a warming, healing soup. Make it if you are feeling low or simply want to fortify your immune system and general sense of well-being. *Note:* Soak barley overnight (p. 31).

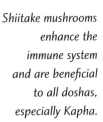

Shiitake mushrooms enhance the immune system and are beneficial to all doshas, especially Kapha.

Sesame oil calms the nervous system, especially for Vata, and is excellent for the skin and hair.

½ cup (125 mL) soaked barley
1 tbsp sesame oil
½ cup (125 mL) chopped onions and/ or sliced leeks
3 cups (750 mL) chopped mushrooms (shiitake and oyster are my favorite)
  • *To reduce Vata: use 1½ cups shiitake mushrooms only as these are warmer and more pungent than other mushrooms*
½ cup (125 mL) chopped carrots
7 cups vegetable stock

1 bay leaf
1 cup (250 mL) chopped asparagus stalks (if not in season, use zucchini or green beans instead)
½ cup (125 mL) asparagus tips
cayenne, to taste
  • *To reduce Pitta: omit*
good salt, to taste (p. 29)
ground black pepper, to taste
¼ cup (60 mL) finely chopped parsley, for garnish

Drain and rinse barley and set aside. In a large pot on medium-high, heat oil. Add onions, mushrooms, and carrots and sauté for 4–5 minutes. Add vegetable stock, bay leaf, and soaked barley. Bring to a boil then immediately reduce heat to low and simmer for 7–8 minutes. Add asparagus stalks and cook for 3 minutes, then add tips and cook for 4 minutes. Season to taste with cayenne, salt, and pepper and serve garnished with parsley.

Makes 4 servings.

slightly +

-

-

Cauliflower, Broccoli & Kale Soup

*
Cauliflower, broccoli, and kale are excellent sources of fiber and vitamins and, as members of the *Brassica* family of cruciferous vegetables, are known cancer fighters. I love the flavors and textures of this nourishing soup. *To make vegan, replace ghee with good oil (p. 26).

1 tsp good oil (p. 26)
1 tsp ghee (or butter)
¼ tsp whole cumin seeds
½ cup (125 mL) finely diced onions
  • *To reduce Pitta: use ¼ cup (60 mL)*
1 garlic clove, minced
  • *To reduce Pitta: omit*
½ tsp minced ginger
¼ tsp ground turmeric
¼ tsp ground coriander
¼ tsp cayenne

1 cup (250 mL) diced tomatoes
¾ cup (185 mL) diced carrots
1½ cups cauliflower florets
3 cups (750 mL) vegetable stock
1 cup (250 mL) broccoli florets
1 cup (250 mL) chopped kale (I like black kale)
½ cup (125 mL) chopped cilantro
good salt, to taste (p. 29)
ground black pepper, to taste

In a medium pot on medium-high, heat oil and ghee. Drop 1 cumin seed into the oil to test; if it sizzles and turns white, add rest of cumin seeds and let sizzle for 30 seconds. Add onions, garlic, and ginger and sauté for 30 seconds. Then add turmeric, coriander, and cayenne and sauté for another 30 seconds. Add tomatoes and sauté until they soften, then add carrots and sauté for 1–2 minutes. Add cauliflower and stock. When cauliflower has just begun to soften, about 5 minutes, add broccoli and cook for another 3 minutes. Add kale and cilantro and cook for another 2–3 minutes. Season to taste with salt and freshly ground pepper.

Makes 4 servings.

Roasted Fennel, Onion & Potato Soup

This is a gorgeous soup to enjoy on a rainy day.
*To make vegan, replace ghee with good oil (p. 26) and omit yogurt.

2 fennel bulbs, white parts only,
  roughly chopped
1 cup (250 mL) roughly chopped
  onions
1 tbsp good oil (p. 26)
1 tbsp ghee (or butter)
1 tsp good oil (p. 26)

2 leeks, white parts only, sliced
2 tsp minced garlic
6 cups (1.5 L) vegetable stock
4 cups (1 L) diced potatoes
1 cup (250 mL) yogurt
good salt, to taste (p. 29)
ground black pepper, to taste

Preheat oven to 350°F (180°C). Place fennel and onions in a baking pan, drizzle
with 1 tbsp oil, and toss to coat. Roast for 20–25 minutes, until softened.
Remove from oven and set aside. In a large saucepan on medium, heat ghee and
1 tsp oil. Add leeks and sauté for 4 minutes, then add garlic and sauté for 1
minute before adding stock, potatoes, and roasted fennel and onions. Bring to a
boil. Reduce heat and simmer for 20 minutes, until potatoes are soft. Remove
from heat and let cool. With a hand-held blender or in a food processor, purée
until smooth (be careful when blending hot liquids). Stir in yogurt, season to taste,
and serve.

Makes 6–8 servings.

-
-
slightly +

Yam & Pea Soup

* The combination of fresh rosemary, thyme, and grainy mustard adds delicious flavor to this hearty soup.

1 tbsp good oil (p. 26)
1 cup (250 mL) diced onions
4 cups (1 L) vegetable stock
1½ cups chopped yams
1 cup (250 mL) split peas
1 sprig fresh rosemary

1 tsp fresh thyme
1 tsp grainy mustard
1 bay leaf
½ tsp Celtic sea salt
4 whole black peppercorns

In a large pot on medium-high, heat oil. Add onions and sauté on medium heat for about 8 minutes, or until golden brown. Add all remaining ingredients and cook until split peas are soft and yams are tender, about 35 minutes. Remove rosemary, bay leaf, and whole peppercorns before serving.

Makes 4–6 servings.

-

 -

 - # Vegetable Stock

*

I sometimes add 1 tbsp of miso to 1 cup (250 mL) of this stock and enjoy it as an instant energy-boosting snack or appetizer.

¾ cup (185 mL) roughly chopped onions
1 cup (250 mL) roughly chopped carrots
1 cup (250 mL) roughly chopped celery
2 bay leaves
2 cups (500 mL) roughly chopped parsley

2 tsp thyme
2 sage leaves
3 slices fresh ginger (1-in [2.5-cm] rounds, ¼-in [6-mm] thick)
5 whole black peppercorns
8 cups (2 L) water

In a large pot on high, bring all ingredients to a boil. Reduce heat to low, cover pot, and simmer for 1–2 hours. Remove bay and sage leaves, ginger pieces, and peppercorns before serving.

Makes 10–12 cups.

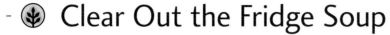
Clear Out the Fridge Soup

This is an easy, nourishing soup with lots of flavor and texture—everything but the kitchen sink!

*To make vegan, replace ghee with good oil (p. 26).

Kale has lots of antioxidants; it's a detoxifier and an anti-inflammatory. Also a good source of vitamins A, B, C, and K, kale is full of iron, manganese, magnesium, and phosphorous, and contains omega-3 essential fatty acids, important for brain health.

1 tsp good oil (p. 26)
1 tsp ghee (or butter)
1 cup (250 mL) diced onions
½ cup (125 mL) sliced leeks, white part only
1 tsp minced ginger
½ tsp minced garlic
2 potatoes, diced
  • To reduce Vata: use sweet potatoes
4 carrots, diced

1 zucchini, diced
5 cups (1.25 L) diced tomatoes, with their juices
1 cup (250 mL) sliced green beans
6 cups (1.5 L) vegetable stock
6 cups (1.5 L) chopped kale
good salt, to taste (p. 29)
ground black pepper, to taste
4 tbsp lemon juice

In a large pot on medium-high, heat oil and ghee. Add onions and leeks and sauté for a few minutes until onions turn translucent. Then add ginger, garlic, potatoes, and carrots and sauté for 3–4 more minutes before adding all other ingredients except salt and pepper and lemon juice. Cook for about 20 minutes, until vegetables have softened. Season with salt and pepper and stir in lemon juice.

Makes 10–12 servings.

Russian Beet Soup

*

This is my vegetarian version of a traditional Russian borscht. I made this on a cool spring evening when my friends Paul and Pauline came over for dinner. Paul, who is of Russian descent, said this was just like the soup his mother made, and Pauline quite delightedly added, "without the heaviness!" I took this as a real compliment, as it satisfied both a traditional and a modern palate. The lemon juice brings out the natural sweetness in the fresh beets.

*To make vegan, omit sour cream.

4 cups (1 L) vegetable stock
6 cups (1.5 L) chopped beets
2 cups (500 mL) chopped carrots
1 cup (250 mL) chopped onions
3 cups (750 mL) chopped green
cabbage
• *To reduce Vata: use 2 cups (500 mL)*

4 tbsp lemon juice
• *To reduce Kapha and Pitta: use less*
¼ cup (60 mL) fresh chopped dill
good salt, to taste (p. 29)
ground black pepper, to taste
8 heaping tbsp sour cream or plain
yogurt, for garnish
2–3 sprigs fresh dill, for garnish

In a large pot on medium-high, bring stock, beets, carrots, and onions to a boil. Reduce heat and simmer for 10 minutes. Add cabbage and simmer for 15 minutes. Stir in lemon juice and chopped dill just before serving. Season with salt and pepper. Serve in bowls garnished with dollops of sour cream and fresh dill sprigs.

Makes 6–8 servings.

+

-

- # Rolanda's Red Pepper Soup

* Rolanda carries Movementglobal, my eco-fashion clothing line, at Harbour Haus in Gibsons, BC. She and her husband Kyle are fabulous cooks—winners of all kinds of awards. She shared with me this lovely, simple recipe that her restaurant guests enjoy. While testing it, I learned that there are many ways to skin a red pepper, and some cooks don't bother peeling them at all, so feel free to do it your way. *To make vegan, omit yogurt.

6 red bell peppers, sliced in half, stalks and seeds removed
2 tbsp good oil (p. 26)
2 cups (500 mL) diced onions
1 tbsp minced garlic
2 cups (500 mL) diced potatoes

4½ cups vegetable stock
good salt, to taste (p. 29)
ground black pepper, to taste
½ cup yogurt or sour cream
6 sprigs fresh cilantro or parsley, for garnish

Preheat oven to 400°F (200°C). On a baking sheet, roast peppers for about 30–40 minutes (time depends on the heat of your oven), until skin is just puckering (check often to avoid burning). Place peppers in a bowl and cover with a cloth until cool. Peel off skins, dice, and set aside. In a medium pot on medium high, heat oil. Add onions, reduce heat to medium, and sauté until golden about 8–10 minutes. Add garlic and sauté for 30–60 seconds until garlic just begins to turn golden: don't let it burn. Add potatoes, roasted peppers, and stock and simmer for 15–20 minutes until potatoes are cooked. Purée with a hand-held blender until smooth. Season with salt and pepper, drizzle with a little yogurt or sour cream, garnish with cilantro or parsley sprigs and serve.

Makes 6 servings.

+ + - Amrita's Variation: Omit potatoes and add 1 cup (250 mL) diced celery, 1 cup (250 mL) diced tomatoes, and ½ tsp Italian chili flakes just after sautéing garlic. Cook until tomatoes soften. Add roasted peppers and stock and simmer for 15–20 minutes before puréeing.

–

slightly +

slightly + # Raw Carrot Ginger Soup

*

I enjoy this soup as a quick lunch—or even breakfast. In the winter, I heat the soup to "just before boiling" (to preserve the enzymes) and sprinkle it with ¼ tsp cinnamon or garam masala to make it a warming soup. *Note:* Soak cashews overnight (p. 31).

2 carrots, roughly chopped
2 stalks celery, roughly sliced
1 cup (250 mL) soaked cashews
1 tbsp minced raw ginger
1 cup (250 mL) freshly squeezed
   orange juice

1 tbsp chopped parsley
¼ tsp Himalayan salt, to taste
¼ tsp garam masala (or cinnamon)

In a blender or food processor, purée all ingredients except garam masala, until smooth and creamy. Sprinkle with garam masala, then serve immediately.

Makes 4 servings.

Fit for a Wedding Feast Biriani (p. 222)

Entrées

In Ayurvedic cooking, a meal rarely consists of a single dish; it usually includes a protein, dal (legume), or bean dish served with rice or other grain, vegetable, condiments (such as plain yogurt or pickles), and something raw, like a salad or sliced vegetables (celery, daikon, carrot, or slices of red pepper) to aid digestion. Some recipes in the section "Rice and Grains" (e.g., West Bay Biriani, p. 208) and Vegetables (Spicy Paneer Bean Pilau, p. 210), as well as many appetizers, soups, and salads in this book can also be served as entrées.

A meal that balances all the doshas ideally includes the six tastes: salty, sour, sweet, pungent, bitter, and astringent. It is important to eat meals that suit your constitution and current state of agni (digestive fire). If your agni is low, choose meals that will gently restore it.

This chapter contains traditional dal dishes as well as healthy versions of more conventional entrées such as pizza and lasagna (in the Rice & Grains section), and a refreshing raw version of pasta (in the Vegetables section) that follow Ayurvedic principles.

Beans & Lentils

Pulses (also known as legumes, and comprised of peas, beans, and lentils) mixed with grains are a staple of many diets all over the world and are an essential component of eating the Ayurvedic way to maintain health and vitality. The combination of pulses with grains (usually rice), which add the essential amino acids that pulses lack, forms a complete protein. The most beneficial serving ratio of rice to pulses for optimal complete protein content is about 2:1; e.g., 1 cup (250 mL) of rice to ½ cup (125 mL) of lentils.

In India, beans and lentils are known as gram (the larger, whole pulse) and dal (the smaller, split pulse), respectively. The chickpea, which is also known as the garbanzo bean in the West, is channa in India, so when you are shopping at Indian or specialty markets and see a package labeled "channa dal," you'll know it is split chickpeas!

Incorporating more beans and lentils (along with rice or other grains) into your meals is a great way to improve your health as they are known to decrease blood fats and hardening of the arteries, lower cholesterol levels, and promote a healthy heart. Pulses are a good source of iron and B vitamins and are high in fiber and low in fat; they are also inexpensive and can be stored for a long period of time without refrigeration. Some people find beans and lentils difficult to digest; those who do, or those who do not already eat them regularly, should introduce them into their diet slowly (about once or twice a week) to give the digestive tract time to adapt.

Before cooking, it is best to soak dried beans and lentils overnight as it helps to break down the starches and their notorious gassy properties—some pulses do not require soaking (see chart on p. 182 for details). Plus, soaking shortens the cooking time while increasing their protein and vitamin C content. Pre-soaking, or "sprouting," pulses also increases their nutritional value (up to an amazing forty times!) as it brings the seed that was dormant back to life. For more information on sprouting, see p. 30.

After soaking, beans and lentils must be cooked thoroughly to ensure easy digestion. You'll know they are done when they are tender in the middle without being mushy—with the exception of the split yellow mung mean and red lentil (also known as Masoor or Egyptian lentil), which inevitably turn mushy and somewhat soupy.

Mung beans are among the easiest to digest, making them beneficial for all the doshas. They are considered cooling and restorative, giving strength and vitality. The cooling qualities of mung beans are best balanced by warm spices, like ginger, green chilies, cumin, and mustard seeds, to aid digestion. Additionally, the sour tastes of lemon or Tamarind Chutney (p. 279) will further help to stimulate agni, the digestive fire. Kidney beans and chickpeas are more difficult to digest and should only be eaten when agni is high, a common attribute of Pitta. If you want to calm excess Vata, look for recipes with urad dal (black lentils). Kaphas will benefit from recipes with channa dal and masoor dal.

Cooking Beans & Lentils

Here is a general recipe for cooking most beans and lentils. Note that you should use about 1 cup beans or lentils for every 3–4 cups of water for cooking. You may need to add more water depending on the altitude you live in and the stove and pots you use. Keep in mind that the longer you soak the beans and lentils, the less cooking time they require.

TYPE OF BEAN OR LENTIL	AMOUNT OF DRIED BEAN OR LENTIL	AMOUNT OF WATER FOR SOAKING	SOAKING TIME	AMOUNT OF WATER FOR COOKING	COOKING TIME	YIELDS AMOUNT OF COOKED BEANS AND LENTILS
All beans and lentils, except ones listed below	1 cup	2–3 cups	6–8 hours	3–4 cups	40–60 minutes (dependent on soaking time)	2 cups
Azuki beans	"	"	"	"	"	3 cups
Black beans	"	"	"	"	"	2¼ cups
Kidney beans	"	"	"	"	"	2¼ cups
Red, brown, and green lentils	"	Not required	Not required	"	20 minutes	2½ cups
Split yellow mung beans	"	Not required	Not required	"	20 minutes	2 cups
Tur dal	"	2–3 cups	1–2 hours	"	40–60 minutes (dependent on soaking time)	2 cups

To drain or not to drain soaking water? We drain and rinse beans to get rid of many of the hard-to-digest sugars. But I had heard that Punjabi women prize the black chickpea (kala channa) soaking water, claiming it contains many nutrients. I asked a nutritionist about this, who told me that, over time, as our bodies get more used to digesting beans, we can slowly use more of the soaking water in these recipes. Listen to your own body, and you be the judge!

1 cup (250 mL) dry beans or lentils
2–3 cups (500–750 mL) water
  (for soaking)
3–4 cups (750 mL–1 L) water
  (for cooking)
¼ tsp ground turmeric
1 tsp good salt (p. 29)
2 slices fresh ginger

1 6-in (15-cm) stick kombu
1 fresh green chili, sliced in half
  lengthwise, leaving end intact
  • *To reduce Pitta: omit*
1 tsp good oil (p. 26)
  • *To reduce Kapha and Pitta: omit*
⅛ tsp hing (optional)

In a large pot or bowl, soak beans or lentils overnight in water for no more than 12 hours; lentils require a minimum of 4 hours (see chart on p. for exceptions). Drain soaked beans or lentils. In a large pot, combine water and beans or lentils and bring to a boil. A froth may rise to the surface; skim off as much as possible with a slotted spoon. Add all remaining ingredients. Reduce heat to medium-low and simmer; make sure there is always enough water to prevent drying or burning. Beans or lentils are done when the center is tender but not mushy. Discard kombu, ginger, and chili (if used) before serving.

Additional tips for cooking beans and lentils:

• Make sure you start with dried pulses that are fresh. Old pulses take a long time to cook and may have lost some of their nutrients. Dried pulses keep for up to a year when stored in a cool dark place. Always rinse them before cooking and pick out stones and debris.

• Don't soak split mung and red lentils, as they become mushy.

• Once pulses have been soaked, drain them and cook in fresh water.

• Bean and lentil dishes are often prepared in two stages. First, the pulses are cooked, and then the vagar (a blend of spices) is sautéed and added to the cooked beans and lentils before serving. The vagar not only enhances the flavor of mild-tasting pulses, it also aids digestion.

Cooking Beans & Lentils, *continued*

- Pulses cook slower when salt or anything acidic is added during their cooking process, so some people add the salt at the end. I prefer to have the pulses absorb the salt, so I add it earlier.

- Cooking pulses with fresh ginger aids their digestibility, as does adding kombu and hing.

- Kombu is a dried, black seaweed available at health-food stores and Japanese grocers. Indians traditionally use ginger and hing when preparing beans and lentils. Using kombu instead is a contemporary, cross-cultural touch; kombu is also full of minerals and nutrients. Kombu should not be eaten, so ensure you discard before serving.

- Hing (asafetida) is spice made from dried resin that comes ground or in rock form and is available in Indian markets. A small jar will last a long time as you need only ⅛ tsp in your beans.

- Simmering means liquid continues to bubble occasionally. This usually requires medium or medium-low heat; however, you should always adjust the heat to ensure bubbling is at its lowest point.

- Removing the froth that appears on the surface helps to prevent flatulence.

slightly +

slightly +

Creamy Urad Dal

I love the light, creamy flavor of this dal and how simple it is to prepare. It is very nourishing and satisfying. Serve on a bed of rice or with chapatis (p. 224) and yogurt. *Note:* Soak dal overnight (see p. 30).

To peel tomatoes: bring a pot of water to a boil. Add tomatoes and remove after 10 seconds. When cool to the touch, skins should come off easily.

1 cup (250 mL) soaked urad dal (black whole lentils)
2 cups (500 mL) water
2 slices ginger, 1-in (2.5-cm) rounds, ¼-in (6-mm) thick
¼ tsp ground turmeric
1 tsp good salt (p. 29)
2 cups (500 mL) peeled and chopped tomatoes, with juices

2 tbsp tomato paste
¼ tsp ground turmeric
1 tsp ground cumin
1 tsp ground coriander
½ tsp garam masala
¼ cup (60 mL) chopped fresh cilantro, for garnish
½ cup (125 mL) yogurt, for garnish
1 lemon, sliced in wedges

Drain and rinse soaked dal. In a pot on medium-high heat, bring soaked lentils, water, ginger, 1¼ tsp turmeric, and salt to a boil. Reduce heat to medium and simmer for 5 minutes. Skim off foam with a slotted spoon and discard. Add tomatoes, tomato paste, another ¼ tsp turmeric, cumin, coriander, and garam masala. Cook for 30–40 minutes or until mung is cooked but not mushy (cooking time depends on how long you soaked them). Adjust seasoning if necessary. Garnish with cilantro and yogurt and serve with lemon wedges to squeeze over individual servings.

Makes 4 servings.

If you have soaked mung beans but don't want to use them right away, you can always sprout them, at least partially. Drain soaked mung in a colander over a large bowl so it can drip, cover it with a damp cloth, and leave it in a dark place. This will begin the sprouting process and increase the nutrients even further. You can then let the mung go through the full sprouting process (p. 30) or cook them at this stage.

Curried Whole Green Mung Dal

This is an easy dal to make and has great flavor. To complete your meal, serve with chapatis or rice and lemon wedges, plain yogurt or raita, and a salad. I leave this dal thicker if I am serving it with chapatis, but if serving it over rice I add a bit more water to thin it out. *Note:* Soak mung overnight (p. 30).

Whole mung beans are prized in Ayurveda because their amino acids balance and nourish all the doshas. They are a good source of potassium, fiber, magnesium, and B vitamins.

Vagar is a group of spices sautéed together to flavor legumes and some vegetable dishes. It aids digestion and is commonly used in Indian cooking.

1 cup (250 mL) soaked whole green mung
3 cups (750 mL) water
1 tsp good salt (p. 29), to taste
1 slice ginger, 1-in (2.5-cm round), ¼-in (6-mm) thick

Vagar:
1 tbsp good oil (p. 26)
1 tsp ground coriander
1 tsp ground cumin
3 garlic cloves, minced
• *To reduce Pitta: use less or omit*

1 green chili, sliced in half lengthwise, leaving end intact (so it appears whole and can easily be removed before serving)
• *To reduce Pitta: use less or omit*
¼ tsp ground turmeric
2 tbsp lemon juice
¼ cup (60 mL) chopped fresh cilantro, for garnish

1 tsp minced fresh ginger
½ tsp cayenne, to taste
• *To reduce Pitta: use less or omit*
½ cup (125 mL) tomato paste

Drain and rinse soaked mung. In a medium pot on high, bring soaked mung and water to a boil. Reduce heat to low. Skim off foam with a slotted spoon and discard. Add salt, ginger, green chili, and turmeric, and simmer for 30–40 minutes. In a medium saucepan on medium-high, heat oil. Add coriander, cumin, garlic, ginger, and cayenne. Sauté for 1 minute, then stir in tomato paste. Cook until the oil starts to come to the surface, about 4 minutes. Add vagar to pot of mung and stir to mix well. Cook until dal is soft but not mushy, about 10 minutes. Add more water if too thick. Stir in lemon juice, sprinkle with fresh cilantro, and serve.

Makes 4 servings.

Yellow Split Mung & Spinach Dal

I love this dal because it is quick and delicious. Make the vagar as soon as you put the dal on. Mung balances all the doshas. Spinach adds great flavor, nourishment, and color.

Dal:

1½ cups (375 mL) split yellow mung

5 cups (1.25 L) vegetable stock

3 slices ginger, 1-in (2.5-cm) round, ¼-in (6-mm) thick

¼ tsp ground turmeric

3 cups (750 mL) chopped spinach

4 tbsp lemon juice

¼ cup (60 mL) chopped fresh cilantro

1 lemon, sliced in wedges

Vagar:

2 tbsp coconut oil

4 dried red whole chilies

  • *To reduce Pitta: use less or omit*

1 tsp black mustard seeds

3 cups (750 mL) chopped tomatoes

4 tbsp tomato paste

½ tsp ground turmeric

1 tbsp ground cumin

1 tsp good salt (p. 29), or to taste

1 tbsp minced ginger

1 tbsp minced garlic

  • *To reduce Pitta: use less or omit*

In a medium saucepan on high, bring mung, stock, ginger, and turmeric to a boil. Immediately reduce heat and let simmer, covered, for about 25–30 minutes. Meanwhile, in a frying pan on medium-high, heat oil. Add dried chilies. When they blacken, about 2 minutes, add mustard seeds and cover pan while they pop, about 30 seconds. Add tomatoes, tomato paste, turmeric, cumin, salt, ginger, and garlic. Cook until oil comes to the surface, about 5 minutes, stirring from time to time and adjusting heat. Stir vagar into dal (once it's cooked) and continue cooking for about 10 minutes. Add spinach in the last 10 minutes of cooking dal. Stir in lemon juice. Garnish with cilantro and serve with lemon wedges to squeeze over individual servings.

Makes 4–6 servings.

+ slightly - -   Variation: Use Swiss chard instead of spinach. Also add, at the same time as chard: ¾ cup (185 mL) finely chopped red bell pepper and ¾ cup (185 mL) finely chopped yellow bell pepper.

+

-

- # Andy's Dal

 (vegan) My friend Andy Blick is a ceramicist who often makes dal in his crockpot at work. I happened to visit him around lunchtime one day and enjoyed the combination of textures, color, and flavors in this hearty dal.

2 tbsp good oil (p. 26)
1½ cups diced onions
2 cups (500 mL) chopped tomatoes
2 tsp tomato paste
1 tsp ground coriander
2 tsp ground cumin
½ tsp ground turmeric
1 tsp garam masala
3 tbsp minced ginger
1 tbsp minced garlic
  • *To reduce Pitta: omit*
1½ cups (375 mL) red lentils
  • *To reduce Pitta: use yellow split mung*

4 cups (1 L) red bell pepper soup
  (p. 175) or vegetable soup stock
  (p. 172)
6 carrots, chopped
2 parsnips, chopped
12 Brussels sprouts, halved
2 cups (500 mL) shelled edamame
  beans
good salt (p. 29), to taste
ground black pepper, to taste

In a large pot on medium-high, heat oil. Add onions and sauté for 1–2 minutes, until they become translucent. Add tomatoes, tomato paste, coriander, cumin, turmeric, garam masala, ginger, and garlic and cook until tomatoes soften. Then add lentils, red pepper soup or stock, and all remaining vegetables and beans. Add enough water to cover vegetables by ¼ in (6 mm). Bring to a boil, then reduce heat to medium-low and simmer for 35–40 minutes. Add salt and pepper to taste and more water if dal seems too thick.

Makes 8–10 servings.

Crockpot variation: Add all ingredients to the crockpot just before you leave for work in the morning and cook on low setting so it will be ready when you return in the evening.

–

 +

 –

Spice Wimp Dal

My friend Pauline, who can't eat spicy foods, wrote a song about this called "Spice Wimp." I created this recipe for her and others like her—and they love it. (You'll find a spicier version on p. 186.) Cilantro balances all the doshas, and the cinnamon and pepper make it warmer for Vata and easier to digest for Kapha.

1 cup (250 mL) split masoor dal (red lentils)
1 cup (250 mL) vegetable stock
1 cup (250 mL) chopped celery
3½–4 cups (830 mL–1 L) chopped tomatoes, with their juices
1½-in (1-cm) piece cinnamon bark (available in Indian grocery stores)

5 whole black peppercorns
1 cup (250 mL) water
1 cup (250 mL) chopped fresh cilantro
good salt (p. 29), to taste
1 tbsp lemon juice

In a large pot on medium, add all ingredients except cilantro, salt, and lemon juice and bring to a boil. Reduce heat and simmer for about 20 minutes. (If it's too thick, add more water or stock.) Add cilantro and cook for another 5 minutes. Season to taste with salt, and stir in lemon juice just before serving.

Makes 4 servings.

Red Lentils with Vegetables

Red lentils store easily and cook quickly for a tasty, nutritious meal.

You can use a reusable cloth teabag or square of cheesecloth tied with string for the bouquet garni of ginger, cinnamon, peppercorns, and cloves; this makes it easier to remove the spices before serving.

Dal:
2 cups (500 mL) split masoor dal (red lentils)
4 cups (1 L) vegetable stock
4 cups (1 L) water
1 cup (250 mL) diced celery
3 slices ginger, 1-in (2.5-cm) rounds, ¼-in (6-mm) thick

Vagar:
1 tbsp good oil (p. 26)
4 dried whole red chilies
1 tbsp black mustard seeds
4 tomatoes, chopped
4 tbsp tomato paste
¼ tsp ground turmeric
3 tsp ground cumin

1 piece cinnamon bark, 2-in (5-cm) long
12 whole black peppercorns
2 whole cloves
¼ tsp ground turmeric
good salt (p. 29), to taste
1 cup (250 mL) chopped fresh cilantro
2 tbsp lemon juice

3 tsp ground coriander
1 tsp good salt (p. 29)
1 tbsp minced ginger
1 tbsp minced garlic
1 tbsp Tamarind Chutney (p. 279)
¼ cup (60 mL) fresh cilantro, for garnish

Red lentils are skinned and split masoor lentils, sometimes known as pink lentils. They turn yellow once cooked!

In a large pot on high, bring lentils, stock, water, celery, ginger, cinnamon, peppercorns, cloves, turmeric, and salt to a boil. Reduce heat to medium-low and simmer for 20 minutes. In last 5 minutes of cooking dal, stir in 1 cup (250 mL) cilantro and lemon juice.

In a frying pan on medium-high, heat oil. Add dried chilies. When they blacken, add mustard seeds and cover while they pop, about 30 seconds. Immediately add all remaining vagar ingredients, except chutney and garnishes. Cook about 8–10 minutes (oil will come to the surface). Stir vagar into dal. Stir in chutney, garnish with ¼ cup (60 mL) cilantro, and serve.

Makes 6 servings.

+

-

- # Baked Falafel

 Enjoy falafel (ground chickpea patties) in pita bread drizzled with tahini salad dressing (p. 137), sliced cucumbers, and tomatoes, or as a satisfying snack on their own. Falafel has become my favorite food to take with me on the ferry to Vancouver, as it is so easily portable and has great flavor. I also serve these patties at Indian tea parties with coconut, green, and tamarind chutneys (see pp. 276–79), much the same way I would pakoras. Note: Cook chickpeas before preparing this recipe.

1 packed cup (250 mL) fresh cilantro, washed and well dried

3 cups (750 mL) roughly chopped onions

3 garlic cloves, roughly chopped
• *To reduce Pitta: use less or omit*

1 green chili, sliced in half lengthwise, leaving end intact
• *To reduce Pitta: use half or omit*

4 cups (1 L) cooked yellow chickpeas

2 tbsp lemon juice

2 tsp ground cumin

1 tsp ground coriander

1 tsp good salt (p. 29)

1 tsp baking powder

good oil (p. 26) spray (or use pastry brush to lightly apply oil)

½–1 cup (125–250 mL) spelt flour

Preheat oven to 350°F (180°C). In a food processor, purée cilantro. Add onions, garlic, and green chili and purée again. Add chickpeas 1 cup (250 mL) at a time, blending well before adding next cup. Add all remaining ingredients except oil and spelt flour. Spray a baking sheet with oil. By hand, add just enough spelt flour to the chickpea dough to allow you to form 2-in (5-cm) wide patties from each tbsp of mixture. (Amount of flour will depend on how dry chickpeas are once drained.) Place individual patties onto baking sheet. Spray each patty or brush with oil. Bake for 15 minutes, flip, then bake for another 15 minutes. Ayurveda does not recommend freezing; however, these can be frozen and used for lunches and snacks.

Makes about 30 patties.

Black Chickpeas with Red Peppers & Zucchini

My friends who tasted this dish told me how much they liked the robust flavor of the black chickpeas—and that they were easy to digest. *Note:* Soak black chickpeas overnight (p. 182).

Many people prefer the taste of kala channa or black chickpeas and find them easier to digest than the conventional yellow kind. While this recipe will still work with the yellow chickpeas, it is easy to find kala channa at your local Indian grocery store.

2 cups (500 mL) kala channa (black chickpeas)
6 cups (1.5 L) water
3 slices ginger, 1-in (2.5-cm) round and ¼-in (6-mm) thick
1 green chili, sliced in half lengthwise,

Vagar:
⅓ cup (80 mL) good oil (p. 26)
2 cups (500 mL) chopped red onions
1 serrano chili, minced
4 tsp minced ginger
1 tbsp minced garlic
1 tbsp ground cumin
1 tbsp ground coriander
¼ tsp ground turmeric

leaving end intact (so it appears whole and can easily be removed before serving)
¼ tsp ground turmeric
1½ tsp good salt (p. 29)

⅛ tsp garam masala
1 cup (250 mL) chopped red bell peppers
1 cup (250 mL) sliced zucchini (1-in/2.5-cm thick rounds)
2 cups (500 mL) peeled (p. 185) and diced tomatoes, with juices
3 tbsp tomato paste

Drain and rinse soaked chickpeas. In a large pot on high, bring chickpeas and water to a boil. Reduce heat to medium-low, skim off foam with a slotted spoon and discard. Add ginger, chili, turmeric, and salt. In a medium pot on medium, heat oil. Add onions, serrano chili, and ginger and sauté for 4 minutes. Add garlic, cumin, coriander, turmeric, garam masala, bell peppers, and zucchini and sauté for another 4 minutes. Add tomatoes and tomato paste and continue to cook for 10 minutes. Stir vagar into the chickpeas and cook until they are soft, about 1 hour.

Makes 6 servings.

 - -
slightly

Variation: Add 1 cup (250 mL) coconut milk after chickpeas have cooked for about 50 minutes.

Amrita's Rajma with Vegetables

Rajma was one of my favorite dishes at a great Indian restaurant that opened for a short while on Bowen Island. Lots of people asked me to include the recipe in this cookbook, so here is my version. *Note:* Soak beans overnight (p. 182).

2 cups (500 mL) uncooked rajma
   (kidney or azuki beans)
   • *To reduce Vata and Kapha: use 6 cups
   (1.5 L) cooked azuki beans*
6 cups (1.5 L) water
3 slices ginger, 1-in (2.5-cm) rounds,
   ¼-in (6-mm) thick

¼ tsp ground turmeric
1 green chili, sliced in half lengthwise,
   leaving end intact (so it appears
   whole and can easily be removed
   before serving)

Vagar:
1 tbsp coconut oil
3 cups (750 mL) chopped onions
1 tbsp minced ginger
1 tbsp ground cumin
½ tsp ground turmeric
cayenne, to taste
3 cups (750 mL) chopped tomatoes,
   with their juices

2 cups (500 mL) chopped red or
   yellow bell peppers
3 packed cups (750 mL) roughly
   chopped spinach
good salt (p. 29), to taste
4 tbsp lemon juice
½ tsp garam masala (optional)

Drain and rinse soaked beans. In a large pot, bring beans and water to a boil. Skim off foam with a slotted spoon and discard. Add ginger, turmeric, and chili. Reduce heat to medium-low and simmer for about 1–1½ hours. Drain beans, reserving the cooking water, and set aside.

In another large pot on medium, heat oil. Add onions and caramelize for about 12 minutes. (If you are in a hurry, you can do this on higher heat in about 5 minutes, but you won't get all the sweetness of the slowly caramelized onions.) Halfway through, add ginger, cumin, turmeric, and cayenne. Once onions are caramelized, add tomatoes and cook for 5 minutes. Add bell peppers, spinach, salt, and cooked and drained beans. Stir to mix well and cook about 10–15 minutes. If extra liquid is needed, add reserved cooking water, 1 tbsp at a time. Stir in lemon juice, sprinkle with garam masala, and serve.

Makes 6–8 servings.

+

+

-

Fawn's Spicy Rajma

Fawn is, in her own words, "addicted" to rajma. She owns a gym on Bowen Island and says she feels replenished when she eats this dish after a workout. Fawn's primary dosha is Pitta, and she loves this dish even though it is spicy! Remember that we don't have to decrease spices in our foods unless we are out of balance. *Note:* Soak and cook beans before preparing recipe.

1 tbsp good oil (p. 26)
1 tsp whole cumin seeds
3 cups (750 mL) chopped yellow
  onions
4 tsp minced ginger
  • *To reduce Pitta: use less or omit*
2 tbsp +1 tsp minced garlic
  • *To reduce Pitta: use less or omit*
1 green chili, minced
  • *To reduce Pitta use less or omit*

4 cups (1 L) chopped tomatoes
2 tsp ground coriander
1 tsp ground cumin
1 tsp garam masala
¼ tsp ground turmeric
4 cups (1 L) cooked red kidney beans,
  rinsed and drained
  • *To reduce Vata: use azuki beans*
3 cups (750 mL) warm water

In a large saucepan on medium-high, heat oil. Drop 1 cumin seed into the oil to test; if it sizzles and turns white, add rest of cumin seeds and let sizzle for 30 seconds. Add onions, ginger, garlic, and chili, and sauté until onions are browned, about 4 minutes. Add chopped tomatoes and remaining spices and stir-fry until fragrant. Add cooked beans and water and simmer for about 20 minutes, until sauce thickens.

Makes 6 servings.

+

-

slightly +

Mountain High Quesadilla Pie

The Doukhobors originated in Russia in the late 1700s and eventually spread across the Russian Empire. They were united by their belief in universal brotherhood.

To make your own refried beans, cook 1 cup (250 mL) soaked kidney or black beans in 2 cups (500 mL) water until soft, about 1½–2 hours. Mash beans and sauté in good oil with 1 diced onion and half a green bell pepper, diced, salt and pepper to taste, and hot pepper (optional). You may also purée the bean dip recipe on p. 76.

Stenya moved to Bowen Island to work with me at my eco-clothing store, Movementglobal, soon after we met last summer. She grew up in a Doukhobor community, has been vegetarian all her life, and always enjoyed making this easy impressive dish with her mother. Serve it with organic plain yogurt or sour cream. Stenya says you can save the leftovers in the refrigerator for a tasty lunch later.

2 cups (500 mL) refried kidney beans
  • *To reduce Kapha: use black beans*
½ cup (125 mL) tomato salsa (p. 81)
2 cups (500 mL) ricotta cheese
3 packed cups (750 mL) chopped spinach
1–3 garlic cloves, minced
  • *To reduce Pitta: use less*
8–10 medium whole-wheat tortillas

1 tomato, sliced
1 cup (250 mL) grated old cheddar cheese
  • *To reduce Kapha: use mozzarella*
1 cup (250 mL) organic plain yogurt or sour cream
  • *To reduce Kapha: use yogurt*

Preheat oven to 375°F (190°C). In a bowl, combine refried beans and salsa and set aside. In another bowl, combine ricotta cheese, spinach, and garlic.

On a lightly oiled cookie sheet or pizza pan, place 1 tortilla and spread with thin layer of the bean/salsa mix. Then place another tortilla over it and spread with thin layer of cheese/spinach mixture. Alternate until all ingredients are used. You will have built an impressive pie at this point. Place the sliced tomatoes on top layer and sprinkle with cheese. Bake for about 30 minutes, or until cheese melts. Remove from oven, let cool for 5 minutes, then slice in wedges and serve each wedge with a dollop of yogurt or sour cream.

Makes 4–6 servings.

+

-

slightly +

Mary's Bodacious Bean Burritos

Mary is the owner of Positively Fit, a gym on Bowen Island where I teach yoga twice a week. I asked her for one of her favorite vegetarian recipes and she offered this gem. Not only are these burritos delicious, inexpensive, and healthy, but they are easy to prepare in advance. They freeze well (even though Ayurveda does not recommend frozen food) and do not need to be individually wrapped. I really enjoyed them topped with yogurt, salsa, and sliced avocadoes, accompanied by a salad—it made a lovely, easy meal. Thanks, Mary!

4 cups (1 L) cooked kidney beans
  • *To reduce Vata: use a cooked azuki beans*
3 tbsp Mexican chili powder
1 tbsp ground cumin

1 cup (250 mL) chopped fresh cilantro
2 tbsp lime juice
1½ tsp good salt (p. 29)
12 sprouted-grain large tortillas
12 oz (340 g) mozzarella cheese

Preheat oven to 375°F (190°C). In a food processor, purée all ingredients except tortillas and cheese. Slice cheese evenly into 12 pieces. Place one slice on each tortilla. Top with puréed bean mixture. Fold tortillas in half, place on an ungreased baking sheet, and bake for 25 minutes.

Makes 12 burritos.

Rice & Grains

Almost every Ayurvedic meal includes a rice or grain dish. White basmati rice, known for its fragrance and delicious flavor, is eaten most often, as it is calming to all doshas and easy on the digestive system. When cooked al dente, basmati rice is low on the glycemic index. Brown rice is high in fiber, B and E vitamins, and contains some protein and iron; however, it can aggravate Pitta and Kapha because of its heavier, moist qualities. If you feel you need to increase your fiber intake, use brown rice, but take note of how it affects your body and digestion. If your body type is mostly Kapha, eat brown rice in moderation.

I have included some barley and quinoa recipes as these grains offer so much nourishment and flavor. Barley is generally more balancing for Pitta and Kapha, but if you add oil and spices, it becomes more calming for Vata. Quinoa is most beneficial for Kapha.

Kitchari with Vegetables

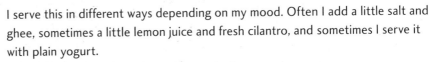

I serve this in different ways depending on my mood. Often I add a little salt and ghee, sometimes a little lemon juice and fresh cilantro, and sometimes I serve it with plain yogurt.

*To make vegan, replace ghee with good oil.

Turmeric is a blood purifier and aids digestion of complete proteins. It reduces flatulence and inflammation and is soothing for a sore throat. It also adds a lovely yellow color to the rice.

1 tbsp ghee (or butter)
1 tsp ground cumin
1 tsp ground coriander
1 tsp grated ginger
1 tsp ground turmeric
1 tsp good salt (p. 29)
½ cup (125 mL) diced carrots

½ cup (125 mL) diced celery
1 cup (250 mL) basmati rice
½ cup (125 mL) split green mung dal
  (yellow split mung with husks on)
2 tbsp freshly squeezed lemon juice,
  to taste (optional)
¼ cup (60 mL) chopped fresh cilantro

In a medium saucepan on medium-high, heat ghee. Add spices and salt and sauté for 1 minute. Add carrots and celery and sauté for 2 minutes. Add rice, split mung, and enough water to cover by 1 in (2.5 cm). Bring to a boil. Reduce heat to low, cover with a tightly fitting lid, and simmer about 20–25 minutes, until rice is cooked. Garnish with lemon juice and cilantro.

Makes 4 servings.

Variation 1: Prepare without the vegetables or spices, except salt, as in The Modern Ayurvedic Cookbook, p. 170, and serve with 1–2 tsp ghee (or butter).
Variation 2: Use urad dal, which have black husks. These are grounding and restorative for Vata.

Kitchari (sometimes spelled kichri) is Indian comfort food. Cooking the rice longer than 20 minutes will soften it further and make it even easier on the digestive system. It can be a good source of nourishment when cleansing, or when our agni (digestive fire) is low and we want to eat something simple. The lentils and rice make a complete protein, providing essential amino acids. The ghee calms the nerves and is a restorative in small amounts for all the doshas, particularly Vata.

-
-
slightly + # West Bay Biriani

My friend and co-worker Stenya and I created this dish together after a blissful summer evening swim. Dinner guests kept on heading for seconds until it was all gone! I love how festive it looks with the saffron-yellow rice border and the variety of mixed vegetable textures piled on top. Serve with lemon wedges.

Biriani (sometimes spelled biryani) originated in Persia; it is a spiced rice dish served with vegetables, meat, or fish. In India and throughout Asia, you will find dozens of regional variations.

1 cup (250 mL) basmati rice
2 cups (500 mL) water
½ tsp good salt (p. 29)
½ tsp saffron strands
1 piece cinnamon bark, 2-in (5-cm) long
1 whole clove
2 cardamom pods, slit open at ends
3 whole black peppercorns
1½ cups (375 mL) enoki mushrooms, whole with stems, roots removed
2 cups (500 mL) sliced carrots
2 cups (500 mL) chopped broccoli florets and stems
2 cups (500 mL) chopped cauliflower florets and stems

3 cups (750 mL) chopped kale
1 cup (250 mL) chopped runner beans (2-in/5-cm pieces)
1 tsp ghee (or butter)
1 tsp good oil (p. 26)
3 whole dried red chilies
 • *To reduce Pitta: use 1 or omit*
1 tsp black mustard seeds
2 cups (500 mL) finely cubed paneer (p. 28)
½ tsp ground turmeric
¼ tsp cayenne powder, to taste
 • *To reduce Pitta: omit*
good salt (p. 29), to taste

Preheat oven to 350°F (180°C). In a medium saucepan, combine rice, water, salt, saffron, cinnamon bark, clove, cardamom, and peppercorns. Bring to a boil on high heat. Reduce heat to low and let simmer, covered with a tightly fitting lid, for 20 minutes, until rice is cooked.

Wrap mushrooms in foil or place in ovenproof pan with 2 tbsp water and bake for 10 minutes. Set aside.

In a large steam basket in a large pot with water on high, steam remaining fresh vegetables for 8–10 minutes.

In a large wok or frying pan on medium-high, heat ghee and oil. Add red chilies and char them (let them blacken). Immediately add black mustard seeds and cover pan with lid while they pop, about 30 seconds. Add paneer, turmeric, and cayenne. Reduce heat to medium and stir occasionally for about 2–4 minutes, until paneer browns. Add steamed vegetables to pan and stir to combine until well mixed. Cook for another 5 minutes. Remove blackened chilies. Season with salt.

Carefully arrange saffron rice on a large platter. Place vegetables in the center of the rice, leaving a 2-in (5-cm) border of rice. Top with mushrooms and serve.

Makes 6–8 servings.

-

slightly +

+ 🌱 Spicy Paneer Bean Pilau

Paneer absorbs the tasty flavors as it cooks, is a great source of protein and calcium, and makes this an easy meal when served with a salad. Soaking the rice shortens its cooking time and makes it easier to digest.

1 cup (250 mL) brown basmati rice
2 cups (500 mL) water for soaking
1 tsp ghee (or butter)
1 tsp good oil (p. 26)
½ cup (125 mL) chopped onions
1 tsp minced ginger
½–1 tsp minced green chili
1 cup (250 mL) cubed tomatoes,
  with juices
1 tsp tomato paste
1 tsp minced garlic

1 tsp ground cumin
1 tsp ground coriander
¼ tsp ground turmeric
½ tsp garam masala
1 tsp good salt (p. 29)
¾ cup (185 mL) cubed paneer (p. 28)
1 cup (250 mL) chopped runner or
  French beans (2-in/5-cm pieces)
¼ cup (60 mL) chopped fresh cilantro,
  for garnish
1 lemon, sliced in wedges, for garnish

Soak rice in water for 15 minutes. In a medium pot on medium-high, heat ghee and oil. Add onions, ginger, and green chili and sauté for 3 minutes. Add tomatoes, tomato paste, garlic, cumin, coriander, turmeric, garam masala, and salt. Sauté until oil comes to the surface, about 5–7 minutes. Stir in paneer and sauté for 1 minute. Add beans, soaked rice, and enough water to cover by 1 in (2.5 cm). Bring to a boil. Reduce heat and simmer for about 30 minutes, until rice is cooked. Sprinkle with cilantro and serve with lemon wedges.

Makes 2–4 servings.

slightly +

-

- # Cauliflower, Broccoli & Carrot Pilau

* The secret to pilaus is that the vegetable juices and spices infuse the rice with flavor while cooking.

*To make vegan, replace ghee with good oil.

1 tsp ghee (or butter)	¼ tsp ground turmeric
1 tsp good oil (p. 26)	2 cups (500 mL) basmati rice
½ cup (125 mL) finely chopped onions	¾ cup (185 mL) cups chopped broccoli florets and stems
2 tsp minced green chili	
• To reduce Pitta: use ½ tsp	¾ cup (185 mL) chopped cauliflower florets and stems
1 tsp minced ginger	
1 tsp minced garlic	½ cup (125 mL) diced carrots
• To reduce Pitta: omit	4 cups (1 L) vegetable stock
¼ cup (60 mL) chopped fresh cilantro	good salt (p. 29), to taste

In a medium pot on medium-high, melt ghee and oil. Add onions and sauté until they become translucent, 1–2 minutes, then add chili, ginger, garlic, cilantro, and turmeric and sauté for another 2 minutes, until onions just begin to turn golden. Add rice and toss to coat with spices, then add vegetables and stock. Bring to a boil on high, then reduce to low, cover with a tightly fitting lid, and simmer for about 20 minutes, until rice is cooked. Try not to remove lid and let steam escape, but if mixture looks too dry, add hot water, 1 tbsp at a time.

Makes 4–6 servings.

–

 –

slightly +

Not Just Mushrooms & Rice

* This was inspired by a rice dish I enjoyed at a monthly vegetarian potluck dinner hosted by my friends Marcel and Jlonka in their beautiful garden. It calls for cooked rice, but you can also just cook it while preparing the vegetables.
*To make vegan, omit the ghee and replace with good oil.

2 tbsp ghee (or butter)
• *To reduce Kapha: use 1 tbsp*
1 tsp good oil (p. 26)
2 cups (500 mL) sliced leeks, white parts only
6 cups (1.5 L) chopped mushrooms (mix of shiitake, portobello, brown button)
1½ cups (375 mL) asparagus stalks
½ cup (125 mL) asparagus tips

1 packed cup (250 mL) grated carrots
1 tbsp minced garlic
¾ cup (185 mL) chopped red bell peppers
2 tbsp fresh or 1 tsp dried thyme
good salt (p. 29), to taste
ground black pepper, to taste
2 cups (500 mL) cooked short grain brown rice

In a large frying pan on medium, heat ghee and oil. Add all remaining ingredients, except rice, and sauté for 12 minutes. Add rice, stir to mix well, and serve.

Makes 6 servings.

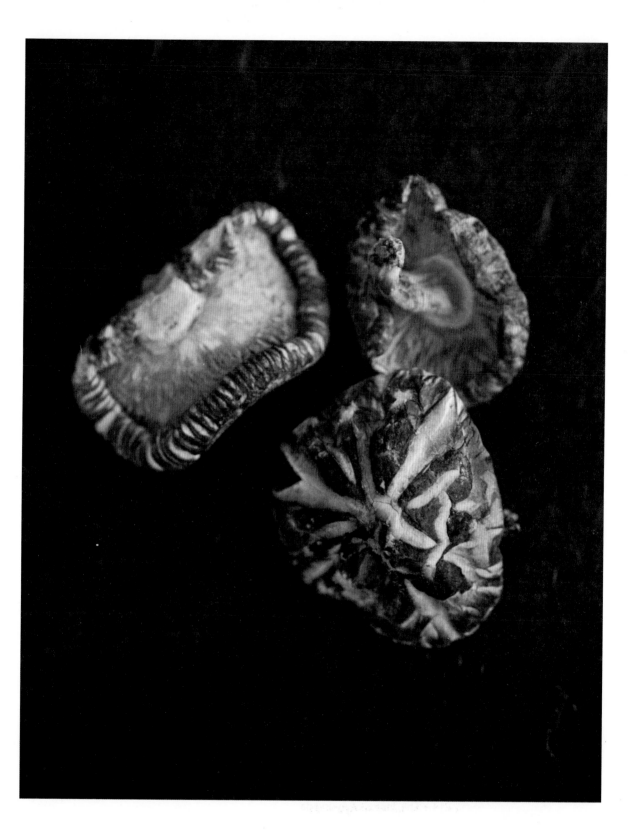

+

-

- # Asian Fusion Quinoa

 This is a great way to use fresh asparagus. The sesame oil adds flavor and calms Vata.

1 cup (250 mL) quinoa
2 cups (500 mL) water
½ tsp good salt (p. 29)
½ cup (125 mL) diced celery
10 diced asparagus stalks
1 tsp toasted sesame oil
1 cup (250 mL) sliced leeks, mostly
  white parts

2 tsp minced garlic
2 tsp minced ginger
2 cups (500 mL) sliced mushrooms
1 cup (250 mL) sliced red bell peppers
10 asparagus heads, sliced in half
1 tbsp tamari

In a medium pot on medium-high, bring quinoa, water, salt, celery, and asparagus to a boil. Reduce heat to low, cover pot with a tightly fitting lid, and simmer for 15 minutes, until quinoa is cooked. In a medium frying pan on medium-high, heat oil. Add remaining ingredients except tamari in order of list above. Stir to mix well and sauté for 1–2 minutes, then add tamari and cover. Let vegetables cook in their own steam for about 4 minutes. Stir cooked quinoa into vegetables until well mixed and serve.

Makes 4–6 servings.

- + + Variation 1: Add 1 cup (250 mL) toasted cashews pieces.

- + + Variation 2: Add ¼ cup (60 mL) sesame seeds.
  slightly   slightly

+

 +

 –

Yammy Quinoa with Sautéed Veg

This can be eaten warm or cool. The finely chopped yam cooks with the rice in one pot. You'll be amazed by how much the flavors of the vegetables are brought out by cooking them in their own steam, and you don't lose a drop of goodness, as it is all tossed with the quinoa.

Soy sauce, or shoyu as it is called in Japan, is a derivative of fermented soy beans and may contain wheat as a thickener, so if you're avoiding wheat, read the label. Tamari is slightly thicker than soy and shoyu, but both have a delicious salty flavor and contain some B vitamins.

1 cup (250 mL) quinoa
½ cup (125 mL) finely chopped yams
2¼ cups (530 mL) water
1 tsp good salt (p. 29)
1 tbsp good oil (p. 26)
¼ cup (60 mL) chopped onions
1½ cups (375 mL) sliced mushrooms
2 garlic cloves, minced
• *To reduce Pitta: use less or omit*

1 cup (125 mL) chopped kale
1 cup (125 mL) sliced red cabbage
tamari, to taste
¼ cup (60 mL) chopped parsley or cilantro, for garnish
¼ cup (60 mL) pumpkin seeds, for garnish

In a large pot, bring quinoa, yams, water, and salt to a boil. Reduce heat to low, cover with a tightly fitting lid, and let cook about 15 minutes, until quinoa is cooked. In a large frying pan on medium-high, heat oil. Add onions and mushrooms and sauté for 4 minutes. Then add garlic, kale, and cabbage, cover pan, and let vegetables cook in their own steam for 4 minutes. Add tamari. If mixture looks too dry, add 2–3 tbsp water. Stir vegetables into quinoa and mix well. Sprinkle with parsley and pumpkin seeds and serve.

Makes 3–4 servings.

– – + Variation 1: Use basmati rice instead of quinoa.

+ – – Variation 2: Use barley instead of quinoa.

+
−
− # Rebecca's Roast Veg & Quinoa

(vegan) This is so delicious, you'll make it often once you've tasted it! I can still hear my friend Rebecca in her Aussie accent describing the delectable combination of spices, lemon juice, and roasted vegetables, and telling me to use every drop! Rebecca puts her turmeric in a salt shaker so she can sprinkle it easily.

Buy a spray bottle that works on a vacuum principle and fill with oil. These bottles make it easy to spray veggies lightly with oil so you don't oversaturate them.

1 cup (250 mL) quinoa
2 cups (500 mL) water
1 tsp good salt (p. 29)
2 red bell peppers, sliced thickly
1 large zucchini, sliced (½-in/1-cm thick rounds)
2 carrots, sliced (1/4-in/6-mm thick rounds)

good oil spray (p. 26), or about 1 tsp oil
• To decrease Vata, add more; to decrease Kapha, use less
¼ tsp ground turmeric
¼ tsp cayenne
4 tbsp lemon juice
2 tsp fresh or 1 tsp dried oregano or thyme
good salt (p. 29), to taste

Preheat broiler. In a small pot, bring quinoa, water, and salt to a boil. Reduce heat to low and simmer, covered with a tightly fitting lid, for about 15 minutes, until quinoa is cooked. Place veggies on baking pan in a single layer. Spray or brush lightly with oil. Sprinkle with turmeric, cayenne, lemon juice, oregano, and salt. Place under broiler with oven door open for about 5 minutes—don't let it burn. Flip vegetables over and broil for another 4–5 minutes. Once you see slight charring, remove from broiler. Stir roasted vegetables into cooked quinoa and mix well. If any liquid remains in bottom of baking pan, pour over quinoa and veggies.

Makes 2–4 servings.

Green Bean Quinoa Pilau

Blackening (or charring) the chilies, popping the mustard seeds, and sautéing them with onion and cumin gives this pilau a wonderful traditional South Indian flavor.

3 tbsp coconut oil	1 tsp ground cumin
2 dried whole red chilies	1½ cups (375 mL) quinoa
1½ tsp black mustard seeds	3 cups (750 mL) vegetable stock
¾ cup (185 mL) minced onions	¾ cup (185 mL) diced green beans

In a medium pot on medium-high, heat oil. Add chilies and cook until they start to blacken. Add mustard seeds, cover pot until they pop, about 30 seconds, then add onions and cumin. Sauté for 2 minutes. Add quinoa, vegetable stock, and green beans. Bring to a boil then reduce heat and simmer, covered with a tightly fitting lid, for 15 minutes, until quinoa is cooked.

Makes 4 servings.

slightly +

-

slightly + # Quinoa Zucchini Boats

These are always a hit—delicious and fun to eat. *Note:* This recipe calls for quinoa that's already been cooked.

3 medium zucchinis
1 tsp good oil (p. 26)
1 tsp ghee (or butter)
¾ cup (185 mL) chopped onions
2 cups (500 mL) chopped mushrooms
  (mix of shiitake, oyster, portobello)
1 tsp minced garlic
2 tbsp finely chopped fresh basil
½ tsp good salt (p. 29), to taste
½ tsp ground black pepper, to taste

1 tbsp pumpkin seeds
1 tbsp sunflower seeds
3 eggs
½ cup (125 mL) grated Parmesan
  cheese
1 cup (250 mL) cooked red quinoa
½ cup (125 mL) grated Parmesan
  cheese
1 cup (250 mL) yogurt or sour cream,
  for garnish

Preheat oven to 350°F (180°C). Slice zucchinis in half lengthwise and scoop out pulp. Chop pulp finely and place in a bowl. Place hollowed zucchini "boats" on a lightly oiled baking dish. In a large frying pan on medium-high, heat oil and ghee. Add onions and cook for 4 minutes, then add zucchini pulp, mushrooms, garlic, basil, and salt and pepper, and sauté for another 5–6 minutes. Sprinkle with pumpkin and sunflower seeds. In a medium bowl, beat eggs, then stir in ½ cup (125 mL) Parmesan cheese. Gently toss egg mixture into pot of cooked quinoa, then add to sautéed vegetables and mix well. Stuff zucchini boats generously with mixture. Sprinkle stuffed boats with remaining ½ cup (125 mL) Parmesan and bake for 35 minutes. Serve garnished with dollops of yogurt or sour cream.

Makes 6 servings.

ø + - Variation: For a spicier version, add 1 minced green chili with the onions and use cilantro instead of basil.

slightly +

−

− # Pearl Barley with Cherry Tomatoes

* I created this recipe from tidbits of a "foodie" dinner conversation I had with James, a chef from Australia. I love the delicate flavors of the lemon rind and basil. *To make vegan, omit ghee and replace with good oil. *Note:* Soak barley overnight (p. 31).

1 cup (250 mL) soaked pearl barley
2 cups (500 mL) water, for cooking
1 tbsp grated lemon rind
¾ cup (185 mL) halved cherry
  tomatoes

1 tsp ghee (or butter)
1 tsp good salt (p. 29)
½ tsp ground black pepper
½ loosely packed cup (125 mL)
  chopped fresh basil

In a large pot, bring barley, cooking water, and all remaining ingredients to a boil. Reduce heat to low and let simmer, covered with a tightly fitting lid, for about 15 minutes, until barley is cooked.

Makes 2-4 servings

Ode to Julia Barley Pilau

There is so much hearty goodness in this dish. My friend Marcel, who is a scientist and fabulous French chef, enjoyed it for dinner and said it's like a barley version of risotto. Soaking the barley overnight makes it quick to cook and easy to digest. Slow-cooking the vegetables really brings out their natural flavors. *Note:* Soak barley overnight (p. 31).

Barley is an ancient grain known to give strength and mental clarity. It also helps tone and detoxify the liver.

2 tbsp good oil (p. 26)
1 cup (250 mL) chopped onions
1 cup (250 mL) sliced leeks, white
    parts only
1 cup (250 mL) grated carrots
1 cup (250 mL) diced celery
4 cups (1 L) sliced mushrooms (mix of
    shiitake, oyster, portobello)
2 cups (500 mL) diced red bell
    peppers

2 cups (500 mL) sliced green beans
    (1-in/2.5-cm pieces)
3 cups (750 mL) soaked barley
6 cups (1.5 L) vegetable stock
4 tsp fresh or 2 tsp dried thyme
good salt (p. 29), to taste
ground black pepper, to taste

In a large pot on medium, heat oil. Add onions, leeks, carrots, celery, and mushrooms and sauté for 10–15 minutes. Stir in all remaining ingredients and bring to a boil. Reduce heat to low, cover with tightly fitting lid, and simmer for about 15 minutes, until barley is cooked.

Makes 8 servings.

–

slightly +

+ # Fit for a Wedding Feast Biriani

 You will need four stove burners going at once to make this healthy version of a Muslim wedding feast dish—one for the rice, one for the mung, one for crispy onions, and one for the vagar—but it's well worth the effort! Remember to take the time to layer the ingredients carefully to show off their colors and textures. *To make vegan, replace ghee with good oil. *Note:* This recipe calls for sprouted mung.

You can also find prepared fried onions in Indian grocery stores.

Rice:

2 cups (500 mL) basmati rice

4 cups (1 L) water

1 tsp saffron strands

1 cinnamon stick, broken into 2–3 pieces

6 whole black peppercorns

2 whole cloves

3 cardamom pods, slit open at ends

1 tsp good salt (p. 29)

In a large saucepan, bring all ingredients to a boil. Reduce heat to low, cover with a tightly fitting lid, and simmer for 20 minutes, until rice is cooked. Remove whole spices before serving.

Mung:

4 cups (1 L) mung bean sprouts

In a large pot, bring mung and enough water to just cover to a boil. Reduce heat to low and simmer for about 10 minutes, until mung are cooked.

Crispy onions:

1 tbsp + 2 tsp ghee (or butter)

1 tsp good oil (p. 26)

1½ cups (375 mL) onions (sliced lengthways, then in half)

In a medium frying pan on medium, heat ghee and oil. Add onions and fry until crisp and brown (about 25–30 minutes). Set aside to drain on paper towel.

Vagar:

1 tbsp ghee (or butter)
1 tsp good oil (p. 26)
1½ cups finely chopped onions
2 tsp minced garlic
1 tsp minced ginger
4 cups (1 L) chopped tomatoes,
  with juices

2 tbsp tomato paste
¼ tsp ground turmeric
2 tsp ground cumin
2 tsp ground coriander
1 tsp cayenne

In a medium frying pan on medium-high, heat ghee and oil. Add onions and sauté for 3–4 minutes, until golden brown. Add all remaining vagar ingredients and cook until oil comes to the surface, about 10 minutes.

To assemble and garnish:
¼ cup (60 mL) chopped cilantro
1 tomato, thinly sliced (optional)

On a large serving platter, evenly distribute saffron rice. Place vagar in center, leaving a 2-in (5-cm) wide border of rice around edge, and top with cooked mung. Sprinkle crispy onions around mung to create a border. Garnish platter with cilantro and tomato slices.

Makes 8–10 servings.

 + + Variation: Sprinkle ¼ cup (60 mL) toasted pistachios and ¼ cup (60 mL) dried cranberries around onion layer for another border.

-
-
+

Spelt Chapatis

Although spelt is a close relative of wheat, many people with wheat intolerances can digest it, as it has a low gluten content. (More chapati recipes may be found on p. 226 and in *The Modern Ayurvedic Cookbook*.)

Spelt is an ancient grain and although it is a close relative of wheat, most people with wheat intolerances can digest it due to its low-gluten content. Spelt has 15–20 percent protein content and more complex carbohydrates than wheat. Spelt flour does not rise quite as high as wheat flour and needs slightly less liquid to bind it.

2 cups (500 mL) spelt flour
½ tsp good salt (p. 29)
½ cup warm water
1½ tsp melted ghee (or butter) or good oil (p. 26)
• *Vata can add 1 tbsp more*

In a large bowl, combine flour and salt. Add water and mix together with hands. Knead to form a firm, smooth dough. If too sticky, add more flour, 1 tbsp at a time; if too dry, add more water, 1 tbsp at a time. Cover and let sit for 5 minutes. Pour melted ghee over dough and knead again. Divide dough into 10 same-sized balls. On a lightly floured surface with a rolling pin, roll out each ball evenly into a 7-in (18-cm) circle.

In a dry heavy-bottomed or non-stick frying pan on medium-high heat, cook each chapati by placing it top-side down into the pan (side you've just rolled). When it begins to bubble, after about 1 minute, gently press edges with a non-metal spatula to allow it to gather air or rise. Flip and cook the other side for 1 minute. Set aside in an ovenproof dish. Repeat with remaining dough. If pan gets too hot, reduce heat. Experiment to determine optimal heat to cook chapatis; the more they bubble and rise, the lighter they are. Stack chapatis on top of each other in dish, separated with wax paper or coated with a little ghee, to prevent sticking. Cover dish with lid so they don't dry out, and keep in a warm oven until ready to serve.

Makes 10 chapatis.

+

+

- # Quinoa Chapatis

 I heard that some Indian cooks were successfully making chapatis from quinoa, so I experimented and came up with this delicious version. Serve with dals and or curries. These are heartier and more filling than traditional chapatis and once cooled work well as crackers to serve with dips.

1 cup (250 mL) cooked quinoa, cooled
¾ cup (185 mL) cornmeal
¼ tsp good salt (p. 29)
¼ cup (60 mL) good oil (p. 26)
½ cup (125 mL) water
3 tsp good oil
2 tbsp good oil (about 1 tsp per
  chapati), for frying

In a food processor, pulse cooked and cooled quinoa until it becomes crumbly, about 1 minute. In a large bowl, combine quinoa, cornmeal, and salt. Make a well in the center and pour in ¼ cup oil and water. Work mixture with your hands until dough clumps together into a ball, about 4 minutes. Cover and let chill in refrigerator for 30 minutes.

Divide the dough into 6 evenly sized balls. Pour 3 tsp oil into a small bowl. Dip your fingers in oil and rub onto each ball, then knead in your hands as if making a snow ball. On a lightly floured surface, flatten each ball with your hands. If ball starts to crumble, dip your fingers into oil and knead again, then flatten. With a rolling pin, roll out each ball into a 6-in (15-cm) circle, about ¼-in (6-mm) thick. In a hot frying pan or griddle, heat 1 tsp oil. Fry 1 chapati at a time, about 2 minutes total on each side, until they are golden. Adjust heat as you cook, and add oil as necessary.

Makes 6 chapatis.

- - + Variation 1: Use corn flour instead of spelt flour.

 Variation 2: Add ¼ cup (60 mL) chopped cilantro, ½ minced green chili, and ½ tsp cumin to dough.

-
-
+ # Thierry's Brown Rice Savory Muffins

Residents and visitors to Bowen Island are still gloating over their good luck that Thierry Mohrbach, French chef and baker extraordinaire, landed on our shores direct from France and became part-owner of Artisan Eats restaurant. I often have lunch there, as it's a few doors from my store. He made this recipe especially for his customers on gluten-free diets. These muffins make a nice portable snack or meal.

2 tbsp good oil (p. 26)
2 cups (500 mL) roughly chopped
   mixed vegetables (mushrooms, red
   bell peppers, zucchini)
4 cloves sliced garlic
   • *To reduce Pitta: use less or omit*
2 tsp dried rosemary or Italian
   seasoning

1 tsp paprika
1 cup (250 mL) brown rice flour
½ tsp baking soda
¼ tsp good salt (p. 29)
3 eggs
½ cup (125 mL) butter, room
   temperature

Preheat broiler to high. In a large bowl, drizzle oil over vegetables and garlic. Toss with rosemary and paprika to coat. On a baking sheet, spread vegetables in a single layer. Roast under broiler for about 5 minutes, then turn and roast other side for 4–5 minutes (peppers should be charred). In a bowl, set vegetables (except peppers) aside and let cool. Place peppers in a bowl, keep covered until cool, then peel. Dice all vegetables, including peppers.

Reduce oven to 350°F (180°C). In a large bowl, mix flour, baking soda, and salt. In a small bowl, beat eggs. Add to dry ingredients. Cream in softened butter. With a spatula, gently fold vegetables into batter. Pour into lightly greased muffin tray and bake for 25 minutes, until a toothpick inserted into center of muffin comes out clean.

Makes 10–12 muffins.

ø

-

slightly + # Hockey Night in Canada Lasagna

I invited my friend Pauline to a potluck at my house to watch the finals of the 2011 Stanley Cup hockey playoffs between Vancouver and Boston. Pauline hadn't watched a hockey game in forty years, but she prepared something that was as fast and exciting as the game itself (but much tastier).

6 brown rice lasagna noodles
¼ cup (60 mL) fresh or 1 tsp dried
  mixed basil and thyme
1½ cups (375 mL) ricotta cheese

3¾ cups (890 mL) tomato sauce
  (p. 260)
5 cups finely chopped (1.25 L) kale
4 cups (1 L) shredded mozzarella
  (Pauline likes goat mozzarella)

Preheat oven to 350°F (180°C). In a large pot on medium-high, cook noodles according to package instructions, until al dente. In a bowl, combine basil and thyme with ricotta cheese and mix well. In a 7 x 11-in (2 L) baking dish, spread a thin layer of tomato sauce. Cover with 3 lasagna noodles, side-by-side. Top with 2½ cups (625 mL) kale, 1¼ cups (310 mL) tomato sauce, half of ricotta mixture, and 2 cups (500 mL) shredded mozzarella. Cover with remaining 3 lasagna noodles and remaining kale, tomato sauce, ricotta, and mozzarella, in that order. Bake uncovered for 45 minutes. Let stand 15 minutes before cutting into squares and serving.

Makes 6 servings.

Pauline's Delicious Pizza Topping

* (vegan) Pauline likes to keep a whole wheat pizza crust in her freezer, which makes preparing this recipe very easy. As Ayurveda does not recommend eating frozen food, I have included a recipe for pizza crust so you can make yours fresh (p. 231).
*To make vegan, omit cheese.

4 tsp good oil (p. 26)
2 cups (500 mL) sliced shiitake
  mushrooms
1 cup (250 mL) sliced green onions
1 tsp good oil (p. 26)

¼ cup (60 mL) Pesto Sauce (p. 259)
2 cups (500 mL) finely chopped kale
1 cup (250 mL) sliced red bell peppers
1 cup (250 mL) crumbled goat feta
  cheese

Preheat oven to 400°F (200°C). In a large frying pan on medium, heat 4 tsp oil. Sauté mushrooms and green onions for about 8–10 minutes, until mushrooms start to soften. Set aside. Spread 1 tsp oil around edges of pizza crust (recipe follows). Spread pesto sauce evenly over crust. Sprinkle with kale, onion/shiitake mixture, bell peppers, and cheese. Bake for about 10–15 minutes.

Makes 4 servings.

Rolanda's Spelt Pizza Dough

Rolanda has been using this recipe every Wednesday evening to make pizza for her family on British Columbia's Sunshine Coast. She suggests baking it on a pizza stone.

1 tbsp dry yeast (Rolanda uses
   Fleischmann's)
1¼ cups (310 mL) warm water

2 cups (500 mL) spelt flour
2 tbsp good oil (p. 26)
1 tsp good salt (p. 29)

In a small bowl, combine yeast and warm water and let yeast dissolve. Let sit 10 minutes. In a large bowl, combine spelt flour and dissolved yeast mixture. Add oil and salt and mix well, without overhandling, until it forms a dough. Place dough in a bowl. Wet a clean dish towel, squeeze it out, and place over bowl of pizza dough. Let sit in a warm dry place until it doubles in size, 1–2 hours.

Preheat oven to 450°F (230°C). Sprinkle a little flour over a flat surface and roll out pizza dough. Place on cookie sheet or pizza stone and bake for 3 minutes, until dough is slightly crisp. Remove from oven. Layer with pizza toppings (see p. 230 or choose your own). Bake for 10–12 more minutes.

Makes 1 pizza crust.

Cauliflower & Rainbow Chard Curry (p. 235)

Vegetables

In Ayurvedic cooking, vegetable dishes, often served in combinations of two or more, are an essential part of a meal. I have included a variety of dishes, some spicy and a few milder recipes, which you can use to take advantage of what you have growing in your backyard garden or find at ethnic or farmers' markets. I hope you enjoy foraging for your ingredients as much as I do!

slightly –

+

– # Simple Eggplant Baji

* When eggplant is soft and delicately spiced—as it is in this recipe—it is one of my all-time favorite vegetables.

*To make vegan, use good oil (p. 26) instead of ghee.

Bajis are a medley of sautéed Indian vegetables in which the whole becomes greater than the sum of its parts. This makes them very delicious; it's true alchemy.

1 tbsp ghee (or butter)
1 tbsp good oil (p. 26)
½ tsp cumin seeds
½ tsp mustard seeds
1½ cups (375 mL) minced onions
⅛ tsp hing (asafetida)

¼ tsp ground turmeric
3 cups (750 mL) diced eggplant
½ tsp garam masala
1 garlic clove, minced
½ tsp good salt (p. 29), or to taste

In a large saucepan on medium-high, heat ghee and oil. Drop 1 cumin seed into the oil to test; if it sizzles and turns white, add rest of cumin seeds and the mustard seeds and let sizzle for 30 seconds. Cover pan while mustard seeds pop, about 30 seconds. Add onions, hing, and turmeric. Reduce heat to medium and sauté until onions are golden brown. Stir in eggplant, garam masala, garlic, and salt. Cook until eggplant is soft, about 30 minutes. Watch this carefully for the first 5 minutes, and stir until eggplant softens. Make sure garlic doesn't burn. If mixture looks too dry, add water 1 tbsp at a time.

Makes 2–4 servings.

+

-

- # Cauliflower & Rainbow Chard Curry

 I wanted a new recipe for the fresh Swiss chard growing on my balcony, so I came up with this quick and easy dish that my guests really enjoyed.

"Rainbow" chard is Swiss chard with yellow, white, and red stems.

1 tbsp good oil (p. 26)
1 tsp whole cumin seeds
4 cups (1 L) cauliflower florets
½ tsp ground turmeric
¼ tsp cayenne, to taste
   • *To reduce Pitta: omit*

1 tsp good salt (p. 29), to taste
½ tsp ground black pepper
4 cups (1 L) chopped Swiss or rainbow chard
   • *To reduce Pitta: use 2 cups (500 mL)*
1 tbsp lemon juice

In a large pot on medium-high, heat oil. Drop 1 cumin seed into the oil to test; if it sizzles and turns white, add rest of cumin seeds and let sizzle for 30 seconds. Then add cauliflower, turmeric, cayenne, salt, and pepper. Toss to coat well with spices. Add 1 tbsp water. Reduce heat to medium, cover pot with tightly fitting lid, and cook for 3–4 minutes. Add chard and cook for another 3–4 minutes, covered, so vegetables can cook in their own steam. When cauliflower is tender, remove from heat. Stir in lemon juice and serve.

Makes 4–6 servings.

ø

-

- # Garden Fresh Swiss Chard

 You will be surprised at how much flavor this packs for the small amount of time it takes to cook. Chard is easy to grow, even in a container garden. It is rich in vitamins, antioxidants, and chlorophyll and has the "bitter" taste so prized in Ayurveda.

Vegetables with the bitter taste help detoxify and cleanse the liver.

¼ cup (60 mL) good oil (p. 26)
1 tbsp whole cumin seeds
2 tbsp minced ginger
6 cups (1.5 L) roughly chopped Swiss chard

¼ tsp ground turmeric
¼ cup (60 mL) lemon juice

In a wok or frying pan on medium-high, heat oil. Drop 1 cumin seed into the oil to test; if it sizzles and turns white, add rest of cumin seeds and let sizzle for 30 seconds. Add ginger and Swiss chard. Sprinkle with turmeric and toss to coat well. Cover with lid and cook for 3–4 minutes, until chard wilts. Stir in lemon juice and serve.

Makes 4 servings.

+

-

- # Braised Red Cabbage

 Jennifer, my yogini/horseback-riding teacher, and I do yoga on her horse, Moz. After she described the flavors in this recipe to me, I had to include it in this book. The ume plum vinegar is good for the digestive fire (agni).

1 tbsp good oil (p. 26)
1½ cups (375 mL) sliced red onions
1 medium head red cabbage, shredded
½ cup (125 mL) ume plum vinegar

⅓ cup (80 mL) granulated gur or
   panela or unrefined cane sugar
1 tsp whole cumin seeds

In a large pot on medium, heat oil. Add onions and sauté for 8–10 minutes, until soft and slightly browned. Add cabbage and sauté for about 25 minutes, stirring occasionally. Reduce heat to low. Stir in vinegar, gur, and cumin seeds. Cover pot and cook for another 20 minutes.

Makes 6–8 servings.

Gur, also called jaggery, is the first derivative of sugar cane with just the fiber and water removed, thus preserving its rich mineral and nutrient content—including iron, magnesium, and potassium. It has a strong flavor like molasses and resembles a semi-solid form of brown sugar. You can buy granulated gur, which is much easier to use, in Indian grocery stores. Panela is the Latin American equivalent and may be purchased in most health-food stores. If you can't find gur or panela, you can use unrefined cane sugar.

+

-

- # James's Star Brussels Sprouts

 (vegan)

James, a chef from Australia, shared this tasty recipe with me. Starring the sprouts (scoring a cross in the stem) allows them to quickly absorb the steam, so they take only 4 minutes to cook. Be careful not to overcook them!

12 Brussels sprouts
1 tbsp good oil (p. 26)
1 tsp crushed coriander seeds
2 fresh red chilies, minced
 • *To reduce Pitta: use less or omit*

2 tsp minced garlic
 • *To reduce Pitta: use less or omit*
1 cup (250 mL) minced red onions
⅓ cup (80 mL) diced tomatoes
dash tamari

Score the stem of each Brussels sprout by making a shallow crosswise incision. In a large pot, steam Brussels sprouts for 4 minutes, until tender. Drain and rinse in cold water to stop cooking process. Slice each sprout into three pieces. In a frying pan on medium-high, heat oil. Add coriander seeds, chilies, and garlic, and sauté for 1 minute. Add onions and sauté for 3 minutes. Add chopped Brussels sprouts and sauté for 2 minutes before adding the tomatoes and a dash of tamari. Cook until liquids have almost evaporated, about 4 minutes.

Makes 4 servings.

+

-

- # Stuffed Portobello Mushrooms

The rich flavor of baked portobello mushrooms inspired me to create this dish when my friends spontaneously came for dinner. These mushrooms are enticing to the eye, simple to make, and delectable to eat. Serve this as a main course with a side salad or soup, as a side dish to an entrée, or as an appetizer.

To test the heat of a serrano or jalapeño chili, smell it or taste the tip of it (have a spoonful of yogurt nearby to cool your tongue!).

4 portobello mushrooms, stems removed and reserved
good oil (p. 26) spray or about 1 tsp oil
1 tsp ghee (or butter)
1 tsp good oil (p. 26)
¾ cup (185 mL) finely diced onions
2 garlic cloves, minced or pressed
  • *To reduce Pitta: use 1 or omit*

½ cup (125 mL) finely diced red bell peppers
1 cup (250 mL) finely diced zucchini
1 tsp minced serrano or jalapeño chili
  • *To reduce Pitta: halve or omit*
¼ cup (60 mL) chopped cilantro or parsley
¼ cup (60 mL) grated Parmesan cheese

Preheat oven to 450°F (230°C). Lightly spray or brush both sides of mushroom caps with oil and place, tops down, in baking dish. Bake for 5 minutes, or until mushrooms begin to sweat. Remove from oven and set aside (but leave oven on). Finely dice mushroom stems and set aside. In a frying pan on medium-high, heat ghee and oil. Add onions and sauté until they become translucent. Then add garlic, bell peppers, zucchini, chilies, and diced mushroom stems. Cover pan and cook until vegetables start to soften, about 5 minutes. Turn mushroom caps over and evenly fill with vegetable stuffing. Sprinkle each mushroom with cilantro and Parmesan cheese. Bake for another 5–7 minutes until cheese begins to melt, and serve.

Makes 4 servings.

slightly +

- # ❀ Kate's Beets with Goat Cheese

This fresh delectable dish was served at a veggie potluck organized by members of the Bowen Island hiking group after we had all climbed to the top of Mount Gardiner. It was made with beets freshly picked from Kate Koffee's backyard garden.

Beets are rich in folic acid, which is beneficial to the female reproductive system. They are also good for alleviating hemorrhoids and constipation.

4 cups (1 L) peeled and chopped beets
½ cup (125 mL) chopped soft goat cheese

¼ cup (60 mL) chopped dill
sprig of fresh dill, to garnish

In medium pot on medium-high, bring beets and enough water to cover them to a boil. Reduce heat and simmer for 30 minutes, until beets are soft. Drain beets (saving water to add to soup or shake, or simply to drink) and add to salad bowl with remaining ingredients. If you want goat cheese to melt slightly, add when beets are still warm. Garnish with sprig of dill and serve.

Makes 4 servings.

ø # Granny's Bhindi

*

My grandmother always served this at our Sunday lunches. When she taught me how to cook, she told me not to be afraid of adding salt! I remember standing beside her in the kitchen in Mombasa, hearing her strong voice and hearty laugh. This dish is great served with dal, chapatis, and yogurt.

*To make vegan, use good oil instead of ghee.

3 tsp ghee (or butter)	3½ cups (830 mL) sliced fresh okra
1 cup (250 mL) sliced onions	½–1 tsp good salt (p. 29)
3 tsp minced ginger	½ tsp ground turmeric
1 green chili, sliced in half lengthwise, leaving end intact (so it appears whole and can easily be removed by the stem before serving) (optional)	

In a large frying pan, heat ghee. Sauté onions, ginger, and green chili for 2 minutes. Add okra, salt, and turmeric. Mix well and sauté for about 25 minutes.

Makes 2–4 servings.

+ - - Variation: Add 1 medium potato, thinly sliced in 1-in (2.5-cm) strips after sautéing onions and before adding okra.

Okra with Cumin

Cumin warms the cooling okra, making this dish calming for all the doshas. Serve with chapatis or pita bread and yogurt.

*To make vegan, use good oil instead of ghee.

3 tsp ghee (or butter)
¾ cup (185 mL) sliced onions
3 cups (750 mL) whole okra, ends trimmed

2½ tsp ground cumin
1 tsp good salt (p. 29)
¼ tsp ground black pepper

In a large frying pan on medium, heat ghee. Add onions, okra, cumin, salt, and pepper, stirring to mix well. Sauté for about 25 minutes, stirring occasionally.

Makes 4 servings.

-

 -

-
Okra with Tomatoes & Spices

*

I made this for a goodbye dinner for Aussie friends who had come to Bowen Island to help Kim and Jason build their hemp house. We sat at the Tunstall Bay Clubhouse and ate this with chapatis while watching the sunset over distant islands and ocean. My guests loved this dish and polished off each and every bite!
*To make vegan, use good oil instead of ghee.

Okra's superior fiber content alleviates constipation and acid reflux and regulates blood sugar and cholesterol.

1 tbsp good oil (p. 26)
1 tbsp ghee (or butter)
2 cups (500 mL) okra, sliced
   lengthwise, leaving tops intact
2 cups (500 mL) thinly sliced potatoes
   • *To reduce Vata: omit*
1 tbsp minced fresh ginger
1 tsp ground cumin
1 tsp ground coriander

½ tsp ground turmeric
½ tsp cayenne, to taste
   • *To reduce Pitta: use less*
1 tsp minced garlic
   • *To reduce Pitta: omit*
3 cups (750 mL) chopped tomatoes,
   with juices
   • *To reduce Pitta: use half*
1 tsp good salt (p. 29), to taste

In a large frying pan on medium-high, heat oil and ghee. Add okra, potatoes, ginger, cumin, coriander, turmeric, and cayenne and sauté for about 5 minutes, until potatoes get a bit crisp. Add garlic, tomatoes, and salt and cook for another 10–15 minutes, until potatoes and okra are soft.

Makes 4–6 servings.

Ajwan New Potatoes

*

Ajwan seeds have been used for centuries in India as a detoxifying spice. They look like small caraway seeds and are available in Indian grocery stores.

*To make vegan, use good oil instead of ghee.

1 tsp ghee (or butter)
1 tsp good oil (p. 26)
½ tsp ajwan seeds
4 cups (1 L) quartered new potatoes
¼ tsp ground turmeric

¼ tsp cayenne
 • *To reduce Pitta: omit*
¾ tsp Himalayan salt, to taste
⅓ cup (80 mL) chopped cilantro leaves

In a large frying pan on medium-high, heat ghee and oil. Add ajwan seeds and let them sizzle for about 30 seconds. Then add potatoes, turmeric, cayenne, and salt and cook for about 15 minutes, stirring frequently. If mixture looks too dry, add water 1 tbsp at a time. Sprinkle with cilantro and serve.

Makes 6 servings.

 Yams with Caramelized Onions

 Jennifer, my yogini and horseback-riding teacher, shared this delicious recipe with me. It is always popular at Thanksgiving or Sunday dinners.

3 tbsp good oil (p. 26)
1 cup (250 mL) thinly sliced onions
1 cinnamon stick, broken into 2–3
   pieces
4 large yams, cut into 1-in (2.5-cm)
   cubes

¼ cup (60 mL) water
½ cup (125 mL) raisins
⅓ cup (80 mL) granulated gur, panela,
   or unrefined cane sugar

In a large pot on medium, heat oil. Add onions and cinnamon stick and sauté for 8–10 minutes, until onions are golden. Reduce heat to medium-low and add yams. Sauté for 5 minutes or until yams are golden and onions a rich brown. Stir in water, raisins, and gur. Reduce heat to low, cover pot, and cook for 10–15 minutes, until yams are soft.

Makes 6–8 servings.

South Indian Roasted Sweet Potato Curry

In Mombasa, Kenya, where I grew up, we used to eat sweet potatoes roasted by street vendors, simply peeling off the skins. We would gather at "the Lighthouse" to socialize and watch the African sunset over the ocean. Here is a sweet potato curry that is nice on its own, or you can take it up a notch and serve it with Tamarind Chutney (p. 279).

*To make vegan, use good oil instead of ghee.

Curry leaves are available in Indian grocery stores. They are used in soups for their distinct flavor and healing properties. In Ayurveda, curry leaves are known to be detoxifying, cooling, and bitter. Personally, I like to leave them in the curry as they continue to add flavor, but if you do, warn your guests not to eat them!

2 tsp ghee (or butter)
1 tsp good oil (p. 26)
½ tsp black mustard seeds
1 sprig fresh curry leaves (about 6 leaves) (available at Indian grocery stores)
¼ tsp hing (asafetida)
1 cup (250 mL) finely chopped red onions

4 sweet potatoes, peeled and chopped
¼ tsp cayenne, or to taste
¼ tsp good salt (p. 29), or to taste
2 whole cloves
3 whole black peppercorns
1 cinnamon stick
¼ tsp ground turmeric

In a saucepan on medium-high, heat ghee and oil, then add mustard seeds and cover pan while they pop, about 30 seconds. Add curry leaves, hing, and onions and sauté until onions become translucent, 3–4 minutes. Add sweet potatoes, cayenne, salt, cloves, peppercorns, cinnamon stick, and turmeric and stir to mix well. Add about ¼ cup (60 mL) water (enough to just cover sweet potatoes). Cover pot and lower heat to medium. Cook for 5 minutes, uncover pot, cook for another 3–4 minutes. Discard whole spices before serving.

Makes 6–8 servings.

Curry leaves

Sindhi Baji

A delicious way to get your vegetables and protein in one dish—and calming for all three doshas. Although Ayurveda emphasizes eating fresh foods, this dish freezes well. I like serving it with chapatis, plain yogurt, and freshly sliced daikon radish. *Note:* Soak channa dal overnight (p. 182)

2 tbsp oil
¾ cup (185 mL) chopped onions
1½ tsp minced ginger
1 tsp minced green chili, or to taste
  • *To reduce Pitta: use less*
1½ cups (375 mL) diced tomatoes
  • *To reduce Pitta: omit*
½ tsp ground turmeric
½ tsp ground cumin
good salt (p. 29), to taste
¾ cup (185 mL) sliced carrots
4–5 cups (1–1.25 L) roughly chopped
  spinach

1 medium eggplant, cubed
1 cup (250 mL) chopped potatoes
1 cup (250 mL) cauliflower florets
1 cup (250 mL) broccoli florets
¼ cup (60 mL) soaked channa dal
  (chickpea split lentils) or use
  yellow split peas
½ cup (125 mL) water
3 tbsp lemon juice
good salt (p. 29), to taste
pepper, to taste

In a large pot on medium-high, heat oil. Add onions and sauté until they are caramelized, about 8 minutes. Add ginger and green chili and sauté for 1 minute. Add tomatoes, turmeric, cumin, and salt and cook until tomatoes soften, about 5 minutes. Add all remaining vegetables, reduce heat to medium, cover pot, and cook for 10 minutes. Vegetables will cook in their own steam; however, if too dry, add water 1 tbsp at a time. Add channa dal and water and reduce heat to low. Cook for about 30 minutes, until dal is soft. Mash with fork (or use food processor or hand-blender to lightly purée); leave some vegetable chunks. Add lemon juice, season with salt and pepper, and serve.

Makes 8 servings.

+

-

ø # Zucchini & Kale Medley

 Quick and easy, this is a summertime favorite.

1 tbsp sesame oil
2 cups (500 mL) chopped zucchini
2 tsp minced ginger

4 cups (1 L) chopped kale
1 tbsp tamari
1 tbsp aged balsamic vinegar

In a wok or large frying pan on medium-high, heat oil. Add zucchini and ginger and sauté for 1 minute. Add kale, tamari, and vinegar. Toss to mix well and cover. Cook until kale is just wilted, about 4 minutes.

Makes 4 servings.

ø

ø # Japanese Spinach with Toasted
- Sesame Seeds (O-Hitashi)

 This flavorful simple dish has been made since ancient times in Japan. It is traditionally served in Japan topped with bonito (tuna) flakes, but this is a vegetarian version. Shoyu is Japanese soy sauce.

¼ tsp good salt (p. 29)
8 cups (2 L) baby spinach leaves
2 tbsp shoyu

2 tbsp water
1 tbsp sesame seeds

Fill a large pot with water, add salt, and bring to a boil. Add spinach and blanch for 20 seconds. Drain in a colander and immediately place under cold running water to stop cooking process. Squeeze out excess water by hand. Divide spinach among 6 small serving bowls or place on a platter. In a small jug, mix shoyu and water, pour over spinach, and set aside. Add sesame seeds to a frying pan on medium heat and stir (don't let them burn), until they just start to pop. Immediately remove from heat and let cool slightly. Sprinkle over spinach and serve.

Makes 6 servings.

Spinach with Tamari & Ginger

When I am craving greens and don't have a lot of time to cook, this is always a great choice.

1 tsp good oil (p. 26)
6 cups (1.5 L) spinach leaves
3 slices ginger, 1-in (2.5-cm) round,
  ¼-in (6 mm) thick
2 tbsp tamari

In a wok or large frying pan on medium-high, heat oil. Add spinach and ginger and toss until spinach is just wilted. Remove from heat, sprinkle with tamari, toss again, and serve.

Makes 4–6 servings.

+

-

-  # Ameeta's Enoki Mushroom Bake

* I love the flavor and simplicity of this dish, which is enhanced when served with umeboshi plum paste, a condiment easily found in Japanese grocery stores. Umeboshi plum paste has a delicious salty-sour flavor and gets the digestive fire (agni) going. *To make vegan, use good oil instead of ghee.

3 cups (750 mL) enoki mushrooms
  (leave them in long bunches, without
  roots)
1 tbsp ghee (or butter)
  • *To reduce Kapha: use 1 tsp*

2 tbsp lemon juice
1 tbsp tamari

Preheat oven to 400°F (200°C). Arrange mushrooms on a 12 x 12-in (30 x 30 cm) piece of foil. Dab with ghee and sprinkle with lemon juice. Wrap foil to seal mushrooms. Bake for 10 minutes. Unfold foil package (be careful, as contents will be hot and steaming), and place mushrooms and their juices in serving dish. Sprinkle with tamari and serve.

Makes 2–4 servings.

- slightly +

Katrina's String Beans

When Katrina saw the big crop of string beans in my container garden, she gave me this recipe. Katrina uses a string bean cutter to slice her beans, while I simply slice them with a good kitchen knife

3 cups (750 mL) sliced string beans
¾ cup (185 mL) raw cashews
  • To reduce Pitta and Kapha: use less
2–3 tbsp balsamic vinegar

¾ cup (185 mL) dried cranberries
  • To reduce Vata: use soaked raisins
good salt (p. 29), to taste

In a medium pot on medium-high, bring beans and enough water to just cover them to a boil. Reduce heat and simmer for about 4 minutes. Drain beans and place in a serving bowl. In a dry frying pan on medium-high heat, toast cashews, stirring frequently. When they start to turn brown, remove from heat and set aside. Toss beans with vinegar, then add cashews and cranberries and toss again to mix well. Season to taste.

Makes 4–6 servings.

Cashews are not as rich and oily as other nuts and are considered to have a sweet and astringent taste in Ayurveda. They are a good source of protein, magnesium, phosphorus, and potassium. Toasting cashews not only brings out their flavor, it also makes them easier to digest.

+

-

-  # Oyster Mushroom Sauté

* In the fall when I walk in the forest with Reidun, who knows the difference between poisonous and edible mushrooms, I have found clusters of oyster mushrooms growing on moss-covered logs. (Of course, be wary of any wild mushrooms you pick on your own unless you are an expert.) The mushrooms should be cooked soon after being picked. I created this delectable easy side-dish to use up my harvest.

*To make vegan, use good oil instead of ghee.

½ tsp good oil (p. 26)
1 tsp ghee (or butter)
¼ cup (60 mL) diced onions
1 garlic clove, minced
1 cup (250 mL) diced oyster
  mushrooms

¼ cup (60 mL) chopped fresh cilantro
good salt (p. 29), to taste
Japanese pepper or ground black
  pepper, to taste

In a frying pan on medium-high, heat oil and ghee. Add onions and garlic and sauté for 30 seconds. Add mushrooms and sauté until they soften, about 4 minutes. Add cilantro, salt, and pepper, sauté for 1 minute, and serve.

Makes 2–3 servings.

Pasta with Broccoli

This is a delicious way to eat your broccoli. Vata and Pitta should use brown rice pasta with bran. Kapha should use buckwheat noodles (soba).

3 cups (750 mL) water
1 tsp good salt (p. 29)
1 cup (250 mL) brown rice penne or
  buckwheat noodles
2 cups (500 mL) broccoli florets
½ tsp good oil (p. 26)

¼ tsp dried chili flakes
  • *To reduce Pitta: omit*
⅓ cup (80 mL) shaved fresh
  Parmesan
  • *To reduce Kapha: use less or omit*
good salt (p. 29), to taste

In a large pot, bring water and salt to a boil. Add pasta and cook, according to instructions, for al dente. Add broccoli to pot 4 minutes before pasta is cooked. Drain pasta and broccoli. In a serving bowl, toss with oil and dried chili flakes. Add Parmesan, season with salt, and serve.

Makes 2 servings.

-
-
slightly +

Zucchini Pasta with Pesto Sauce

*

I love the simplicity of this dish, especially when I can make it using basil and parsley grown on my balcony and local garlic.
*To make this raw, don't toast the pine nuts.

"Pasta"
4 medium zucchinis

Pesto sauce:
4 cloves garlic
  • *To reduce Pitta: use only 2 cloves*
3 packed cups (750 mL) fresh basil
  leaves
¾ cup packed (185 mL) fresh parsley

1 cup (250 mL) pine nuts
½ cup (125 mL) olive oil (p. 26)
¼ cup (60 mL) sundried tomatoes in oil
4–6 sprigs parsley, for garnish
2 tbsp toasted pine nuts, for garnish

Using a potato peeler, create long thin strips of "pasta" from the zucchini. Include the peel to add color and extra nutrients. (If you have a spiral slicer, you can create even more interesting strips.) In a food processor, blend pesto ingredients until smooth, adding more oil, 1 tbsp at a time, if necessary. Toss with zucchini "pasta," garnish with parsley and pine nuts, and serve.

Makes 6–8 servings.

-

 +

slightly +

Zucchini Pasta with Raw Tomato Sauce

 raw

 vegan

This is a gorgeous raw dish, full of bursts of flavor that will surprise and impress guests.

"Pasta":
2 medium zucchinis
1 tsp good salt (p. 29)

Tomato sauce:
1 garlic clove
⅓ cup (80 mL) chopped onions
½ loosely packed cup (125 mL) fresh
   basil leaves
2 tbsp extra virgin olive oil
1 tbsp lime juice
ground black pepper, to taste

½ serrano chili (optional)
3 cups (750 mL) chopped fresh
   tomatoes
½ tsp good salt (p. 29)
4–6 sprigs fresh basil, for garnish

Using a vegetable peeler, create long thin strips of "pasta" from the zucchini and place in a bowl. Sprinkle evenly with salt and toss. In a blender or food processor, mince garlic and onions. Add remaining sauce ingredients, except sprigs of basil, and blend until smooth. Let sit for ½ hour, so the flavors can marry. Pour sauce over zucchini "pasta" in individual bowls. Garnish with basil sprigs, and serve.

Makes 4–6 servings.

 - + + Variation: Lightly toast ¼ cup (60 mL) pine nuts in a frying pan for a few minutes. Leave whole or mince slightly, then sprinkle a little on top of each serving.

Mint Raita (p. 265)

Condiments

Including a condiment in every meal makes it easy to get the six essential tastes of Ayurveda. Condiments need only be eaten in very small amounts (2 or 3 tbsps of the raitas, 1 or 2 tsp of the chutneys and pickles) to get our digestive juices going (or, as it is said in Ayurvedic terms, activate agni). They can also be a simple way to get some raw food into every meal, as encouraged by Ayurveda. Serve a few condiments in small bowls placed decoratively on the table—they add appetizing colors as well as sensational flavors to the meals they accompany. All of the recipes included here are relatively simple to prepare; in some, the vegetables, fruits, and spices are cooked lightly or simply marinated.

Homemade Yogurt

Yogurt replenishes the beneficial bacteria in our intestinal systems that aid digestion, kill some harmful bacteria, and help keep us healthy. Freshly made yogurt is so delicious and easy to make, you will wonder why you ever used store-bought. People who have difficulty digesting milk often find freshly made yogurt much easier to digest. Use only organic ingredients when preparing your homemade yogurt. And don't forget to save some to create your next batch!

Here is an Indian remedy for an upset stomach: ¼ cup (60 mL) fresh yogurt and ¼ tsp whole cumin seeds, crushed.

4 cups (1 L) whole milk
2 heaping tbsp yogurt (room
   temperature)

In a pot on medium, heat milk until it foams up. Remove from heat and allow to cool. Test with your finger; when it feels lukewarm (about 100°F/38°C), pour milk into a very clean or sterilized bowl. Whisk in the yogurt. Cover bowl and let sit in a warm place where there is no draft (such as in the oven with the light on) for 8–12 hours.

Makes 4 cups (1 L).

–

slightly +

+ # Mint Raita

The mint in this raita is refreshing and the paprika gives a wonderful sprinkling of color. See *The Modern Ayurvedic Cookbook* for more varieties of raitas.

1½ cups (375 mL) plain yogurt
¼ cup (60 mL) loosely packed, chop-
    ped fresh mint leaves
¼ tsp Himalayan salt
⅛ tsp paprika, for garnish
1 small sprig mint, for garnish

In a bowl, mix yogurt, mint, and salt. Let marinate for at least 15 minutes. Stir again. Sprinkle with paprika and garnish with mint sprig.

Makes about 1¾ cups (415 mL).

Raitas are yogurt-based condiments that add flavor to a meal and aid digestion. There are dozens of varieties of raitas, which are eaten in small quantities (about 2–3 tbsp) as an accompaniment to a meal. Raitas can help to cool down a spicy dish; however, their rasa, or taste, which is sour in Ayurveda, warms up the body.

-

+

slightly + # Okra Raita

The fresh and dry spices in this raita mixed with the crispy okra are so delicious, it'll be hard not to polish it all off before you get the whole meal on the table! Enjoy this raita with chapatis or any other lentil or curried dish.

Okra is said to lubricate the joints and alleviate arthritis and osteoporosis.

2 tsp coconut oil
3 cups (750 mL) sliced okra (½-in/1-cm)
1½–1¾ cups (375–415 mL) plain yogurt
2 green chilies, sliced in half lengthwise, leaving end intact
  • *To reduce Pitta: omit*

⅔ cup (160 mL) chopped fresh cilantro
2 tsp coconut oil
2 whole dried red chilies
  • *To reduce Pitta: omit*
½ tsp black mustard seeds
½ tsp whole cumin seeds
6 curry leaves (can be left on stem)

In a medium heavy-bottomed saucepan on medium-high, heat 2 tsp oil. Add okra and sauté until it softens and turns slightly crispy and brown, about 15 minutes. In a serving bowl, combine yogurt, green chilies, cilantro, and cooked okra and set aside. In a small saucepan on medium-high, heat 2 tsp oil. Add dry red chilies and cook until they start to turn black. Add mustard seeds, cover pot, and let them pop, about 30 seconds. Uncover pot, add cumin seeds, and let them sizzle for 10 seconds. Add curry leaves, reduce heat to medium, and toss for another 30–60 seconds. Don't let them burn. Pour spice mixture into yogurt mixture, adding every scrap of spice, which makes this dish intensely flavorful. Stir to mix well. Marinate in refrigerator for at least 30 minutes. Just before serving, remove red and green chilies and curry leaves.

Makes about 4 cups (1 L).

-
-
slightly +

Tzatziki Dip

Serve with crudités, falafel, or as a side to curries and dals.

2 cups (500 mL) grated English
  cucumber
½ tsp good salt (p. 29)
¼ cup (60 mL) extra virgin olive oil
1 tbsp apple cider vinegar
4 garlic cloves, minced
  • To reduce Pitta: use less or omit

½ tsp good salt (p. 29)
4 cups (1 L) yogurt (the thicker the
  better)
1 tsp minced fresh dill
1 sprig fresh dill, for garnish

In a colander, combine grated cucumber and salt. Place over a bowl for 1 hour, so liquid can drain from the cucumber. Squeeze cucumber with hands to extract more water. In a bowl, combine cucumber with remainder of ingredients (except garnish). Chill in refrigerator for 2 hours, garnish with dill, and serve.

Makes about 5½ cups (1.3 L).

-

+

-  # Daikon, Carrot & Watercress

raw

vegan

This crunchy, simple salad refreshes the palate. Daikon (white radish) is a great blood cleanser. If you can't find daikon (they look like giant white carrots), red radishes are a good substitute.

⅓ cup (80 mL) julienned daikon
⅓ cup (80 mL) julienned carrots
⅓ cup (80 mL) chopped watercress
1 tbsp rice wine vinegar

In a bowl, toss all ingredients together.

Makes 1 cup (250 mL).

−

 +

 −
Carrot & Raw Mango Pickle

 Enjoy this pickle with vegetable curries or dals and get your digestive juices going.

1 tsp good salt (p. 29)
½ tsp ground turmeric
¾ tsp cayenne
½ tsp ground coriander
½ tsp ground cumin
1 tsp fenugreek seeds
1 tbsp + 2 tsp lemon juice
1 tbsp good oil (p. 26)

2 dried whole red chilies
1 tsp yellow mustard seeds
2 tsp minced garlic
4 cups (1 L) julienned carrots
2 cups (500 mL) thinly sliced unripe
    mangoes
4 green chilies, thinly sliced

In a large bowl, combine salt, turmeric, cayenne, coriander, cumin, fenugreek, and lemon juice. Mix well and set aside. In a medium pan on medium-high, heat oil. Add red chilies and cook 1–2 minutes, until they start to blacken. Add mustard seeds, cover pan, and let pop for 30 seconds. Add garlic and sauté for 10 seconds. Remove from heat and pour this mixture into bowl of spices. Add carrots, mangoes, and green chilies. Stir to mix well; vegetables should be well-coated in spices. Marinate at least 1 hour (a few hours is better) before serving. Store in glass jar with lid.

Makes about 6¼ cups (1.5 L).

-
-
+

Cucumber Lime Pickle

Here is a simple, tasty pickle that will add lots of flavor and offer the raw food component that completes a balanced Ayurvedic meal.

1 cup (250 mL) diced English
  cucumber
½ tsp good salt (p. 29)
¼ tsp ground turmeric (optional)

2 slices ginger, 1-in (2.5 cm) rounds,
  ¼-in (6-mm) thick
¼ tsp cayenne
2 tbsp lime juice

In a large jar, combine all ingredients. Marinate for at least 30 minutes. Shake jar to mix ingredients before serving.

Makes about 1 cup (250 mL).

-

 +

 -

Red Hot Roasted Tomato Chutney

 This chutney gives you both sweet and sour tastes, and roasting brings out the full flavor of the tomatoes.

1 cup (250 mL) halved cherry tomatoes
1 tbsp extra virgin olive oil, or olive oil spray

¼ cup (60 mL) chopped fresh cilantro
1 green chili, finely chopped
1 tbsp lime juice

Preheat oven to 450°F (230°C). Place tomatoes on an ungreased baking sheet. Drizzle or spray with olive oil. Bake for 15 minutes, until tomatoes are slightly charred. In a decorative serving bowl, combine tomatoes with remainder of ingredients and let marinate for at least 15 minutes before serving.

Makes 1 cup (250 mL).

- + - Variation: Add 1 clove minced garlic and ¼ cup (60 mL) diced red onions.

-

+

slightly + # Tomato & Cucumber Cachumber

 This is a colorful accompaniment to falafels, dals, and other curries.

1 cup (250 mL) chopped tomatoes
¾ cup (375 mL) chopped cucumber
½ cup (125 mL) sliced onions
½ cup (125 mL) chopped cilantro

1 tsp minced green chili
  • *To reduce Pitta: omit*
2 tbsp lime juice
¼ tsp good salt (p. 29)

In a decorative bowl, combine all ingredients and let marinate for at least 15 minutes before serving.

Makes about 2½ cups (625 mL).

–

+

+

Simple Tahini

Tahini, made from sesame seeds, is a good source of calcium. It is delicious served as a sauce with falafel or, thinned with a bit of water, as a dressing for vegetable dishes and salads. I sometimes pour tahini over steamed mixed vegetables and brown rice for a quick and nourishing supper.

4 cups (1 L) white sesame seeds
¼ cup (60 mL) extra virgin olive oil

Preheat oven to 350°F (180°C). Spread sesame seeds evenly onto 2 baking sheets (2 cups per sheet) and bake for about 5–10 minutes, stirring so they toast evenly and ensuring they don't burn. When they turn golden, remove from oven, let cool slightly, and place in blender. Pour in olive oil and blend. Add more oil if needed to make a smooth paste.

Makes about 4 cups (1 L).

Pumpkin Seed Butter

Pumpkin seeds calm all doshas when eaten in small amounts. Try spreading a little pumpkin butter on celery sticks for an easy, quick, and tasty snack. The addition of a liquid sweetener is optional.

Toasting the pumpkins seeds makes them tastier and more digestible.

2 cups (500 mL) raw pumpkin seeds
¼ cup (60 mL) extra virgin olive oil
¼ cup (60 mL) sweetener: honey (for Vata and Kapha) or maple syrup (for Pitta)
¼ tsp good salt (p. 29)

Preheat oven to 350°F (180°C). Spread pumpkin seeds evenly on 2 baking sheets (1 cup per sheet). Bake for about 15 minutes, stirring so they toast evenly and ensuring they don't burn. Once they turn slightly golden, remove from oven and cool. In a food processor, pulse toasted seeds until crumbled. Add olive oil, sweetener, and salt. Keep pulsing until mixture achieves the consistency of a smooth butter, about 5–8 minutes. Vata and Pitta may add more oil; Kapha should add sparingly.

Makes about 1 cup (250 mL).

 - -

Variation: Omit sweetener. This tastes good on fruit slices (e.g., apples) that are already naturally sweet.

Green Cilantro Mint Chutney

Our family always has a jar of "green chutney" in the refrigerator. We use it for flavor as the "under layer" on our grilled cheese sandwiches or to accompany other dishes and snacks. It is balancing to all the doshas.

To preserve chutney, place in a container and add 1–2 tsp olive oil on top before sealing well. It will last up to 2 weeks in the refrigerator as long as you keep it topped off with a layer of oil and do not contaminate it. Ayurveda always recommends using fresh food, but this chutney freezes well (for up to 1 month).

1 bunch fresh cilantro leaves (about 6 cups [1.5 L])
1 bunch fresh mint leaves (about 3 cups [750 mL])
2 tsp good salt (p. 29), or to taste
3 tbsp extra virgin olive or grapeseed oil

• To reduce Kapha: use a light oil

6 tbsp lime juice (1–2 limes) (may use lemons)
1 tbsp agave nectar (optional)
1–2 tsp extra virgin olive oil (for preserving, see sidebar) (optional)

In a blender or food processor, combine all ingredients and blend to a pulp. If chutney is too chunky, while blending add an additional 1–2 tbsp olive oil (will reduce Vata) or lime juice.

Makes 1½ cups (375 mL).

Green Cilantro Garlic Chutney

 This second of two green chutneys (see p. 276) offers a delicious and pungent combination of flavors. Be careful, though—this chutney is addictive.

4–5 cloves garlic
  • *To reduce Pitta: use 2 or omit*
1–3 fresh green chilies
  • *To reduce Pitta: omit*
2 bunches fresh cilantro leaves (about ¼ lb/115 g)

2 tsp good salt (p. 29)
3 tbsp extra virgin olive oil
5 tbsp lime (or lemon) juice
1 tbsp agave nectar (optional)

In a blender or food processor, combine garlic and green chilies. Add all remaining ingredients and blend to a pulp.

Makes 1–1½ cups (250–375 mL).

   Variation: Cilantro Garlic Coconut Chutney

slightly

Add 2–3 tbsp grated coconut to the above mixture. The chutney should have a paste-like consistency; if it needs more liquid, add 1–3 tbsp lime juice. Serve with Dosas (p. 49), Inspired Pakoras (p. 90), or Baked Falafel (p. 195).

Tamarind Chutney

Tamarind pods, which grow on the tamarind tree—a large evergreen native to tropical Africa—contain a pulp that has a distinctly rich, sour flavor; it is mouthwateringly delicious and enhances digestion. Tamarind chutney is a great addition to any meal and is wonderful served with Inspired Pakoras (p. 90), Dosas (p. 49), or Baked Falafel (p. 195) or added to dals.

½ cup (125 mL) tamarind pulp (see below)
2 cups (500 mL) water

½ cup gur or brown sugar
2–2½ tsp chili powder, to taste
¼ tsp ground cumin

Rinse tamarind pulp once under running water and then, in a bowl, soak in water for 30 minutes. In a medium pot on high heat, bring tamarind pulp and water to a boil. Reduce heat to low and simmer. Add remainder of ingredients. Simmer for 5 minutes and remove from heat. Once cooled, rub mixture through a sieve with the back of a spoon into a bowl. Store in a sealed container in the refrigerator for up to 2 weeks.

Makes 1½ cups (375 mL).

Tamarind pulp is available in Indian grocery stores or specialty markets. Make sure you rub as much tamarind juice as you can out of the pulp. Discard pits and threads. The flavor of this chutney is slightly sweeter when made with brown sugar instead of gur.

–

 slightly +

 +

Papaya, Mint & Red Pepper Chutney

 raw

 vegan

Mint has a cooling taste, which complements the sweet and sour flavors in this fresh chutney.

2 cups (500 mL) peeled and diced papaya
1 tbsp minced fresh ginger
1 cup (250 mL) diced red bell peppers
¾ cup (185 mL) chopped red onions
1 green chili, minced
• *To reduce Pitta: use less or omit*

½ cup (125 mL) chopped fresh mint
2 tbsp granulated gur, panela, or unrefined cane sugar
½ cup (125 mL) lime juice
2 tsp Himalayan salt

In a bowl, toss all ingredients together and marinate for at least 15 minutes before serving.

Makes about 4 cups (1 L).

slightly – # Raw Date & Currant Chutney

Just a little will add sweet and sour tastes to any dish. A small jar of this home-made chutney makes a great hostess gift.

Dates are a good source of B vitamins and essential minerals, plus they're a great way to add the sweet taste to dishes without using sugar.

1 cup (250 mL) chopped dates
½ cup (125 mL) unsulfured currants
1 cup (250 mL) boiling water
½ tsp cayenne (or to taste)

½ tsp ground cumin
½ tsp Himalayan salt
2 tbsp + 2 tsp fresh lime juice

In a bowl or jar, soak dates and currants in water for 2 hours, then drain. In a food processor, blend soaked dates and currants with all remaining ingredients until smooth. Stir to ensure spices are well mixed; serve at once or store in an airtight jar in the refrigerator.

Makes about 1½ cups (375 mL).

+ - # Green Mango Chutney

Just thinking of the tasty flavors of this chutney makes my mouth start to water. When you see unripe mangoes, buy a couple to make this recipe.

1 cup (250 mL) diced green (unripe) mangos
2 tsp apple cider vinegar
½ tsp minced ginger

¼ tsp cayenne
¼ tsp good salt (p. 29)
2 tsp granulated gur, panela, or unrefined cane sugar

Add all ingredients to a jar with lid and shake. Marinate for at least 15 minutes, shake again, and serve immediately, or store in an airtight container in refrigerator.

Makes about 1 cup (250 mL)

 - - # Apple Raisin Chutney

This is a fabulous recipe to make with apples from your garden (or a friend's) or those you find fresh at the farmer's market.

2 apples, peeled, cored, and chopped
¼ cup (60 mL) raisins
½ tsp ground cinnamon
1 tsp minced ginger

⅓ cup (80 mL) lemon juice
¼ tsp good salt (p. 29)
1 tbsp granulated gur, panela, or unrefined cane sugar

In a saucepan, combine all ingredients and bring to a boil. Reduce heat and simmer until fruit has softened, about 25 minutes, stirring occasionally. If it looks too dry, add more water, 1 tbsp at a time. Serve immediately, or store in an airtight container in refrigerator.

Makes about 1½ cups (375 mL).

Roasted Fennel Seeds

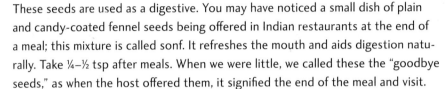

These seeds are used as a digestive. You may have noticed a small dish of plain and candy-coated fennel seeds being offered in Indian restaurants at the end of a meal; this mixture is called sonf. It refreshes the mouth and aids digestion naturally. Take ¼–½ tsp after meals. When we were little, we called these the "goodbye seeds," as when the host offered them, it signified the end of the meal and visit.

You can find more delicious condiment recipes in The Modern Ayurvedic Cookbook.

½ cup (125 mL) fennel seeds

Preheat oven to 350°F (180°C). Spread ¼ cup (60 mL) fennel seeds on a baking sheet. Roast for about 20 minutes, or until the seeds start to turn slightly brown. Cool, then mix with unroasted seeds in an airtight jar or container.

Quinoa Dark Chocolate Cake (p. 288)

Desserts & Sweets

According to Ayurveda, lovers who feed something sweet to each other on their wedding day will ensure that sweetness exists in their marriage. This taste is said to bring us bliss or divine essence (*amrita*). Just a little bit of the sweeter, heavier desserts will go a long way, especially for Kapha. Too much dessert, especially right after a main course, can inhibit digestion and create an imbalance in our bodies.

In this chapter, I offer a variety of sweets, from completely guilt-free fruit dishes and lighter desserts that can be enjoyed even while on a cleanse, to heavier desserts that nevertheless use healthy and wholesome ingredients. These recipes use a variety of flours, including quinoa, spelt, buckwheat, and nut—and offer many gluten-free options. You will also find recipes that call for granulated gur, panela, or unrefined cane sugar, which contain natural nutrients. I also recommend organic ingredients whenever possible, and baking powder that is aluminum-free.

Quinoa Dark Chocolate Cake

Serve this with strawberries and whipped cream for a sumptuous dessert. If you are a dark chocoholic, this is your cake! Quinoa gives it a great taste and texture and won't spike blood-sugar levels. I omitted the oil in this recipe by mistake once, and it still tasted moist, rich, and chocolaty—great for Kapha.

4 eggs
1 tsp vanilla extract
½ cup (125 mL) almond milk
2 cups (500 mL) cooked and cooled red quinoa
½ cup (125 mL) melted and cooled coconut oil

1½ (375 mL) cups panela, granulated gur, or unrefined cane sugar
1¼ (310 mL) cup raw cocoa powder
1 tbsp baking powder
½ tsp good salt (p. 29)

Preheat oven to 350°F (180°C). Lightly grease an 8-in round (1.2-L) baking pan and line with parchment paper. In a food processor, pulse eggs, vanilla, milk, and cooled quinoa to blend. Add coconut oil and blend until smooth. In a large bowl, combine dry ingredients. Pour wet ingredients (quinoa mixture) into dry and stir well to mix. Pour batter into baking pan and cook for about 50 minutes, or until a toothpick inserted into the center of the cake comes out clean.

Makes 8 servings.

Variation 1: Omit oil.
Variation 2: Add 1 tbsp grated orange rind and omit oil.

Raw unadulterated cocoa powder is what foodies call cacao, as chocolate is from the seed of the cacao tree. Cocoa is high in magnesium, which helps maintain normal muscle and nerve function (and thus prevents cramping), keeps our heart rhythms steady, and our bones strong, and supports a healthy immune system. Chocolate contains caffeine, so if you're eating it at night, go easy!

slightly +

ø

ø # Rolanda's Buckwheat Cake

My Italian-Swiss friend Rolanda gave me this recipe from her mother in Italy. This cake, which always transports me to a European café, looks enticing and elegant with icing sugar sprinkled over it. It's filled with jam—use your favorite (mine's strawberry). The buckwheat, ground almonds, and eggs make it so wholesome that I sometimes have it for breakfast!

6 eggs, separated
1 cup (250 mL) butter, room
  temperature
½ cup (125 mL) unrefined cane sugar
1 cup (250 mL) buckwheat flour

1 cup (250 mL) ground roasted
  almonds
⅓ cup (80 mL) jam
¼ cup (60 mL) icing sugar

Preheat oven to 350°F (180°C). In a bowl, with hand held egg beaters or a stand mixer, beat egg whites until stiff peaks form. Set aside. In a large bowl, beat egg yolks, butter, and sugar until light and fluffy, then add buckwheat flour and ground almonds. Fold in egg whites. Pour batter into greased 9-in round (1.5-L) cake pan. Bake for 50 minutes or until a toothpick inserted into the center comes out clean. Let cake cool. Slice into 2 layers and spread bottom layer with jam. Replace top layer of cake and smooth sides. Using a sifter, sprinkle icing sugar over top and serve.

Makes 8–10 servings.

-
-
+ # Joanie's Lemon Loaf

The lemon rind adds so much flavor to this loaf, and the sauce makes it truly sumptuous. Joan Santopinto, my friend and private trainer extraordinaire, serves it as a treat to her clients with blueberries and whipping cream.

When honey is heated to the boiling point, it becomes tamasic (toxic) in Ayurveda. When at room temperature or warmed, it is full of healing benefits and helps us to digest grain. Honey is balancing for Kapha in small amounts.

Cake:

½ cup (125 mL) butter, room
  temperature
1 cup (250 mL) panela or unrefined
  cane sugar
2 eggs
grated rind of 1 lemon

1½ cups (375 mL) sprouted spelt flour
  (found in health-food stores;
  unsprouted will also work)
1 tsp baking powder
⅛ tsp good salt (p. 29)
⅔ cup (160 mL) buttermilk

Sauce:

3 tbsp lemon juice
⅓ cup (80 mL) panela or unrefined cane sugar
¼ cup (60 mL) raw unpasteurized honey

Preheat oven to 350°F (180°C). In a stand mixer or large bowl with a hand-held blender, whip butter, gradually adding panela or sugar. Add eggs 1 at a time. Add grated lemon rind. In a separate bowl, mix flour, baking powder, and salt. Alternating with buttermilk, add dry ingredients to wet ingredients. Pour into a greased 8 x 4-in (1.5-L) loaf pan and bake for 55–60 minutes or until a toothpick inserted into the center of the cake comes out clean. Remove loaf from pan when cool and let sit while you make the sauce. (If you bake this in a 9 x 5-in [2-L] loaf pan, it will take 50 minutes to bake and be shorter and broader.)

In a small saucepan on medium, combine lemon juice, panela, and honey until warm, not hot—do not let this boil. Pierce loaf evenly with a skewer or toothpick and pour sauce all over it.

Makes 6–8 servings.

-
ø
+ # Pistachio Ginger Banana Muffins

I took these muffins to warm a gathering of friends who had gone swimming at night off Bowen Island in the phosphorescence, and everyone was delighted by the subtle and surprising flavors. Although Ayurveda recommends eating foods when fresh, these muffins freeze well for up to 2 weeks.

½ cup (125 mL) coconut oil, melted
  and cooled but still liquid
¾ cup (185 mL) granulated gur, panela,
  or unrefined cane sugar
2 eggs
1¾ cups (415 mL) mashed ripe bananas
1 tsp vanilla extract
1¼ cups (310 mL) spelt flour (also nice
  with sprouted flour)

¼ cup (60 mL) wheat germ
1 tbsp ground flax seeds
1 tsp baking soda
1 tsp baking powder
⅓ cup (80 mL) chopped pistachios
2 tbsp finely chopped candied ginger

Preheat oven to 350°F (180°C). Lightly grease a muffin tray. In a large bowl, combine oil, gur, eggs, bananas, and vanilla extract. Stir until just mixed. Fold in flour, wheat germ, flax seeds, baking soda, and baking powder, until just combined. Stir in pistachios and ginger. Pour batter into muffin tray. Bake for 45–55 minutes, until toothpick inserted into center of a muffin comes out clean. This also works well in a 9x5 loaf pan.

Makes 12 muffins.

-

ø

slightly + # Sugarless Bran 'n' Pecan Muffins

These muffins are delicious, hearty, and nourishing—and don't spike blood sugar. The secret ingredient? Dates. *Note:* Soaking spelt flour in buttermilk overnight makes them moist and easy to digest.

Soaking the spelt flour in buttermilk neutralizes phytic acid and increases the absorption of nutrients.

1 cup (250 mL) spelt flour
1 cup (250 mL) buttermilk
2 cups (500 mL) wheat bran
¼ cup (60 mL) wheat germ
2 tsp baking soda
½ tsp good salt (p. 29)
1 cup (250 mL) chopped dates

½ cup (125 mL) chopped pecans
1 tbsp grated orange rind
¾ cup (185 mL) buttermilk
 • *To reduce Pitta: use milk*
⅓ cup (80 mL) melted unsalted butter
⅓ cup (80 mL) molasses

In a bowl, mix spelt flour and 1 cup buttermilk and leave in a warm place overnight or for up to 24 hours.

Preheat oven to 400°F (200°C). Lightly grease a muffin tray. In a large bowl, combine wheat bran, wheat germ, baking soda, and salt and stir to mix well. Add dates, pecans, and orange rind. Toss lightly to separate and coat dates. In a small bowl, mix ¾ cup buttermilk, butter, and molasses. Add soaked spelt flour and buttermilk and stir to blend well. Add wet mixture to dry ingredients and stir until just blended. Pour batter into muffin tray. Bake for 20–25 minutes or until tooth-pick inserted into center of muffin comes out clean.

Makes 12 muffins.

Andrea's Apple & Cheese Muffins

These muffins have great texture and flavor and lots of wholesome ingredients that make them a fortifying meal or snack. Andrea (a fellow Bowen-Islander) says this recipe is a great way to use up aged cheese.

1 cup (250 mL) sprouted spelt (found in health-food stores) or whole wheat flour

¼ lightly packed cup (60 mL) unrefined cane sugar

1 tsp baking soda

1 tsp ground cinnamon

½ tsp ground nutmeg

1 egg

1 cup (250 mL) plain yogurt

⅓ cup (80 mL) olive or grape seed oil

2 cups (500 mL) cored, peeled, and diced apples

½ cup (125 mL) shredded aged cheddar cheese

Preheat oven to 375°F (190°C). Lightly grease a muffin tray. In a large bowl, combine flour, sugar, baking soda, cinnamon, and nutmeg. In another bowl, combine egg, yogurt, oil, apples, and cheese. Add wet mixture to dry ingredients and stir until just blended. Pour batter into muffin tray. Bake for 20 minutes or until toothpick inserted into center of muffin comes out clean.

Makes 12 muffins.

Andrea's Wickedly Good Coconut Cake

When I ran into my friend Daniella at the post office and told her I was writing the desserts chapter of my book, she said, "You have to get Andrea's Coconut Cake in there. It is wickedly good!" I immediately called Andrea who said, "I'll give you the recipe, because it is just nasty delicious!" Here goes!

1 cup (250 mL) unsalted butter, room temperature
2 cups (500 mL) granulated gur, panela, or unrefined cane sugar
4 eggs
3 cups (750 mL) whole-wheat pastry flour

1½ tsp baking powder
½ tsp good salt (p. 29)
1 cup (250 mL) coconut milk
¾ cup (185 mL) shredded coconut
Coconut Butter Icing (p. 295)

Preheat oven to 350°F (180°C). Lightly grease a 9-in (1.5-L) round pan. In a stand mixer or in a bowl with hand-held blender, cream butter until fluffy. Add sugar and blend for 6–8 minutes (get it seriously fluffy!). Add eggs 1 at a time. In separate bowl, combine flour, baking powder, and salt. Add coconut milk and flour mixture alternately to butter mixture, beginning and ending with flour. Pour batter into pan from a height of a few inches, gently drop pan onto counter a few times to get air bubbles out of batter. Bake for 25–30 minutes, or until a toothpick inserted into center of cake comes out clean. Let cool completely and ice with Coconut Butter Icing. Sprinkle with shredded coconut.

Makes 8–10 servings.

-
-
+ Coconut Butter Icing

1 cup (250 mL) unsalted butter, room
   temperature
⅛ tsp good salt (p. 29)
4 cups (1 L) icing sugar
¼ cup (60 mL) coconut milk
½ tsp vanilla extract

In a large bowl, beat butter with salt until smooth. Beat in icing sugar alternately
with coconut milk, adding a ⅓ of the sugar at a time and ½ of the coconut milk
at a time. Beat in vanilla extract.

Makes about 3 cups (750 mL).

-

 +

 -

Chocolate Chia Pudding

 raw

 vegan

This is as tasty as it is nourishing and uses only one bowl. Make it about 11 hours before serving so the chia seeds have time to expand.

2½ tbsp raw cocoa powder
3 cups (750 mL) almond milk
1 cup (250 mL) chia seeds
6 tbsp agave nectar
1 tsp vanilla extract
⅛ tsp good salt (p. 29)
1 kiwi fruit, peeled and sliced thinly, for
  garnish

In a dessert serving bowl, whisk cocoa with almond milk to blend well. Add chia seeds, agave nectar, vanilla, and salt and whisk again. Leave to chill in refrigerator for at least 8 and preferably 11 hours. Decorate with kiwi slices just before serving.

Serves 4.

- - -

Variation: Omit cocoa and add ¼ tsp ground cardamom and 2–4 drops of rosewater.

- + slightly

Berries with Cashew Cream

 raw

For this delicious dessert, Mother Nature did most of the work!

 vegan

1 cup (250 mL) blueberries
1 cup (250 mL) raspberries

1 cup blackberries
1 cup (250 mL) Cashew Cream (p. 298)

Toss berries together in decorative bowl and serve with Cashew Cream.

Makes 2–3 servings.

 + +  slightly

Cashew Cream

 vegan

This vegan classic is delicious and quiets the nervous system, so it's good for calming Vata. Serve over fresh berries instead of whipping cream. Feel free to adjust the amounts of lemon juice and sweetener to your taste. *Note:* Soak cashews for 7–8 hours or overnight (p. 31).

1½ cups (375 mL) raw cashews
½ cup (125 mL) water

2 tsp lemon juice
2 tbsp maple syrup

Drain soaked cashews. In a food processor or blender, pulse cashews to break up into crumbly bits. Add water, lemon juice, and maple syrup and purée until completely smooth.

Makes about 1¼ cups (310 mL).

 # Fruit Kebabs

These colorful fruit kebabs can be combined in a way to satisfy each dosha (see suggested combinations, below). Strawberries and grapes are easy to thread on whole; kiwi, pineapple, and mangoes need to be peeled and chopped first. *Note:* You'll need a packet of wooden skewers for these kebabs.

2 cups whole strawberries, hulled
1 pineapple, peeled, cored, and sliced into bite-sized chunks
2 cups (500 mL) whole grapes, green or red or both

2 cups (500 mL) peeled, seeded, and chopped ripe mangoes
2 kiwi fruits, peeled and cut into chunks

Thread fruit on skewers for each dosha, below. Serve on platter separated into sections by doshas.

Makes 10–12 servings.

Tridoshic
strawberries
grapes
mangoes

Vata
strawberries
pineapple
grapes
mangoes

Pitta
pineapple
grapes
mangoes
kiwis

Kapha
strawberries
grapes
mangoes
kiwis

Peaches with Mint &

Candied Ginger

Try this recipe the next time you find fresh peaches. This is one of those simple dishes where any individual ingredient would be satisfying, but the combination is exhilarating. My sister-in-law Sona's latest favorite summer dessert, she got the recipe from Daniel, a fashion designer living in Mauritius.

4 sweet juicy peaches, peeled and
  chopped
¼ cup (60 mL) finely chopped fresh
  mint leaves
½ cup finely chopped candied ginger

In a serving bowl, combine all ingredients well and serve.

Makes 4 servings.

+

-

- # Almost Raw Apples & Walnuts

 raw

 vegan

I wanted to get the most out of the apples my friend Jeto gave me from her tree, so I cooked them on the lowest setting in my convection oven, which brought out their sweetness while retaining their nutrients. I shared this recipe with my friend Julie, who now makes it every week, topping it with ice cream for an easy dessert or taking it with her as a trail mix.

¼ cup (60 mL) water
½ cup (125 mL) granulated gur, panela, or unrefined cane sugar

4 apples, peeled, cored and diced
½ cup (125 mL) chopped walnuts
¼ tsp ground cinnamon

Preheat oven to 175°F (70°C). In a bowl, mix water with gur. Add apples and toss to mix well and coat apples. Spread apples on a baking sheet and bake for 2 hours. After 2 hours, add walnuts. Sprinkle with cinnamon and bake for another 2 hours. Let cool, then store in an airtight container for about a week.

Makes 4–6 servings.

+

-

- # Applesauce

Karen grew up harvesting boxes and boxes of apples from her family's trees, so I knew she was the right person to test this recipe with. She told me that she always makes applesauce with imperfect apples, cutting out the bruised or insect-eaten parts. (By the way, this almost always proves that the apples haven't been sprayed with pesticides!) Serve in small bowls for a light dessert.

Apples are high in pectin, which helps flush out toxins and enhances radiance of the skin.

½ cup (125 mL) water
4 cups (1 L) peeled, cored, and diced apples
1 tbsp gur, panela, or unrefined cane sugar (optional)

1 tbsp lemon juice (optional)
¼ tsp cinnamon powder (optional)

In a medium pot on medium heat, bring water and apples to a boil. Reduce heat to low and simmer for about 10 minutes, stirring frequently, until apples have softened. Cooking time will vary with apple variety and ripeness. Taste before adding cinnamon, sweetener or lemon juice to see if you need it.

Makes about 3 cups (750 mL).

slightly +

slightly +

Rhubarb & Applesauce

Rhubarb is full of vitamins and minerals, is an aid for digestion, an anti-inflammatory, and lowers blood pressure as well as being an excellent source of fiber. Remember to use only the stalks—the leaves are poisonous! This sauce is great served on its own, with a dollop of yogurt, or as a filling for Almond Pie Crust (p. 305). *Note:* Soak raisins overnight (p. 30).

4 cups (1 L) chopped rhubarb stalks
2 cups (500 mL) cored, peeled, and
  finely chopped apples

1 cup (185 mL) soaked raisins or chopped dates
1 cup (185 mL) granulated gur, panela, or unrefined cane sugar

In a large pot on medium-high, bring all ingredients and enough water to just cover to a boil. Reduce heat to low and simmer until rhubarb and apples have softened, about 25 minutes.

Makes 6 servings.

- + +
slightly

Variation: Use 1–2 cups (250–500 mL) strawberries instead of apples.

-

 +

 +

Almond Pie Crust

Use this delicious gluten-free crust with your favorite filling, like Rhubarb & Apple-sauce (p. 304), and serve topped with ice cream.

1 cup (250 mL) almond meal (finely ground almonds)

3 tbsp butter

⅓ cup (80 mL) panela or unrefined cane sugar

Preheat oven to 350°F (180°C). In a food processor, blend all ingredients just until it binds (don't over process or it will turn into almond butter!). Pat dough into a 9-in (23-cm) pie plate. Bake for 10 minutes, then let cool before filling.

Makes 1 pie crust.

 - - +

Variation: Use room temperature, softened coconut butter instead of butter, and do not bake the crust.

 # Brazil Nut Coconut Balls

These are flavorful and easy to take with you for an energizing snack. Brazil nuts are full of selenium, plus other minerals and antioxidants. The balls are so quick and fun to make that once you start, you won't stop. If you make them for company, double the recipe so you have leftovers. *Note:* Soak Brazil nuts overnight (p. 31).

Eat a Brazil nut a day to get a good serving of the mineral selenium, which is great for the hair, skin, and nails. Selenium also regulates the immune system and supports the thyroid.

½ cup (125 mL) soaked Brazil nuts
½ cup (125 mL) shredded unsweetened coconut
¼ cup (60 mL) agave nectar

½ tsp vanilla extract
⅛ tsp Himalayan salt
¼ cup (60 mL) shredded coconut
8 dried cranberries

In a food processor, pulse Brazil nuts until reduced to a fine grain. Add coconut, agave nectar, vanilla, and salt, and purée. In a shallow bowl, add shredded coconut. Form Brazil nut "dough" into 8 evenly shaped balls with your fingers. Roll each ball in coconut to coat. Press 1 cranberry gently into top of each ball. Let chill on wax paper in refrigerator before serving.

Makes 8 balls.

Variation: Use soaked almonds instead of Brazil nuts.

-
-
+

Tania's Fig & Goat Cheese Sweets

Tania brought these tasty treats to my friend Jeffrey Simon's yoga retreat on Bowen Island. She often serves them after she teaches her yoga classes at Sechelt. Tania loves creating healthy recipes and sharing them with others.

1 cup (250 mL) toasted almonds
1 cup (250 mL) toasted walnuts
2 cups (500 mL) chopped dried figs
2–3 tbsp orange brandy (or water)
⅛ tsp ground cinnamon
⅛ tsp ground nutmeg or cloves

⅓–½ cup (80–125 mL) ground flax seeds
1 tbsp honey
¾ cup (185 mL) finely ground almonds
⅔ cup (160 mL) soft goat cheese
½ tsp ground anise seeds

In a food processor, pulse almonds and walnuts until finely ground. Add figs and continue to blend. Add brandy 1 tbsp at a time to help blend. Add cinnamon and nutmeg and blend to combine. Add enough flax seeds to thicken mixture and give it a dough-like consistency. Roll fig mixture into 1-in (2.5-cm) balls and press with your thumb to flatten. Dip each ball into honey and then roll in finely ground almonds. Place about ¾ tsp goat cheese on top of each. Sprinkle with ground anise seeds.

Makes 25–30 balls.

−

 −

+ # Chocolate Chip & Coconut Bars

(vegan) My friend Carrie, who looks vibrant since she removed wheat and refined sugar from her diet, offered me these "crazy good" bars. When almonds are soaked, blanched, and then ground, they are calming for Pitta and easier to digest for Kapha too, but should be eaten in moderation. Even though Ayurveda does not recommend freezing, these freeze very well.

To make your own ground almonds (almond meal), soak almonds overnight or for 6 hours. Blanch (p. 31) and toast or dehydrate almonds until just dry and crunchy. In a food processor, pulse just until finely ground—but no longer, or you will have almond butter instead!

1¼ cup (310 mL) almond meal
¼ tsp baking soda
¼ tsp good salt (p. 29)
3½ tbsp melted and cooled coconut oil,
1 tsp vanilla extract
¼ cup (60 mL) agave nectar
½ cup (125 mL) unsweetened shredded coconut

¼ cup (60 mL) chopped pecans
½ cup (125 mL) pumpkin seeds
½ cup (125 mL) sunflower seeds
¼ cup (60 mL) chopped raisins
¼ cup (60 mL) dark chocolate chips

Preheat oven to 350°F (180°C). In a large bowl, combine almond meal, baking soda, and salt. In another bowl, mix coconut oil, vanilla, and agave nectar and add to almond meal. Stir in coconut, pecans, pumpkin and sunflower seeds, raisins, and chocolate chips. Grease an 8 x 8-in (20 x 20-cm) baking pan and/or line with parchment paper to make it easier to remove. Press mixture into pan evenly, wetting hands to help pat the dough down firmly. Bake for 20 minutes or until golden brown. Cool before cutting into squares.

Makes 8 bars.

Mixed Nut & Seed Brittle Pak

When I was growing up in Kenya, we would eat these tasty treats, called pak (pronounced "paahk"), on the train we took to get to our boarding school 500 miles away from home in the Rift Valley.

½ cup (125 mL) granulated gur, panela, or unrefined cane sugar
½ cup (125 mL) agave nectar or maple syrup
¼ cup (60 mL) sunflower seeds

¼ cup (60 mL) pumpkin seeds
¼ cup (60 mL) sesame seeds
½ cup (125 mL) blanched almonds
¼ cup (60 mL) almond flour

Preheat oven to 300°F (150°C). Grease a baking tray. In a pot on medium, heat gur and agave nectar but do not boil. Remove from heat and mix in all remaining ingredients. Spread on baking tray and bake for 20 minutes. Cut into squares while still warm, then let cool. Store in airtight jars or tins for about a month.

Makes 16–20 squares.

slightly

Variation:
½ cup (125 mL) granulated gur, panela, or unrefined cane sugar
½ cup (125 mL) agave nectar
½ cup (125 mL) sunflower seeds
½ cup (125 mL) pumpkin seeds
½ cup (125 mL) sunflower seed flour (grind sunflower seeds in clean coffee grinder or blender until pulverized)

Follow instructions as above.

−

 +

 +

Shaheen's Almond Energy Pak

Gum arabic, harvested from wild acacia trees that grow in the Sudan, sub-Saharan areas, and west Asia, has been used for centuries. It is a baking stabilizer and is said to have many healing properties, including benefiting the gums and lowering cholesterol levels. The twigs of the acacia tree are considered in India to be natural toothbrushes and prevent bleeding gums; my grandmother, who always used acacia twigs, had all her teeth until she died when she was in her nineties. Gum arabic is available at Indian grocery stores.

My friend Shaheen, who manages to stay balanced despite her busy schedule, gave me the recipe for this protein-packed energy snack. Nuts are restorative, nutrient-filled, and warming in Ayurveda.

1 tbsp good oil (p. 26)
2 tbsp gum arabic
4 cups (1 L) unsalted butter or ghee
¼ tsp cardamom seeds
¼ tsp ground cardamom
¼ tsp ground nutmeg
¼ tsp saffron
4 cups (1 L) semolina or cream of
   wheat
½ cup (125 mL) granulated gur, panela,
   or unrefined cane sugar
4 cups (1 L) chopped almonds

2½ 14-oz (398-mL) cans (just over 4⅓
   cups [1.02 L]) sweetened condensed
   milk
¾ tsp cardamom seeds
1¼ tsp ground cardamom
¾ tsp ground nutmeg
¾ tsp saffron
1 tbsp ground poppy seeds
3 tbsp slivered almonds, for garnish
3 tbsp slightly crushed pistachios, for
   garnish

In a small frying pan on medium high, heat oil. Add gum arabic and sauté until it swells. Remove and drain on a paper towel or in a colander and set aside. In a large pot on medium heat, add butter and ¼ tsp cardamom seeds, ¼ tsp ground cardamom, ¼ tsp ground nutmeg, and ¼ tsp saffron. When melted, add semolina and cook on low until the mixture turns a golden brown. Add gur and stir to mix well. Remove from heat and fold in almonds until well coated. Add condensed milk and toss to coat all ingredients. Return to stove on medium heat. Add remaining cardamom seeds, ground cardamom, nutmeg, saffron, and gum arabic. Stir for 5 minutes until oil begins to ooze out (do not overheat). Pour onto a greased 18 x 13-in (46 x 20-cm) baking pan and spread evenly. Flatten mixture with back of wide wooden spoon. Sprinkle evenly with poppy seeds, slivered almonds, and pistachios. Use a wide sharp knife to cut into squares. Let sit overnight at room temperature. Carefully remove squares to serve.

Makes about 24 3-in (8-cm) squares.

-
-
+

Traditional Kulfi (Ice Cream)

Kulfi is Indian ice cream; this is the recipe for the traditional version, using kulfi molds (available at Indian grocery stores)—definitely a labor of love. (Two short versions follow, but I had to show you purists the real thing!) *Note:* Soak nuts overnight (p. 31).

Kulfi containers are conical molds made from tin. They have lids that can be screwed on and off to make the ice cream easier to remove. Simply run the kulfi mold under hot water, then shake the ice cream into a serving bowl.

8 cups (2 L) whole milk
8 cardamom pods, slit open at ends
8 tbsp granulated gur, panela, or unrefined cane sugar
1 tbsp soaked, blanched, and finely
  chopped almonds

1 tbsp soaked, blanched, and finely
  chopped pistachios
4 drops rosewater
3 sheets edible silver leaf (vark or varak
  in Hindi), optional

In a heavy-bottomed saucepan on medium-high, combine milk and cardamom pods and bring to a boil. Immediately reduce heat to low and simmer, stirring frequently, for about 2 hours, until the milk has reduced to ⅓ of original amount, about 3 cups (750 mL). Keep stirring in any skin that forms on top. Stir in gur and simmer for 5 minutes, then strain mixture into a heat-proof bowl. Add almonds and pistachios and let cool. Stir in rosewater. Pour into ⅓-cup (80-mL) kulfi molds and freeze for at least 4 hours. Empty molds and decorate with silver leaf.

Makes 9 kulfis or servings.

–

 –

 +

Mango Coconut Kulfi

 *

Quick, easy, and delicious. This kulfi has a fabulous peachy orange color from the mangoes and saffron and great texture from the almonds and pistachios. I served these to my yoga clients at our summer party and it was a big hit. If you don't have kulfi molds, use muffin tins. *Note:* Soak almonds overnight (p. 31).

Saffron strands (or threads) are the dried stigmas from the saffron crocus. They are the world's most expensive spice, but a little goes a long way. They are known to revitalize the blood and circulation, as well as alleviate migraine headaches. Look for brightness in the color.

½–1 tsp saffron strands
1¾ (415 mL) cups coconut milk
½ cup (125 mL) soaked and
 blanched almonds

4 cups (1 L) finely chopped mangoes
½ cup (125 mL) agave nectar
⅛ tsp ground cardamom
¼ cup (60 mL) pistachios

In a bowl, add saffron strands to coconut milk and set aside to dissolve for at least 5 minutes. In a food processor, pulse almonds until finely minced, then add mangoes, agave nectar, cardamom, and coconut milk mixture and purée. Add pistachios and pulse a few times to break them up a little, but do not purée. Pour into kulfi molds (or muffin tray) and freeze for at least 4 hours. Let sit at room temperature for about 20 minutes or briefly place in a shallow bath of boiling water to help loosen kulfi from containers.

Makes 10–12 kulfis or servings.

-
+
+

Banana Chocolate Kulfi

This kulfi looks great garnished with fresh raspberries and mint.
*To make raw, dissolve gur in lukewarm, not boiling, water.

¼ cup (60 mL) granulated gur, panela, or unrefined cane sugar
¼ cup (60 mL) boiling water

2 cups (500 mL) sliced bananas
⅓ cup cocoa powder
⅓ cup (80 mL) pistachios

Mix gur and boiling water in a mug and stir until dissolved. In a food processor, blend all other ingredients until smooth. Add dissolved gur and blend again. Some bits of banana or pistachios may still be visible; don't worry, they give the kulfi a nice texture. Spoon mixture evenly into kulfi molds or a muffin tray and freeze for at least 4 hours. Let sit at room temperature for about 20 minutes or briefly place in a shallow bath of boiling water to help loosen the kulfi from the molds.

Makes 6–8 kulfis or servings.

-
-
+ # Fragrant Sago Pearl Pudding

Making this pudding reminds me of making risotto, as it's necessary to stir steadily for 15–20 minutes. Just put on some good music and enjoy doing one thing at a time! It has many layers of flavor, so savor each bite.

Sago pearls are made from the sago palm and are used in Indian desserts. According to Ayurveda they are cooling and balancing to the body. Desserts made from sago also offer simple good nourishment, especially if recovering from an illness.

1 cup (250 mL) sago pearls (available in Indian grocery stores)
2 cups water (for soaking)
2 cups (500 mL) whole milk
2 cups water (for cooking)
½–¾ cup (125–185 mL) granulated gur, panela, or unrefined cane sugar
3 cardamom pods, slit open at ends

3 slices ginger, 1-in (2.5-cm) rounds, ¼-in (6-mm) thick
¼ tsp saffron threads (optional)
⅓ cup (80 mL) roughly chopped pistachios, for garnish (optional)
edible flowers, such as nasturtiums, for garnish (optional)

In a bowl, combine sago pearls with water and soak for 30 minutes. Drain water, then add soaked pearls to medium pot on medium-high. Add 2 cups (500 mL) water and all remaining ingredients, except pistachios and flowers. Bring to a boil, then reduce heat to medium-low. To prevent lumps, stir constantly for 15–20 minutes. Remove from heat. Put pistachios in paper bag and use a rolling pin to gently crush. Garnish pudding with pistachios and edible flowers.

Makes 4–6 servings.

- - + Variation: Garnish with ⅓ cup (80 mL) black currants.

-
-
+ # Oatmeal Chocolate Chip Cookies

My friend Pauline has been making these yummy cookies with children for years. She always uses organic ingredients to keep them wholesome.

½ cup (125 mL) panela or other unrefined cane sugar
½ cup (125 mL) butter, room temperature
2 eggs
2 cups (500 mL) rolled oats

1¼ (310 mL) cups whole spelt flour
⅔ tsp baking soda
1 cup (250 mL) very dark chocolate chips (or chop up a dark chocolate bar)
1 cup (250 mL) chopped walnuts

Preheat oven to 350°F (180°C). Lightly grease a baking sheet. In a large bowl, beat sugar and butter until well blended. Stir in eggs and mix well. In another bowl, combine rolled oats, flour, and baking soda. Add to butter mixture and mix well. Stir in chocolate chips and nuts. Drop heaping tbsps of dough onto baking sheet. Bake for 10–12 minutes, until cookies are light golden brown.

Makes 24 cookies.

+

 -

slightly +

Andrea's Carob Chip Cookies

Andrea lived in Africa for just over a year and adopted twin boys from Ghana. She says this experience taught her to be grateful for simple things like baking pans and ovens. Enjoy these tasty cookies, which she loves to make for her boys, and think about what you're grateful for. (I have adapted this recipe to follow Ayurvedic principles.)

1 cup (250 mL) unsalted butter, room temperature

1–1½ cups (125 mL) unrefined cane sugar (I like it with just 1 cup, some like it sweeter)

3 eggs

2 tsp vanilla extract

2 cups (500 mL) brown rice flour

1 cup (250 mL) large flake oatmeal (not instant)

½ cup (125 mL) ground flax seeds

½ cup (125 mL) coarsely ground pumpkin seeds

¼ cup (60 mL) coarsely ground sunflower seeds

1 tsp baking soda

½ tsp good salt (p. 29)

1 cup (250 mL) carob chips

½ cup (125 mL) dried cranberries

• *To reduce Vata and Pitta: use raisins*

Preheat oven to 350°F (180°C). Grease 2 baking sheets. In a large bowl, combine butter and sugar, and beat until light and fluffy. Add eggs, 1 at a time, beating until fluffy. Stir in vanilla and mix well. In another bowl, combine dry ingredients. Add to butter mixture and mix until just combined. Stir in carob chips and cranberries. Drop heaping tbsps onto baking sheet roughly 2-in (5-cm) apart. Flatten slightly. Bake for 15–18 minutes or until cookies are firm. Allow to cool and store in an airtight container.

Makes 55–60 cookies.

Aromatic Whole Spice Rooibos Chai (p. 344)

Beverages

Try some of these nourishing hot and cool beverages instead of caffeinated drinks and notice how your well-being improves. Some of the smoothies and shakes in this chapter make sustaining, nutritional snacks and can even be used as an occasional meal replacement. According to Ayurveda, cold beverages suppress the digestive fire (agni) and so are not recommended, especially if the immune or digestive systems are weak. Beverages that are warm or at room temperature are considered healthier. Ayurveda also recommends drinking most beverages, whether hot or cold, between meals, so the liquids do not dilute your digestive juices.

-
-
+ # Almond Milk

A small glass of almond milk is a wonderful way to get your protein and omega-3 oils, which enhance clear thinking and lubricate the skin from the inside out. If you need to reduce Kapha, drink a smaller amount and omit the maple syrup, or use a little honey instead. Note: Soak almonds overnight (p. 31).

You can blanch almonds after soaking them. Drain, then cover in hot water. When the water becomes cool enough to touch, the almond skins will pop off easily.

1 cup (250 mL) almonds
3 cups (750 mL) water
maple syrup or honey, to taste
  (optional)

Drain soaked almonds and blanch them (see sidebar). In a blender or food processor, blend almonds until very smooth. Add water and continue to blend for about 3 minutes. Pour almond mixture through cheesecloth into a pitcher to drain off liquid; squeeze to extract any remaining liquid. Add maple syrup to liquid and mix. Save any leftover almond solids to add to other recipes calling for nuts and seeds or to sprinkle over your breakfast cereal.

Makes 3 cups (750 mL).

-
-
slightly +

Soothing Turmeric Almond Milk

Turmeric, a natural antibiotic, can help ward off sore throats. It's also good for the complexion. It will give a lovely warm yellow color to your almond milk.

4 cups (1 L) almond milk
½ tsp ground turmeric
1 tsp minced ginger

3 tsp unpasteurized honey, to taste
• *To reduce Pitta: use maple syrup*

In a saucepan on medium heat, combine almond milk, turmeric, and ginger. Warm, do not boil, then remove from heat, stir in honey, and serve.

Makes 4 cups (1 L).

-

+

+ # Raw Cocoa Shake

This is a fabulous way to start your day. Cocoa (or cacao) was prized by the ancient Incas, Aztecs, and Mayans for its natural energizing properties. In its raw form, it's considered a superfood, full of antioxidants. Cocoa contains a number of substances that act as stimulants, increasing the activity of neurotransmitters and unleashing endorphins in the brain. *Note:* Soak almonds overnight (p. 31).

½ cup (125 mL) soaked almonds
2 bananas
2 tbsp cocoa powder

¼ tsp good salt (p. 29)
¼ cup (60 mL) agave

Drain and rinse almonds and blanch them (see sidebar, p. 31). In a blender, combine almonds with all remaining ingredients and purée until smooth.

Makes about 3½ cups (830 mL).

-

 +

 + Cashew Cinnamon Nut Milk

This is a delicious, warming drink. Notice how it feeds your brain as well as your nadis (the energy circuits in your body). It is also calming when warmed up a little (do not boil) and consumed just before bed. *Note:* Soak cashews 1–7 hours before making this recipe.

½ cup (125 mL) soaked cashews
⅛ tsp salt
2 cups (500 mL) water

¼ tsp cinnamon
2 tsp agave nectar (optional)

Drain and rinse cashews. In a blender, purée cashews with water, cinnamon, and agave nectar until smooth.

Makes about 2½ cups (625 mL).

- + + Variation: Omit cinnamon.

slightly –

slightly +

slightly + # Blueberry Cashew Smoothie

Enjoy the tantalizing tastes of blueberries, which are an immune booster, and cashews, which are rich in omega-3 oils, vitamins, and minerals.

2 cups (500 mL) blueberries
2 cups (500 mL) cashew milk (use variation in Cashew Cinnamon Nut Milk p. 323)

½ banana

In a blender, purée all ingredients until smooth.

Makes about 3–3½ cups (750–830 mL).

 # Hemp Milk

I like to use this in my rooibos tea (p. 343). Hemp seeds, unlike almonds, do not have to be soaked before blending, so you can make this quickly. You will never run out of milk again as long as you have hemp seeds around!

½ cup (125 mL) hemp seeds
1½ cups (375 mL) water

In a blender, purée hemp seeds with water at high speed until smooth.

Makes about 2 cups (500 mL).

Hemp seeds are one of the best sources of essential fatty acids (EFAs) in the plant kingdom. EFAs give luster to skin, eyes, and hair and are an essential brain food. Hemp seeds do not contain THC (the active chemical in marijuana) but are full of healthy minerals (such as calcium, magnesium, phosphorous, and potassium) as well as protein and vitamin A. Enjoy the subtle, nutty flavor of raw hemp seeds sprinkled on porridge, shakes, salads, and steamed vegetables.

-
+
+ 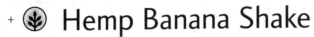 # Hemp Banana Shake

This yummy drink is a great way to start your day, but you can enjoy it any time!

1 cup (250 mL) hemp seeds
4 cups (1 L) water
1 large banana (about 1½ cups
   mashed)

1 tbsp coconut butter
1 tbsp vanilla extract

In a blender, purée all ingredients until smooth.

Makes about 6 cups (1.5 L).

Coconut butter boosts metabolism, regulates the thyroid, gives us lots of energy, and can help us to manage our weight as it contains fats that are easily burned by our bodies. It boosts good cholesterol (HDL) and reduces bad (LDL). Coconut butter is also antibacterial. Ensure that you use raw, unadulterated coconut oil (usually sold in tubs), found in reputable health-food stores.

+

 -

slightly + # Pistachio Coconut Dream

raw

vegan

Rosewater is available in Indian grocers and is potent—do not use more than 2–3 drops. Don't worry about getting all the pistachios completely pulverized; the bits are nice to chew on as you sip it. Serve in clear glasses; shake and swivel each glass to bring the nuts to the surface before drinking.

Rosewater, used since ancient times, has a wonderful fragrance and subtle flavor. It calms Pitta, bringing out his/ her sweetness, is antibacterial, aids digestion, and is rich in flavonoids, vitamins, and minerals. Rosewater also helps lower the risk of bladder infections.

½ cup (125 mL) pistachios
1½ cups (375 mL) coconut water
1 cup (250 mL) almond milk
3 drops rosewater or vanilla extract

In a blender, purée all ingredients until smooth and serve.

Makes 2⅓ cups (552 mL).

+

-

-

Pear, Coconut & Greens Shake

This is a delicious, nourishing drink with an unusual and rich combination of tastes. I like to pick the baby Swiss chard leaves from my garden and use them in this shake. *Note:* Soak chia seeds before preparing recipe.

Soak chia seeds for 11 hours so they expand to their full size. If you soak for less time, drink lots of water; the seeds will expand in your digestive tract and absorb the liquid in your body.

½ cup (125 mL) loosely packed, chopped Swiss chard
1 ripe Bartlett pear, cored
2 tbsp unsweetened finely grated coconut

4–5 cups (1.25 L) coconut water
2 tbsp hemp seed oil
⅓ cup (80 mL) soaked chia seeds
2 tsp (or serving size as directed on your brand) powdered greens

In a blender, combine all ingredients and purée until smooth.

Makes about 6 cups (1.5 L).

-
-
- # Digestive Ginger & Cumin Lassi

 A "lassi" is a natural yogurt drink. This is all about instant nourishment! Increase the salt to ¼ tsp when you're losing body fluids through perspiration in the heat of summer.

1 cup (250 mL) plain yogurt	⅛ tsp salt
1 tsp grated ginger	4 cups (1 L) water
½ tsp ground cumin	

In a blender, purée all ingredients until smooth.

Makes about 5 cups (1.25 L).

- - - Variation: Use 1 cup (250 mL) kefir instead of yogurt.

-
-
+ Classic Mango Lassi

Cardamom is calming to all doshas and adds a wonderful warming flavor. The taste of this drink always takes me back to Africa; I remember sipping it under a mango tree. You'll enjoy this, even if you aren't sitting under a mango tree!

2 cups (500 mL) peeled, seeded, and chopped mangoes
1 cup (250 mL) yogurt
2 cups (500 mL) water

¼ tsp ground cardamom
2 tbsp agave nectar
short stem of bougainvillea or nasturtium, for garnish (optional)

In a blender, purée all ingredients, except bougainvillea, until smooth. Garnish each glass with bougainvillea.

Makes 4½ cups (1.1 L).

Cardamom comes in little white or greenish pods with tiny black seeds neatly packaged inside. These give a wonderful flavor to various dishes or drinks. Use whole pods with the ends slit open, leaving the rest of the pods intact, to infuse dishes with flavor. The pods can then be easily removed before serving. Alternatively, you can remove the outer husk and grind the seeds into a fine powder.

-
-
slightly +

Vegan Mango "Lassi"

This is as delicious as it is colorful and will leave your guests feeling blissful. I often serve this energizing drink at yoga retreats.

2 cups (500 mL) peeled, seeded, and chopped mango
3 cups (750 mL) water
¼ cup (60 mL) almonds
  • *To reduce Pitta: soak first*

¼ tsp ground cardamom
2 tbsp agave nectar, to taste

In a blender, purée all ingredients until smooth.

Makes about 4½ cups (1.1 L).

Mangoes are called the King of Fruits. Sweet mangoes are good for skin and beneficial to all the doshas. They are known as a superfood, as they are very nutritious and full of vitamins A and C. They also generate warmth in the body and are great for soothing sore throats.

-

+

+ # Kefir

Kefir is a traditional beverage that's been enjoyed for centuries in some parts of the world. It is a fermented dairy drink that tastes like a fizzy sour yogurt. Kefir is full of probiotics and aids digestion; as little as 1 tbsp a day can help to restore the digestive tract. Many people who are lactose-intolerant can enjoy kefir, which also has a relaxing effect on the nervous system. It is full of calcium, magnesium, and vitamins A, B, D, and K. Kefir must be eaten raw to preserve all these benefits.

Equipment needed:
1 1-qt/L wide-mouth jar
cheesecloth or fine strainer

1 tbsp kefir grains or powder (available at health-food stores)

2 cups (500 mL) non-homogenized fresh whole milk (raw, if available, is best)

In a fine strainer, rinse kefir grains with filtered water and set aside to drain. In a pot on medium, warm milk until it just begins to froth—not boil—then immediately remove from heat. Pour milk into clean wide-mouth jar. Stir in kefir grains to mix well and cover open jar loosely with a clean tea towel. Leave in a warm place (such as inside of oven with light on) for 12–24 hours. Strain kefir grains through cheesecloth or fine strainer. Store liquid in refrigerator for about 2 weeks. Kefir grains can be re-used to make another batch immediately or rinsed and stored in refrigerator in ½ cup (125 mL) water for up to 2 weeks.

Makes 2 cups (500 mL).

+

-

- # Cabbage Rejuvelac

This drink has a lovely purple color and tastes slightly lemony. It is full of lacto-bacteria, which promote the growth of good intestinal flora. Drink about ¼ cup (60 mL) daily or, if in need of deep healing, ½ a cup, 3 times a day between meals. Check on the Rejuvelac regularly as it ferments. I like to start this on a Friday if I know I will be home on the weekend, so I can keep an eye on it.

Equipment needed:
2 1-qt/L clean wide-mouth jars
cheesecloth
scissors
thick elastic bands that will stretch over
  jar mouths

6 cups (1.5 L) chopped purple cabbage
3½ cups (830 mL) water

In a blender, purée cabbage and water for about 1 minute, until well blended. Pour into clean glass jars. Cover open jars with clean tea towels and let stand at room temperature for 3 days. Monitor the jars for mold, and do not let them sit longer than 3 days, especially in a hot environment. If you find mold in any of the jars, discard the contents and sanitize the jar. After 3 days, cut cheesecloth into squares large enough to cover jar mouths with a 2-in (5-cm) overlap; wrap well with elastic bands. Strain mixture through cheesecloth into large clean bowl. Discard or compost cabbage pulp. Pour liquid into clean jars and keep in refrigerator for up to 1 week.

Makes about 6 cups (1.5 L).

Nimbu Pani (Lemon Refresher)

I remember enjoying this replenishing drink when I was growing up in the tropical beach town of Mombasa, Kenya. Now, my taste buds start warming up just thinking about the delicious sweet and sour flavors combined with the texture and taste of crushed cumin seeds.

Since ancient times, cumin has been used to aid digestion and calm the stomach.

1 cup (250 mL) lemon juice (juice of about 10 lemons)
• *To reduce Pitta: use lime juice*
10 cups (2.5 L) water

½ cup (125 mL) agave nectar, or honey
1 tsp salt
½ tsp crushed whole cumin seeds

In a large jug, add all ingredients and stir until well mixed.

Makes 11½ cups (2.7 L).

Crush whole cumin seeds in a coffee grinder (one you don't usually use for coffee) by pulsing 1 or 2 times, stopping when the seeds are semi-crushed. Don't pulse for too long or seeds will become pulverized. To clean the coffee grinder, grind half a slice of bread into breadcrumbs, then discard.

+

-

slightly - # Lime Refresher

Quench your thirst, refresh your doshas, and please your taste buds with this drink!

½ tsp crushed whole cumin seeds
¼ cup (60 mL) fresh mint leaves
2 tbsp fresh cilantro leaves
1 cup (250 mL) lime juice (juice of about 10 limes)

10 cups (2.5 L) water
3 tbsp agave nectar
1 tsp Himalayan salt
8 lemon slices, for garnish
8 mint sprigs, for garnish

In a blender, combine cumin seeds, mint, and cilantro. Blend until mixture forms a paste. Add lime juice, water, agave nectar, and salt and blend until well mixed. Pour into glasses with lemon slices, garnish with mint springs, and serve.

Makes 8 servings or about 12 cups (2.9 L).

Lemons and limes are said to increase Pitta and Kapha. A small amount is excellent, however, for cleansing the digestive tract and for stimulating agni, digestive fire. Limes are considered lighter than lemons and more calming for Pitta and Kapha.

slightly + # Papaya Drink

I grew up eating a slice of papaya with a squeeze of lime every day to start off my breakfast. Papayas fell off the trees that grew wild in our backyards in my hometown of Mombasa, Kenya.

3 cups (750 mL) peeled, seeded, and roughly chopped or mashed papaya
4 cups (1 L) water

1 tbsp lime juice
agave nectar, to taste (optional)

In a blender, combine all ingredients and purée until smooth.

Makes 7 cups (1.75 L).

Papaya has been used for centuries in Ayurveda to aid agni (digestive fire), relieve constipation, and keep menstruation smooth. If your Pitta is high, avoid papayas or reduce the amount you eat, as they are considered heating. Listen to the signals from your own body.

-

slightly +

+ # Pineapple Papaya Lime Medley

Pineapple is high in bromelain, an important health-promoting enzyme. It is great for digestion and reduces inflammation. This exotic fruit is also full of vitamins B and C and antioxidants. To get the most benefit from this recipe, drink it between meals. (Try it first thing in the morning and wait at least 20 minutes before eating.)

2 cups (500 mL) mashed papayas
1 cup (250 mL) chopped pineapple,
  with juices
¼ cup (60 mL) lime juice

¼ cup (60 mL) fresh mint
4 cups (1 L) water
agave nectar, to taste (optional)

In a blender, combine all ingredients and purée until smooth.

Makes about 7½ cups (1.8 L).

-
-
+ # Pineapple Pistachio Bliss

Try this as a pick-me-up the next time you're tempted by a caffeinated drink.

1 cup (250 mL) chopped pineapple
1 cup (250 mL) water
¼ cup (60 mL) pistachios

2 tbsp coconut oil
¼ cup (60 mL) fresh chopped mint
  leaves

In a blender, combine all ingredients and purée until smooth.

Makes about 2½ cups (625 mL).

-

slightly +

slightly + # Leisha Laird's Hawaiian Special

Enjoy the flavors and healing benefits of this fruit blend. The ingredients will help to balance hormones. As well, this drink cleanses the liver which can be affected negatively by stress. *Caution: Before using bee pollen, make sure you are not allergic to it.*

1 banana
½ cup (125 mL) açai berries (or blueberries)
½ cup (125 mL) chopped mangoes
3 tsp spirulina or chlorella

¼ tsp bee pollen (*caution:* see note
  above)
3 tsp flax seed oil
¼ cup (60 mL) water

In a blender, combine all ingredients and purée until smooth. Drink immediately. Makes about 2½ cups (625 mL).

Leisha Laird is a doctor of Chinese medicine. She says: "Chlorella and spirulina have great anti-inflammatory properties. This drink is great for clearing up imbalanced skin conditions. Chlorophyll (found in spirulina and chlorella, both available at most health food stores) nourishes the liver post-partum and is beneficial for breast-milk."

Leisha Laird's Fertility Smoothie

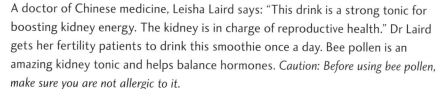

A doctor of Chinese medicine, Leisha Laird says: "This drink is a strong tonic for boosting kidney energy. The kidney is in charge of reproductive health." Dr Laird gets her fertility patients to drink this smoothie once a day. Bee pollen is an amazing kidney tonic and helps balance hormones. *Caution: Before using bee pollen, make sure you are not allergic to it.*

1 cup (250 mL) chopped spinach or kale

1 cup (250 mL) berries, your choice

½–1 banana, sliced

• *To reduce Pitta and Kapha: use less*

1 tbsp lemon juice

4 carrots (if not using a Vitamix or juicer, use 1 cup/250 mL fresh carrot or apple juice)

½ cup (125 mL) water

1 tsp chlorella or spirulina

¼–½ tsp bee pollen (*caution:* see note above)

3 tsp vegetarian omega oil or 1 tsp fish oil

In a Vitamix or juicer, combine all ingredients and juice until smooth. Or, in a blender, combine all ingredients (using carrot juice rather than carrots) and purée until smooth.

Makes about 3½–4 cups (830 mL–1 L).

Stop the Cramps Blackberry Drink

This is a traditional Vietnamese cure for menstrual cramps, given to me by my friend Tammy. Drink this on an empty stomach. It's relaxing and healing for men and women—and delicious as well.

3 cups (750 mL) blackberries
¼ cup (60 mL) agave nectar
1 tbsp chopped fresh lemon balm or
  mint

4 cups (1 L) water
⅛ tsp sea salt

Blackberries help to relax muscles in the stomach, bladder, and uterus, lessening cramps and urinary system spasms. Blackberries are also rich in antioxidants and vitamins and are used to alleviate anemia.

In a blender, combine all ingredients and purée until smooth.

Makes about 7 cups (1.75 L).

Rooibos & Lemon Balm Iced Tea

This is a delicious way to drink rooibos tea, especially in the summer. Ayurveda does not recommend iced drinks, so you may want to drink this tea at room temperature. It is important to steep rooibos tea for 10 minutes before drinking to get the full health benefits.

4 rooibos tea bags (or 4 tbsp loose tea)

1 cup (250 mL) fresh lemon balm, with stalks

8 cups (2 L) water

2 cups (500 mL) ice cubes or 1 cup cold water

3 tbsp agave nectar, or to taste (optional)

1 lemon, sliced

In a pot, bring rooibos tea bags, lemon balm, and water to a boil. Remove from heat. Steep for 10 minutes. When cooled, add to a jug with ice or cold water, agave nectar, and lemon slices. Stir and serve.

Makes about 10 cups (2.5 L).

Rooibos is grown in South Africa, where it's also known as redbush tea. It has a wonderfully calming effect on the body. It contains polyphenols and powerful antioxidants. Rooibos has a low tannin content and no caffeine, so the tea will never taste bitter, no matter how long it steeps. Its unique full-bodied flavor is delicious alone, but it also pairs well with milk, lemon, and/or sweeteners.

Aromatic Whole Spice Rooibos Chai

This is a delicious, full-bodied, spiced tea that is calming to all the doshas. I used to be an avid black tea drinker, but I now find that caffeine-free rooibos is a great substitute and doesn't leave me missing the taste of black tea. If you let it steep and then reheat it, the spices will have infused the tea and to make it even more flavorful. The nutritional value of the rooibos also increases the longer it steeps. Keep in a thermos and drink it throughout the day.

Keep all the dried chai spices in this recipe on your kitchen counter in a glass jar so you can make it any time—their varied shapes and textures of the spices also make a great visual display.

1 dried star anise
1 cinnamon stick
4 whole cardamom pods, slit open at ends
2 whole cloves
5 whole black peppercorns
4 slices ginger, 1-in (2.5-cm) rounds, ¼-in (6-mm) thick

4 rooibos tea bags (or 4 tbsp loose tea)
3 cups (750 mL) water
1 cup (250 mL) almond milk
• *To reduce Kapha: add 1 cup water or rice milk*
• *To reduce Pitta: use cow or goat's milk*

In a large pot on medium-high, combine all ingredients and bring to a boil. Reduce heat to low and simmer for 10 minutes. Strain and serve.

Makes about 4 cups (1 L).

Immune-Boosting Ginger Turmeric Tea

This tea is great for busting a cold before it begins. Ginger warms the body and, like turmeric, is an anti-inflammatory. Turmeric is also a natural antibiotic. A small amount of lemon juice cleanses toxins, purifies the blood, and increases digestive fire (agni) for all the doshas.

Unpasteurized honey has many healing properties that are destroyed if heated beyond 108°F (42°C). Honey should be added to hot drinks just before serving, once they have cooled down a bit, or it can become toxic (ama, in Ayurveda) and lose its beneficial minerals, enzymes, and amino acids. Honey is naturally warming and calms Kapha.

8 slices ginger, 1-in (2.5-cm) rounds, ¼-in (6-mm) thick
8 cups (2 L) water
1 tsp ground turmeric

4 tbsp lemon juice
 • *To reduce Pitta: use lime juice*
2 tbsp unpasteurized honey, or to taste

In a large pot on high heat, bring ginger and water to a boil. Reduce heat and simmer for 10–15 minutes. Remove from heat. Pour into teapot and add turmeric and lemon juice. Let the tea cool slightly (see sidebar) before adding honey.

Makes about 8 cups (2 L).

Variation: Add ⅛ tsp cayenne. Leisha Laird, a doctor of traditional Chinese medicine, gives this tea to all her fertility clients. It's a great drink whether you are trying to become pregnant, detox and cleanse, or simply want to enjoy a delicious cup of refreshing, warming tea. It's so easy to make if you keep turmeric, cayenne, and fresh ginger on hand.

-
+
-

Simplest Ginger Tea

Warming on cool evenings and tasty with or without a touch of sweetener.

3 cups (750 mL) boiling water
2 tsp finely chopped ginger
sweetener (your choice), to taste

- *To reduce Pitta: use maple syrup or gur*
- *To reduce Kapha: use honey*

In a teapot, combine boiling water and ginger. Let steep for 10 minutes or longer. Add sweetener, if desired, strain, and drink.

Makes 3 cups (750 mL).

Variation: Add 1–2 tbsp lemon juice.

Be Now Tea

 Jaime, a yoga teacher from Utah whom I had the pleasure of meeting through my online Movementglobal clothing store, gave me this dosha-calming recipe for a subtly flavored tea. She takes it with her in a thermos and sips it all day. Thanks, Jaime!

1½ sticks lemongrass, cut into 3-in (8-cm) pieces and unraveled
3 tbsp chopped ginger
10 whole cardamom pods, slit open at ends

1 tbsp fennel seeds
8 cups (2 L) boiling water

In a teapot, combine all ingredients. Steep for 20 minutes, strain, and serve.

Makes 8 cups (2 L).

-

 +

 -

Rosemary Tea

My friend Pauline serves this at our singing classes. It is very calming and helps us to overcome our nerves.

Rosemary tea alleviates headaches and fever and aids circulation. The scent of rosemary increases mental clarity.

1 tbsp fresh rosemary leaves
6 cups (1.5 L) boiling water

In a teapot, combine rosemary with boiling water. Let steep for at least 5–8 minutes, strain, and serve.

Makes 6 cups (1.5 L).

Healing Nettle Tea

When I was growing up in Kenya, one of my favorite hobbies was horseback riding. This was how my cousin Sonita and our close friends at boarding school spent our free time. We built secret jumps in the forests of the Rift Valley and cantered across open fields. I loved everything about riding, except getting stung by wild nettles that grew where we rode! Now I know that nettle leaves are very healing—as long as we collect them wearing rubber gloves!

4 cups (1 L) water
½ cup (125 mL) nettles
sweetener (your choice), to taste

• *To reduce Pitta: use maple syrup or agave*
• *To reduce Kapha: use honey*

In a pot on medium-high, bring water to a boil. Add nettles and simmer for 5 minutes. Pour into a teapot and steep for 15 minutes. Strain, sweeten, and serve.

Makes 4 cups (1 L).

Nettle leaves are full of amino acids and vitamins. This tea helps lower blood-sugar levels, which makes it beneficial for diabetes. Nettle has diuretic properties and is antiviral and antibiotic. It also helps alleviate anemia and has anti-inflammatory properties. Nettle tea can be consumed hot or cold.

-
-
- # Mint Tea

My friend Rolanda gives me large bunches of chocolate mint and spearmint from her garden, so I always have a nice fresh supply in the summer.

1 cup (250 mL) loosely packed fresh
  mint or 2 tbsp dried
8 cups (2 L) water

In a large pot on high heat, bring mint and water to a boil. Reduce heat to low and let simmer for 5–10 minutes, depending on desired strength. Strain before serving.

Makes 8 cups (2 L).

Mint tea has long been used to settle an upset stomach. To dry mint, tie the ends of the stems and hang them upside down in your kitchen. Once dry, crumble the leaves into a jar. Seal well and discard stems. Mint grows easily and needs little attention, so plant some in your garden and enjoy your home-grown mint tea year round.

Homemade Dry Mint Tea Bags

Keep these bags handy if you want to make a mug or pot of tea from your home-grown mint without the bother of straining off loose leaves in the teapot.

5 tbsp + 1 tsp dried mint
8 refillable gauze tea bags

Fill each tea bag with 2 tsp mint. Store in a jar. When ready to use, pour boiling water over a tea bag in a mug or pot. Steep for 3–5 minutes.

Makes 8 tea bags.

-
-
- # Raspberry Mint Tea

Raspberry leaves have been known to have medicinal qualities since ancient Roman times. They are full of vitamins A and C as well as potassium, phosphorus, and calcium. To dry, tie the ends of the raspberry stems and hang them upside down in the kitchen. Once dry, crumble the leaves into a jar, seal well, and discard stems. This tea helps to relieve cramps and upset tummies, and can be beneficial in postpartum recovery.

3 tsp dried raspberry leaves
2 tsp dried mint leaves
3 cups (750 mL) water

2 tsp sweetener (your choice),
   to taste

In a pot on high heat, combine herbs and water and bring to a boil. Remove from heat, let steep for 10 minutes, then bring to a boil again. Remove from heat, pour into a teapot, and let steep again for another 3 minutes. Strain, sweeten if desired, and serve.

Makes 3 cups (750 mL).

Relaxing Lemon Balm Tea

This tea has a wonderful lemony aroma and flavor. Lemon balm helps to promote sleep and reduces anxiety. To dry lemon balm, tie the ends of the stems and hang them upside down in the kitchen. Once dry, crumble the leaves into a jar, seal well, and discard stems.

¼ cup (60 mL) fresh or 2 tbsp dried lemon balm

8 cups (2 L) boiling water
sweetener (your choice), to taste

In a teapot, pour boiling water over lemon balm. Let steep for 10 minutes, strain, sweeten if desired, and serve.

Makes 8 cups (2 L).

+

-

- # Clarity & Strength Barley Tea

 Barley is said to give us strength, mental clarity, and fortitude. It is also a detoxifying tonic for the liver and alleviates coughs and sore throats. This tea is a nice way to get the benefits of barley, especially if you are under the weather.

½ cup (125 mL) barley, rinsed well and drained
10 cups (2.5 L) water
honey, to taste (optional)

• *To calm Pitta: use maple syrup or gur*

In a pot on high heat, bring barley and water to a boil. Reduce heat and simmer for 1 hour. Strain, sweeten with honey if desired, and serve.

Makes 10 cups (2.5 L).

 # Fennel Tea

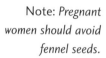

Great for stimulating digestion and calming stomach upsets, fennel (an antibacterial) is also known in Ayurveda to help sharpen eyesight and soothe coughs. Drink 2–3 cups (500–750 mL) daily. Kaphas should drink this only in moderation.

Note: *Pregnant women should avoid fennel seeds.*

2 tsp crushed fennel seeds
2 cups (500 mL) water

½ cup (125 mL) milk (optional)

In a pot on high heat, bring fennel seeds and water to a boil. Reduce heat to low and simmer for 10–15 minutes or steep in a teapot. Add milk if desired, strain, and serve.

Makes 2–2½ cups (500–625 mL).

-
-
-  # Miso Warmer

 Miso has a delicious savory flavor and has been used in Japanese cuisine for centuries. It's a good source of protein and an instant energy replenisher. Serve in small bowls or mugs.

4 cups (1 L) water
1 tbsp miso, to taste

In a pot on high heat, bring water to a boil, then let cool to drinking temperature. Add miso paste and stir well to dissolve.

Makes 4 cups (2 L).

- - Variation: Add 1 tbsp tamari and 1 tbsp chives or green onions.

Appendix

Raw & Living Foods

The raw and living food diet consists of eating vegan or vegetarian uncooked and unprocessed foods. Proponents believe that heating foods above 118°F (47°C) and for more than two minutes destroys digestive enzymes and nutrients. More people are becoming interested in this diet following studies that show the health benefits of consuming raw and living foods. But how does it complement an Ayurvedic diet? According to Ayurveda, the amount of raw foods you should eat depends on your dominant dosha (your individual constitution), the season, and your emotional and physical environments.

Ayurveda has always recommended that some raw foods be eaten at every meal to aid digestion and cleanse the system. The warm Pitta seasons are the best times to eat more raw foods. In autumn, the Vata (wind) season, and in winter, the Kapha (earth) season, Ayurveda recommends eating warming foods. In the cooler seasons, the body has to use energy to stay warm and may not have enough left over for the increased digestive fire, or agni, needed to process a completely raw meal. If agni is low (for example, during an illness), it can be taxing to eat only raw foods and may send the body even further out of balance. Each situation is unique. I have noticed that many pure raw foodists live in warmer climates and often have a Pitta constitution and a strong digestive fire.

If you are considering a raw food diet, consult the table "Food Guidelines for Basic Constitutional Types" on p. 390 and the information on pp. 21–23 for tastes that balance Vata, Pitta, and Kapha, as well as the recipes marked 🌱 throughout the book.

Vata

A completely raw diet is not traditionally recommended by Ayurveda for people with a dominant Vata constitution, as it can aggravate Vata. If Vatas want to follow a completely raw and living foods diet, they should do so during the warm seasons. To keep within Ayurvedic principles and to calm and balance Vata, choose more warming foods (e.g., dill, honey, mustard greens, fennel, horseradish) and grounding foods (e.g., beets, carrots, avocadoes, asparagus, and soaked nuts and seeds). Nuts and seeds should be soaked to reduce their dryness; this will also help reduce flatulence. Using good oils (p. 26) in dressings, and liberally using nut dressings when eating leafy greens or astringent and bitter vegetables helps to balance them for Vata.

As Vatas have a tendency to be dry, they should use watery vegetables such as zucchini, celery, and cucumber. Daikon or other types of radishes also balance Vata, as do cilantro, watercress, basil, tarragon, and a little parsley. Warming spices such as ginger, nutmeg, cinnamon, a little serrano and jalapeño chilies, and cayenne powder are also recommended. Heating some foods to a lukewarm temperature (between 110° and 150°F [43° and 66°C]) is still considered "raw" by some raw food practitioners, as these temperatures do not destroy the food enzymes. Heating foods slightly is good for Vata. Good salt (p. 29) and seaweed help to keep Vata in balance, as do warming teas, like ginger and rosemary. Fruits, especially sweet berries, cherries, plums, and citrus, are usually balancing to Vata.

Juicing vegetables with warming spices makes them easier to digest for Vata; juices can also be warmed, as long as they are not heated for more than 2 minutes and not over 118°F (47°C) so that enzymes are preserved.

Vata should eat meals in warm, cozy environments in which they do not feel rushed or forced to talk or listen to heated discussions. Meditation before meals is encouraged.

Pitta

People with Pitta as their dominant constitution have an easier time on a raw food diet as their agni, or digestive fire, is naturally strong.

Pittas should eat foods that are cool and grounding (as Pittas are naturally fiery). Hot spicy foods should generally be avoided. Pittas should eat in moderation, as they tend to get acid reflux if they overeat. They should reduce garlic and onions and go easy on citrus fruits unless these are very sweet; however, lemons are considered alkaline and purifying to the system and thus should be eaten in small amounts when desired.

Pittas should eat plenty of vegetables and fruits and use spices such as fennel, cumin, cardamom, cinnamon, and turmeric and fresh herbs such as mint, basil, and cilantro. Pittas will thrive on eating leafy greens, cucumber, asparagus, squash, celery, sprouts, okra, cabbage, and Brussels sprouts. Avocadoes used in moderation are balancing and calming for Pitta. A small amount of carrots and beets are beneficial, but too much will imbalance Pitta, especially if already in excess. Pittas can eat more often than Kaphas—including healthy snacks—because of their strong agni (digestive fire.)

Pumpkin and sunflower seeds benefit Pitta and most soaked nuts, in moderation, though too many will create imbalance. Nut milks (used in shakes) are beneficial if watered down and made from soaked, blanched nuts. Coconut water and coconut meat are very calming for Pitta. Sweet fruits, such as melons (when eaten on their own), grapes, sweet pineapples, sweet oranges, apples and berries calm Pitta.

Pittas should eat in a cool, calm environment. During meals, they should avoid over-heated discussions and competitive, judgmental, or overly critical company. They are encouraged to relax and do some deep breathing before meals.

Kapha

A raw food diet can benefit Kaphas, as it lightens them up and gives them more energy. Raw food has a lot of fiber, which helps eliminate toxins and can get a sluggish Kapha system moving.

The best foods for Kapha are light, warm, and dry (as Kaphas are already naturally oily and moist). People with Kapha as their dominant constitution should eat lots of leafy greens and bitter and astringent vegetables or other vegetables that are slightly warmed with pungent spices like ginger, cumin, black pepper, and chilies. Pungent, astringent vegetables, such as sprouts, leafy greens, parsley, cilantro, peppers, spinach, cauliflower, cabbage, carrots, celery, snow peas, and beets, all suit Kapha.

Kaphas can also indulge in onions and garlic and use pungent salad dressings. As they have slower digestive systems than Vatas or Pittas, they should especially take care to completely digest one meal before starting another. Astringent fruits—apples, pears, apricots, cranberries, and pomegranates—suit Kapha.

Flax, pumpkin, and sunflower seeds are good for Kapha when eaten in moderation. Nuts should be eaten in small amounts; too many will tax the typical Kapha digestive system and make Kapha feel too heavy and lethargic. Kapha should eat in a peaceful, loving, and uplifting environment.

Eating for the Seasons

Just as food affects each dosha, so does each season. For example, the Vata season, fall and early winter, tends to be full of movement—leaves are falling and people are going back to their routines after summer vacations. During this time, all doshas should be mindful of being grounded and follow a diet that will decrease Vata, especially Vatas. The Pitta season, late spring and summer, gives Pitta a "double dose" of fire. All body types should follow more cooling recipes and practices during this time, especially Pittas. Winter and early spring have Kapha qualities—cool, moist, and dormant—so every body type should compensate with more warming, Pitta-increasing foods, especially Kaphas. See the guidelines below for more information on balancing your primary doshas throughout the seasons as well as the sections on yoga poses (p. 372) and other alternative Ayurvedic therapies (p. 385).

The Vata season is fall and early winter. This is the time to eat comfort foods and warmer, grounding foods, like cooked root vegetables. Rest and engage in relaxing activities when possible: sit by a warm fire or take a walk in the forest. Decorate your surroundings with earth tones to ground your energy.

The Pitta season is late spring and summer, when the heat is on. Balance by eating lighter, cooling, less spicy foods, as well as more fruits and salads. Decorate your surroundings with cool, soothing colors. Try to rest and relax as much as possible near water or in the shade.

The Kapha season is winter and early spring. Balance by including extra outdoor activities in your regular exercise routine and increase the amount of hot spices in your meals. Eat warm, light foods such as vegetable soups as well as foods that are more pungent, bitter, and astringent. You should also decorate your surroundings with warm, vibrant colors.

Menu Plans

When planning your own Ayurvedic menus, include the six tastes of Ayurveda—sweet, salty, sour, pungent, bitter, and astringent—to calm the doshas and restore the body's natural balance. You can adjust any recipe or meal plan to suit your individual constitution by choosing foods that will balance your particular dosha and omitting those that will aggravate it; follow the dosha symbols accompanying each recipe and read the tips that show you how to modify it. When cooking for guests, you can serve tridoshic dishes (appropriate for all three doshas), or a variety of dishes that will balance each dosha. You also can offer each of the six tastes as condiments or side dishes so guests can adjust meals themselves to suit their constitution. In addition, whether you are dining alone or with others, remember that your surroundings greatly influence the Ayurvedic benefits of food and your ability to properly digest the meal, so pay attention to ambiance: avoid eating while watching television; keep conversation light and amicable; and select background music that will enhance, not stifle, the sensual enjoyment of your meal.

The season and time of day are also important factors when planning a menu. Once you are aware of the general principles of the seasonal and daily cycles, you can fine-tune your food preparation accordingly—for example, serve Pitta-reducing dishes at midday and in the heat of summer, which are common Pitta-aggravating times (see p. 363 for more seasonal tips).

Here is a summary of the seasons and times of day (year-round) that can aggravate (+) each dosha, and therefore require dishes that reduce or calm (–) that dosha:

Vata: Fall and early winter: 2 a.m.–6 a.m. and 2 p.m.–6 p.m.

Pitta: Summer and late spring: 10 a.m.–2 p.m. and 10 p.m.–2 a.m.

Kapha: Winter and early spring: 6 a.m.–10 a.m. and 6 p.m.–midnight

The menu plans that follow suit all doshas and include all six tastes. They should be used as a general guideline so that once you become familiar with the principles of Ayurveda, you will be able to modify and create menu plans that work for you.
In general, an Indian-style party meal should include an appetizer and some chutneys, restorative drinks appropriate to the season, a few vegetable dishes, a protein dish (e.g., a lentil or bean dish), some pickles, a raita, salad, and dessert. For everyday meals, eliminate the appetizer and dessert or really simplify things by choosing a one-pot dish—for example, Hearty White Bean & Barley Stew (p. 166), Amrita's Rajma with Vegetables (p. 198), or West Bay Biriani (p. 208). Add a salad or grain dish for a complete and balanced meal.

Pitta Season: Summer Picnic or Take-out Lunch

To reduce your use of packaging and packaged foods, make your own lunch and take it to work, or to a picnic, in a tiffin, a multi-tiered stainless steel container available at many Indian grocery stores. These are used in India to carry lunches or light meals and are not only functional but will make unpacking your lunch more fun!

Appetizer:
Raw veggies with Tzatziki (p. 268)

Beverage:
Rooibos & Lemon Balm Tea (p. 343)

Entrée:
Baked Falafel (p. 195)

Condiments:
Tahini & Lemon Dressing (p. 137) (use it as a condiment for Falafel), Cucumber Lime Pickle (p. 271), and Tomato & Cucumber Cachumber (p. 273)

Salad:
Brown Rice Mediterranean Salad (Variation 2, p. 105)

Dessert:
Peaches with Mint & Candied Ginger (p. 301)

Vata Season: Warming Autumn Meal

Enjoy this tasty meal that will fortify the body as the seasons change and the cooler weather sets in.

Appetizer:
Spicy Paneer & Zucchini Kebabs (p. 84)

Beverage:
Fennel Tea (p. 355)

Entrée:
Black Chickpeas with Red Peppers & Zucchini (p. 196); Cauliflower & Rainbow Chard Curry (p. 235); Simple Eggplant Baji (p. 234)

Grain:
Basmati rice

Condiments:
Raw Date & Currant Chutney (p. 282); plain yogurt (p. 264)

Dessert:
Fragrant Sago Pearl Pudding (p. 315)

Kapha Season: Winter Evening Meal

This meal will make you cozy and warm on a winter evening. Enjoy it with a crackling fire in the background and lots of candlelight.

Appetizer:
Green Chutney Mushroom Caps
  (p. 91)

Beverage:
Rosemary Tea (p. 348)

Entrée:
Hearty White Bean & Barley Stew
  (p. 166)

Grain:
Your favorite bread

Salad:
Mixed Greens & Crushed Pistachio
  Salad (p. 116) with Lime, Honey &
  Cilantro Dressing (p. 140)

Dessert:
Almost Raw Apples & Walnuts (p. 302)
  served in Almond Pie Crust (p. 305)

Sunday Brunch

This delectable array of goodies will nourish you and your guests at your next brunch.

Appetizer:
Pear, Coconut & Greens Shake (p. 329)

Beverage:
Aromatic Whole Spice Rooibos Chai
  (p. 344)

Entrée:
Sona's Fresh Cilantro, Mushroom &
  Chili Flake Omelette (p. 58),
  Pauline's Travel Scones (p. 67)

Condiment:
Carrot & Raw Mango Pickle (p. 270)

Dessert:
Berries with Cashew Cream (p. 298)

Almost Japanese Breakfast

Enjoy the subtle and complementary flavors of this meal, and relax in the still point that always exists, even in the busiest of days.

Appetizer:
slice of cantaloupe

Beverage:
Green tea and/or miso

Entrée:
Michelle's Yummy Egg on Quinoa
  Breakfast (p. 62)

Condiment:
Daikon, Carrot & Watercress (p. 269)

Everyday Breakfasts

Try some of these satisfying breakfasts any day of the week.

Beverage:
Cashew Cinnamon Nut Milk (p. 323)

Grain:
Quick Oats the Old-Fashioned Way
  (p. 41)

or

Beverage:
Patrick's Strawberry, Coconut & Cacao
  Morning Shake (p. 39)

or

Beverage:
Hemp Milk (p. 325)

Grain:
The Most Delicious Spelt Pancakes
  (p. 66) with strawberries

These are new menu plans I created for a few of the interesting themes we used on the TV series *The Ayurvedic Way*.

Food for Creativity

Prepare this meal ahead of time to free you up for creative activities throughout the day, or make its preparation one of your acts of creation. Simply by trying new things our creative juices start flowing.

Appetizer:
Baby Bocconcini, Basil & Tomato
  Skewers (p. 83)

Beverage:
Simplest Ginger Tea (p. 346)

Entrée:
Mountain High Quesadilla Pie (p. 201)

Salad:
Crunchy Rainbow Salad (p. 113)

Dessert:
Andrea's Carob Chip Cookies (p. 317)

Valentine's Day Dinner

Activate your senses with these tantalizing creations.

Appetizer:
Mango Salsa (p. 80) served with your
  favorite crackers or vegetable sticks

Beverage:
Pineapple Pistachio Bliss (p. 339)

Entrée:
Fit for a Wedding Feast Biriani (p. 222)
  and Garden Fresh Swiss Chard
  (p. 236)

Tea:
Relaxing Lemon Balm Tea (p. 353)

Dessert:
Quinoa Dark Chocolate Cake (p. 288)

Spice Up Your Life

Enjoy this typical Indian meal and add a little zest to your life.

Appetizer:
Spicy Tomato Salsa (p. 81)

Beverage:
Fresh Mint Tea (p. 350)

Entrée:
Red Lentils with Vegetables (p. 194);
  Cauliflower, Broccoli & Carrot Pilau
  (p. 211); Simple Eggplant Baji
  (p. 234)

Condiment:
Okra Raita (p. 266)

Dessert:
Mango Coconut Kulfi (p. 313)

Food for the Brain

Good breakfasts are essential for fueling the brain. The shake has lots of essential fatty acids, and the organic eggs are rich in minerals and full of protein. Eggs also contain choline, which can boost memory. The cabbage in the coleslaw will keep you energized all day, and the walnuts give you even more omega-3 oils. The enzymes in mung beans are excellent for fueling the brain and are delicious paired with spinach, which is also known to boost memory.

Beverage:
Brain Power Blueberry & Almond Shake
  (p. 36)

Breakfast:
Parsi Scrambled Eggs (p. 53)

Lunch:
Power Your Day Coleslaw (p. 122)

Dinner:
Yellow Split Mung & Spinach Dal
  (p. 188)

Food for Me-Time Days

These tasty dishes can all be prepared ahead of time and do not require heating so you can stay well-nourished while you take care of yourself.

Appetizer:
Egyptian Fava Bean Hummus (p. 78)

Beverage:
Leisha Laird's Hawaiian Special (p. 340)

Entrée:
Sabzi (p. 24)

Dessert:
Brazil Nut Coconut Balls (p. 306)

Food for Meditation

This is a cleansing menu that is light and perfect for a day of meditation. Enjoy the practice of mindfulness as you prepare it.

Appetizer:
Go Anywhere Trail Mix (p. 88)

Salad:
Summer Beach Salad (p. 111)

Beverage:
Be Now Tea (p. 347)

Condiment:
Mint Raita (p. 265)

Entrée:
Kitchari with Vegetables (p. 206)

Dessert:
Fruit Kebabs (p. 300)

Cleanses

Why Should I Do a Cleanse?

There are many types of cleanses that restore the body by eliminating toxins, thereby improving our ability to absorb nutrients. After cleansing, people usually find that their digestion improves, resulting in clear skin, more energy, and a healthier weight. Additionally, cleanses can balance moods and improve mental clarity, making you feel clear-headed and present. It is advisable to do a cleanse one to four times a year. Always consult a health professional or doctor before commencing a cleanse.

General tips

Be creative when preparing a cleansing menu. Experiment with various tea recipes. Discover the variety of fruits and vegetables available in your local markets. Make your salads colorful and adventurous; for example, add beets, carrots, avocados, nuts, watercress, dandelion greens, sprouts, radicchio, onions, and/or nuts. Add garlic, ginger, salt, herbs, raisins, dried cranberries, and pomegranate seeds which impart great contrasting flavors. Prepare tasty, invigorating dressings using lemon juice and cold-pressed oils (e.g., olive, flax seed, hemp, or sesame). Always try to incorporate the Six Essential Tastes of Ayurveda: salty, sweet, sour, astringent, pungent, and bitter. Lastly, have fun with the choices you make!

Panchakarma (Cleanse)

This is the name for the Ayurvedic process that deeply cleanses toxins from our cells, regenerates our bodies to maximum health, and rebalances our doshas. Ayurveda holds that as we cleanse our bodies physically, we also clear our emotional bodies. It is important to do panchakarma in the appropriate season and the time when it is right for you personally, as the release of toxins can lead initially to fatigue. Spring is often a good time to cleanse and detox.

Eating the right cleansing foods and getting plenty of rest are essential to a successful cleanse. A daily body massage using oil appropriate for your doshas (see below) is recommended as well as a warm oil massage of the forehead. Here is a simple panchakarma that you can do yourself:

If you are interested in doing a twelve-day cleanse, please see p. 299 in The Modern Ayurvedic Cookbook.

1. Take a three-day break from the world and rest your senses.

2. Turn off the phone and don't watch TV or read newspapers. Listen only to meditative music without words and read only meditative books and literature.

3. Cut out all caffeinated drinks, hot or cold, and other stimulants. Drink herbal teas and pure water. Eat a simple diet of kitchari (p. 206), which is used in Ayurvedic healing as it is tridoshic (balances all our doshas) and nutritious. It is also easy on the digestive system when eaten with a little bit of ghee. Stick to steamed vegetables or nourishing freshly made vegetable or fruit smoothies (without dairy). Eat fruit separately from all other food. *Note:* Eat melon on its own.

Another cleansing treatment to rebalance the digestive system and doshas is therapeutic colonics. A full panchakarma is complex and requires the supervision of a qualified Ayurvedic doctor.

4. Give yourself a daily oil massage. Add a few drops of essential oils to your massage oil. As you are on a panchakarma, spend longer (than the five-minute massage, see p. 370) doing the massage and let the oil soak into your body for at least 20 minutes before you wash it off.

5. Take long walks alone outside in nature (such as in a nearby park, forest, or at a beach), staying out of extreme weather.

6. Practice yoga that suits your doshas (p. 372) twice a day, followed by 10–60 minutes of meditation.

7. Take time to start and end your day with meditation (p. 371).

Five-minute *abhyanga* massage

This invigorating Ayurvedic massage strengthens your immune system and increases circulation, leaving you feeling refreshed. It takes only a few minutes and can be done anywhere; just make sure you do this at least half an hour before eating. If you have more time, you may add oil to this massage: sesame or almond oil for Vata; cold-pressed olive, coconut, or sunflower for Pitta; or corn, mustard, safflower, or almond oil for Kapha.

Start by standing or sitting. Briskly rub the palms of your hands together for 10–20 seconds. Place your left hand over your left ear and right hand over your right ear, then briskly run your hands back and forth over your ears for 10–20 seconds; this touches all the acupressure points (or *nadis*) on the ears that invigorate the entire body. Next, use both palms to lightly wipe or clean the aura around your head using downward movements. Shake your hands as if flicking off water to clear energy from your hands. Next, run your palms down the front and back of your body with downward strokes, using circular motions for all major joints (e.g., shoulders, elbows, knees). Keep shaking your hands to get rid of old energy.

Meditation

The traditional time for meditation is at sunrise or sunset. Do some asanas (poses) appropriate for your body type prior to the meditation so that you feel released from your immediate preoccupations and relaxed enough to be able to sit. Find a comfortable seat where your spine and neck (cervical spine) are straight and your sitting bones are resting. If you need to lean against a wall or use a bolster for added support, this is fine. Eventually you will probably enjoy sitting without back support. Tune the crown of your head upwards to the heavens and root the sitting bones to the earth. Imagine a chord connecting you to the life force, or prana, in both. Become aware that you are connected to this infinite energy source and that this is your birthright. Focus on your breath moving inside your body on inhalation and exhalation. Imagine breathing out old toxins, old attachments, and old ideas. On inhaling, imagine light filling every cell in your body. Know that the more you can let go of the old, the more you can let in new replenishing oxygen and light.

Yoga for the Doshas

Yoga is an integral part of Ayurveda and the holistic healing process. Yoga, which means union, helps to connect mind, body, and spirit. By practicing yoga regularly you will notice an increase in flexibility, your movements will be more graceful, and you will feel more grounded and in the present moment. If you are a beginner, be gentle on yourself; go only slightly past the point where you feel your muscles stretching. Do not strain yourself; pay attention to your body and allow your flexibility to slowly improve over time. Avoid self-judgment, and let your mind clear as the various postures replenish and relax you. It may also be helpful to try beginner yoga classes and/or watch instructional yoga DVDs, particularly to get a better understanding of body alignment principles and modifications for poses. For your own daily personal practice, start with 5–10 minute sessions; over time, you will notice an increase in your ability, endurance, and energy levels.

It is important to begin each yoga session by lying down or sitting comfortably and focusing on your breathing. As you become aware of your inhalations and exhalations, also become aware of your body, mind, and emotions. Replenish yourself with long inhalations. When you exhale, try to release more oxygen than you think you have inhaled, and notice how the length and depth of your inhalations expand. Visualize which parts of your body your breath reaches, dissolving any areas that feel tight or obstructed.

Specific breathing exercises can benefit specific doshas. Breathing to and from the abdomen helps to ground Vata. Breathing in and out from the ribcage will give you a sense of empowerment, and is especially beneficial for Pitta. Complete breaths energize and enliven the entire body, especially for Kapha. To take a complete breath, inhale all the way to the lower abdomen and lower back first, then allow the breath to work its way up, filling the ribcage, then the mid- and upper-back, up to the collarbones and neck; your body should feel completely full of oxygen. Exhale slowly, allowing the breath to release from the upper body first, then the ribcage, followed by the mid-and lower back, and lastly the abdomen.

Breathing is a wonderful tool to bring us back into our bodies and nourish us at any time throughout the day. Take notice of how your breathing patterns may shift during the day and in what situations. According to Ayurvedic and yogic traditions, having control of (or being aware of) your breathing is the same as having control of your life. Exhale to release old toxins, old beliefs, old attachments—anything that is not from the present moment—and use inhalation to replenish every cell of your body with oxygen and light.

While practicing asanas, or yoga postures, continue to be aware of your body, and take note of where and how your breath travels through you. This will deepen your yoga practice and make it far more beneficial than if you only concentrate on alignment, strength, and flexibility.

Just as it is important to begin a yoga session with breath awareness, make sure you end each session in *savasana*, the "just be" pose for 5–10 minutes. Lie flat on your back with legs outstretched and slightly apart and arms at your sides with palms facing up. Close your eyes and imagine your body melting into the floor and while being aware of your breath. Imagine the space that your yoga practice has created in your body and imagine it filling with radiant light. Savasana provides an important cooling-down period when the body, mind, and spirit can integrate the benefits of the yoga session. You may also choose to rest and integrate in a seated meditation pose.

By following these suggestions, your body, mind, and spirit will, over time, radiate with light. Of course there will be ups and downs, but remember that the downs are crucial periods to continue practicing yoga, as these are usually the times when we transition from the past to a new period in life. It takes courage to practice yoga—by doing so, you are opening up your heart, body, and mind, becoming a fully functioning human being in the truest sense.

All body types can benefit from the variety of poses listed under Vata, Pitta, and Kapha. Vata should do the poses slowly; Pitta should do them with inner focus; and Kapha should do them more vigorously.

Vata Poses

Vata benefits from slower, meditative poses that reduce anxiety and create a feeling of safety, warmth, and stability. Balancing poses help quiet the active Vata mind. Holding the poses for 3–6 deep breaths or longer is recommended to calm Vata. The poses demonstrated by Clara Roberts-Oss (Vata being her primary dosha) are especially good for a Vata body type; however, all yoga poses are beneficial for Vata when done slowly and steadily. Make sure to end your yoga session with a long savasana and meditation.

Child's pose

Child's Pose
• promotes a sense of being nurtured and protected
• relaxes back and spine
• rejuvenates the body while calming Vata nerves

Start in Sitting Mountain (p. 378) with knees slightly apart. Bend forward from the lower back. Rest your upper body on your thighs and knees with your forehead touching the mat and your arms outstretched in front of you, palms down. Take a few deep, replenishing breaths here. Then make a pillow on which to rest your forehead by clasping your hands together; this quiets the busy Vata mind and opens the third eye to enhance the inner sense of vision. Take a few long, deep breaths in this position before bringing your arms beside your legs, palms up, resting on the mat. Take a few more long, deep breaths and relax into this pose. Notice that your breath naturally flows into your back in Child's Pose as it brings you back from the outside world into your own body. When you feel replenished, return to a seated position or move into Rabbit, below.

Rabbit pose

Rabbit Pose
• improves the complexion
• increases alertness and clarity of mind

Begin in Child's Pose. Bend forward while clasping your heels with your hands. Place the crown of your head onto the mat and lift the sitting bones slightly off the mat. Take a few breaths here. After a few breaths, return to Child's Pose and repeat.

Lying-Down Twist

- calms anxiety and clears the mind
- rebalances the flow of energy, decompresses the spine, and creates a feeling of spaciousness in the body while opening hips, ribcage, waist, shoulders, and neck
- aids the digestive system

Lie flat on your back on a mat. Take a few deep inhalations and exhalations. Pull your right knee in toward your chest and take a few more deep breaths as you enjoy this leg stretch. With your left hand on your right knee, pull it over your outstretched left leg. Hook your right foot behind your left knee. If your right knee does not touch the ground, you may want to use a bolster or some cushions to support your bent knee. Turn your head to look over your right shoulder. Stretch your right arm out at shoulder-level. Take full, deep breaths in this pose as your body releases and lets go of tension. Stay here for a few breaths, return to center, then repeat on the other side.

Lying-Down Twist

Standing Mountain

A mudra is a gesture, usually made with the hands, that locks and guides energy flow and reflexes to the brain. Become conscious of the flow of energy through your body as you hold this mudra.

Tree

- unites mind, body, and spirit while grounding and lengthening the body

The focus in this balancing pose helps to eliminate the vrittis (a Sanskrit word for waves of thoughts, impulses, or anxieties) to create a centered, balanced feeling. Stand with your weight evenly balanced on both sides of the body in Standing Mountain (tadasana, see photo, left). Imagine creating space in your body as you stand tall with your feet rooted to the ground. Begin to shift your weight onto your right foot while maintaining a squared alignment. Pick up your left foot and place the sole on the inside of your right thigh. If you are a beginner, you can start with your foot on your calf and work your way up over time. Press your right thigh back into your foot to maintain your balance. Bring your hands into the prayer mudra at the center of your chest.

Find a focal point for your eyes (drishti) to help you keep your balance. (If you are an advanced yoga practitioner, try this pose with your eyes closed; this will help to develop your inner sense of balance.) Take several full, deep breaths here. When you feel replenished, return to Standing Mountain, then repeat on other side.

Tree pose (three variations)

Pitta Poses

These poses gently increase flexibility and bring a sense of calm and centeredness to Pitta, who can benefit from a strong energetic practice as they are blessed with stamina and vitality. Pittas will also enjoy the dynamic warrior asanas (poses) for Kapha (see pp. 379–381). The poses shown here are very restorative. Holding the poses for 4–6 deep, long breaths or longer is recommended. The poses demonstrated by Padma Marla Stewart (a predominantly Pitta body type) are good for reducing Pitta; however, all the poses are beneficial if they are done with a relaxed yet alert mind.

Bent-Knee Sitting Side Bend

- allows Pitta to let go of "overdrive" and opens up the entire back area while bringing a sense of calm
- massages the digestive organs and increases (sometimes much-needed) Pitta flexibility

Sit with a straight spine and both legs outstretched in a wide V-shape. Take a couple of deep breaths in this position. Bend your right knee so that the sole of your right foot touches the inside of your left thigh. Take a few deep breaths here. Inhale and raise both arms overhead and exhale as you extend your body and arms over your left leg. Go only as far as you can with a straight back, moving from the sacrum (base of the spine) and reaching with the heart. Less is more, when done correctly. With practice, you will be able to go further as you build flexibility. Hold this pose and take several long, deep breaths, remembering to breathe into your back and exhale fully. Return to center and repeat on other side.

Bent-Knee Sitting Side Bend

Sitting Mountain Pose

• brings a feeling of centered calmness
• restores good posture while opening the quads, shins, and feet

Sit on bent legs with your weight evenly distributed on both knees. If you cannot do this, place a bolster or cushions between your thighs and calves. With practice, you will build more flexibility. Imagine a string of pearls running from the ground up through your spine and neck and emerging from the crown of your head, pulling them erect, while feeling the spaces between the vertebrae. Take long, full, deep breaths and let your shoulders relax and drop, becoming broader and more open. See yourself in the center of your heart, with an inner focus.

Sitting Mountain Pose

Alternate Arm and Leg Lifts in Tabletop

• stabilizes the right and left sides of the body and brain
• builds strength and balance

On a mat, get down on your hands and knees. Come into a "tabletop" position in which you are evenly balanced on all sides. Keep your abdomen lifted. Stretch out your right arm and your left leg, while staying square. Hold for a few breaths. Alternate the pose using your left arm and right leg. Repeat 6 times.

Alternate Arm and Leg Lifts in Tabletop

Kapha Poses

Kaphas benefit from faster, invigorating yoga practiced in warm, dry environments. They should include variety in their yoga routine and dynamic poses such as the Warrior Series shown here, done in sequence, or the Sun Salutation sequence (see *The Modern Ayurvedic Cookbook*, pp. 304–306). The poses demonstrated by Todd Inouye (Kapha being his primary dosha) are especially good for a Kapha body type; however, all poses (including those for Vata and Pitta) are beneficial for Kapha, especially if they are done in an invigorating way.

Warrior 1
• strengthens legs, back, shoulders, and arms while opening chest and heart
• develops stability and stamina in the whole body
• increases flexibility

Start by centering yourself in tadasana or Standing Mountain. Move right leg into a forward lunge, back knee off the ground. Make sure your knee is positioned directly over your ankle at a 90-degree angle and your back foot is at a 45-degree angle. Keep your back leg straight and square your hips to the front. Sweep both arms overhead, hands clasped in prayer position with fingers pointing up. Lean back slightly as you gaze up at your hands. Engage your quadriceps. Enjoy this chest stretch that opens the heart while lengthening the spine, and hold this pose for a few breaths. Repeat with the left leg forward.

Warrior 1

Warrior 2

Warrior 2

- opens the hips while stretching the arms
- develops stamina, focus, and grounding

Start in the forward lunge position, right leg forward, with your back knee off the ground. Sweep your arms up sideways at shoulder height, parallel to your mat, palms down. Face forward and stay rooted in your back leg as you feel your hips open. Gaze at your front fingertips as you center your torso over your hips. Stay grounded and don't lean forward. Hold this pose for a few deep breaths, then repeat on the other side. *Note:* If you are in a safe environment, this is a great pose in which to belt out a warrior's "ahhhhh." Use this sound to open the energy circuits in your body.

Head to Knee Pose

- stretches the hamstrings in a delicious way
- calms the mind
- stretches the spine

Start in the forward lunge position: right leg forward with your back knee off the ground. Straighten the front leg (back leg is already straight). Moving from your sacrum and leading with your heart, bend forward and place your hands on either side of your front foot. You may need a pair of blocks (or two piles of books of the same height), on the outside of each foot to place your hands on to stay square and open, not compressed. Bring your head toward your knee or shin with a straight back. Again, less, done correctly, is more. You should feel a hamstring stretch in your front leg as you stay rooted in the back leg. Take a few deep breaths here. To get an even deeper stretch, flex your front foot so that your weight is on your heel, and pull your toes toward you. Take a few more breaths. When you feel that the stretch has loosened your hamstrings, repeat on the other side.

Head to Knee Pose

Standing Side Twist

• develops stability and strength while energizing the whole body
• increases flexibility
• improves digestion
• massages our organs

Begin in the forward lunge position (see Warrior 2), right leg forward, back knee off the ground. With your hands pressed together in prayer position, twist your arms until your left elbow is resting on your right knee. Look up toward your right shoulder. Take a few long, deep breaths here. When you feel released and complete on this side, repeat on the other side.

Standing Side Twist

Workplace poses to calm the doshas

The simple poses outlined here can be done in most office or workplace settings. When they are done with inner focus and consciousness, they improve the health of our nervous systems, enhance our moods, and aid clear thinking. These postures can relieve stress and bring health and vitality to the work we do alone and in relationships with others.

Neck Rolls

• releases tension in the neck and shoulders
• rebalances the thyroid
• reconnects the mind with the body and spirit

Sit or stand with your back and head straight. Take a couple of deep breaths. While exhaling deeply, drop your head so your chin touches your neck at the level of your thyroid gland. Slowly roll your head to the right so that your ear drops toward your right shoulder. Take some deep breaths, releasing tightness on the exhalations. Return chin to center and repeat on your left side.

Shoulder Lifts and Rolls

• good for all doshas, especially for focusing Vata's sometimes scattered energy, centering and directing positive resolve in Pitta, and energizing Kapha
• releases tension held in the neck and shoulders
• brings energy to the whole body
• stretches arms, back, and shoulders

Sit or stand with your back and head straight. Take a few deep breaths. Shrug your shoulders up tightly toward your ears and hold, then release as you drop your shoulders. Repeat a few times until you feel a nice release of tension.

Sit or stand with your back and head straight. Take a few deep breaths. Roll both shoulders from front to back 3–6 times as you feel them loosen and release. Then roll them from back to front 3–6 times. Repeat until you feel relaxed and energized.

Standing Half Moon

- strengthens and lengthens the arms and sides of our bodies
- trims and tones our waistlines
- re-aligns the spine and pulls us out of our joints (this position actually "de-cranks" us, as when we get stuck in our joints, we also get cranky!)

Start in Standing Mountain (p. 376), with your weight evenly balanced on both sides of the body. Keep your feet parallel and close together. Stretch your arms overhead with fingers locked and index fingers pointing straight up. Imagine creating space in the body as you stand tall with your feet rooted to the ground. Take a few long, deep breaths here as you concentrate on using the breath to expand any of the tight places in your body. Slowly bend to the right as you stretch your body to the side. Take a few long deep breaths, then bring your body back to center. Repeat on the other side.

Arms Clasped Forward Bend

- releases stress and old stuck energy
- loosens shoulders, arm, back, and spine
- lengthens hamstrings and releases limbs from our joints (another "de-cranking" pose)

Stand with your weight evenly balanced on both sides of the body in Standing Mountain. Clasp your hands behind you and stretch them out and up. Bend slowly from the waist with a straight back, dropping your head and lifting your outstretched arms up toward the back of your head. Take a few breaths, then return slowly to standing position. Repeat a few times.

Standing Half Moon

Arms Clasped Forward Bend

Arm Front Twist

Arm Front Twist

• opens up the back of the shoulders and releases tension there

Stand with your weight evenly balanced in Standing Mountain. Raise your arms straight out in front of you. Place your right arm over the left, crossing over at the elbow. By twisting the right forearm up, clasp your hands together, opening the shoulders. To get a deeper stretch, pull the arms out from your body at shoulder level while maintaining an erect posture. Take a few deep breaths here, releasing tension in your shoulders as you exhale. Repeat, crossing your arms in the opposite direction (left arm over right).

Chair Sitting Twist

• refreshes, re-energizes, and detoxifies

Sit on a chair with your back and head straight. Your feet should be parallel and firmly planted on the ground, hip-width apart. Put your left hand on the outside of your outer right thigh. Place your right hand on the back of the chair, behind your spine, and turn your head to look over your right shoulder. Gently twist from your waist up while your hips are stable, squared, and facing forward. Take some deep breaths here, return to center, then repeat on the other side.

Chair Sitting Twist

Chanting Om

• calms all the doshas
• clears stuck energy and creates a feeling of peace and at-oneness with our surroundings

Sit with a straight spine. Pull the crown of your head up toward the ceiling and keep the sitting bones firmly planted on the edge of your chair. Imagine your spine lengthening and the spaces between each vertebrae increasing. Take a deep breath in and chant "om" as you breathe out. This can be done quietly and softly in an office; if you are alone or with a group, you can chant louder. Repeat 3 times.

Meditation

• slows the mind, reduces blood pressure and heart rate, and increases clarity, peace, and serenity

Begin with Chanting Om in the sitting position described above. Imagine an egg-shaped space all around you that extends 3 feet (about 1 m) in every direction. Only you are in this space. This is the you that always knows who you are, never ages, never changes, and does not need a name. Start by following the breath on the inside of your body. Follow the breath by noticing which organs it might be touching and the ones it might not be touching. Imagine any obstacles to breath melting away. Keep expanding your breath to fill every part of your body, and on exhaling, imagine releasing old toxins, attachments, and beliefs. Do this for 5–10 minutes.

Vastu Veda: The Song of Our Surroundings

When we walk into a room where the concepts of vastu (which has been described as Ayurvedic feng shui) have been mindfully applied, we experience a feeling of ease and harmony. We start to feel tranquil; stress and anxiety seem to vanish almost magically. Vastu harmonizes and increases our prana (life force) when used throughout our homes and work areas. It utilizes the five essential constituent elements of all things: earth, ether (or space), air, fire, and water. Simple changes to your home, furniture arrangements, and color selections can create harmony for the doshas. Here are some guidelines:

• Keep the entrance to your home elegant and open.
• Use only natural materials and avoid synthetic materials.
• Keep the center of the room uncluttered; this allows prana to move outwards from this sacred center to all areas of the room, creating a feeling of spaciousness, peace, and harmony.
• Put your heaviest, most grounding furniture in the southwest area of the room; place lighter pieces in the northeast.
• Use brighter, more yang (male) colors in the east, the direction that represents the sun and yang energy.
• Use lighter, softer, and more yin (female) colors in the northwest, the direction that represents the moon and yin energy.
• Use colors to balance the doshas.

⊙ Vata can be balanced with white, green, violet, magenta, turquoise, and red.

🔥 Pitta can be balanced with white, green, deep ocean blue, violet, magenta, pale pinks, and turquoise. (Avoid strong colors such as red and black.)

🌿 Kapha can be balanced with red, orange, and magenta. Turquoise and green are also beneficial.

For a list of colors and their properties, see *The Modern Ayurvedic Cookbook*, p. 316.

• Position the head of your bed in the east or south.

• Keep things simple. Get rid of clutter and anything that does not inspire you or you don't truly love or use. There are lots of places to recycle and lots of people in need who could use what's lying static and dormant in your sacred space, creating ama or toxins.

• Burn candles, use aromatherapy (see *The Modern Ayurvedic Cookbook*, p. 314), and air out your home regularly to get rid of old "stuck" energy and lift your mood.

• Play harmonious meditative music; this changes the vibration of a home and the objects within it.

• Create a *sattvic* (pure) place to live and work to maximize your fullest *dharma* (potential).

Balcony Vegetable Gardening

In May 2011, it was reported that watermelons in China had exploded in the field after an application of the wrong chemical fertilizer. After this incident, many more Chinese citizens took to zealously growing some of their own fruits and vegetables, no matter how small their balconies or backyards were. When I heard about the Chinese "balcony farmers," it inspired me to start my own balcony garden. My friend and yoga client Julia Hadrill helped me set it up; we planted a lovely edible container garden of runner beans, cherry, heirloom, and yellow pear-shaped tomatoes, Swiss chard, miniature strawberries, and an herb garden. I also planted a variety of lettuces in different flavors, colors, and textures so I could create fabulous prana-filled salads. In fact, I was inspired to create some of the recipes in this book by the ingredients growing on my balcony. I also enjoy cooking with food I buy at the local farmer's markets and with bountiful produce gifts from my friends' gardens.

In return for a Sunday brunch of Spelt Pancakes with Berry Compote (p. 64) and Rooibos Chai (p. 344), Julia shared with me the following thoughts on growing your own food:

• Just get started; don't be fearful. Ask questions of experienced gardeners. The first time you grow a vegetable garden, view it as an experiment. You will learn from your mistakes. Enjoy the process!

• Herbs are the easiest thing to start growing. Next, try a few greens like Swiss chard, kale, spinach, and lettuce.

• By growing vegetables, you are not necessarily forgoing flowers. Runner beans, for example, have gorgeous red flowers!

• The quality of your soil is extremely important, as is the quality of the seeds and plants with which you start. Buy soil for container gardens that is pre-mixed, organic, and sterilized. Make sure the soil you buy is correct for the plants you will be growing. Avoid chemical fertilizers and pesticides.

- Be conscious of your seed source; there are some giant industrial and chemical corporations that are beginning to patent and own many crop seeds. Grow only heritage tomatoes, as you can save the seeds and grow plants from them annually, without having to buy packaged seeds every year. If we stop supporting multinationals that are genetically modifying our food, we will be helping to protect and preserve the environment.

- Over time, seeds can get more "intelligent" about the location in which they are grown; they become healthier and sturdier plants. Some gardeners prefer to buy seeds developed in the climate in which they are going to grow.

- What you can grow depends on the site. Will it be mostly in the sun or shade? Is it windy? These are some of the factors that affect the watering needs and growth of your plants. For example, tomatoes need lots of sun, but leafy greens grow well in the shade.

- Containers should be light so that they are movable. They should be big enough to give the plants room to grow. A good size—one that will hold water and not dry out too quickly—is 12-in (30-cm) square and 18-in (26-cm) deep. To a certain extent, plants will grow to fit the size of the container; plants in smaller containers will remain small.

- With container planting, it's best to grow the plants vertically as much as possible. For example, some people put netting over their squash or zucchini and make little slings where the fruits start to form so they have a place to "rest" in, instead of letting the plant spread horizontally on the ground.

- An advantage of container gardening is that there are fewer destructive bugs to deal with than in a garden plot.

- A successful garden will have the correct moisture balance for the plants (the right soil and amount of water). Plants will tell you when they are flagging: when the leaves turn yellow, give them more water. As plants grow, they drink more water; when flowering, they need even more. Larger containers hold more water and give the roots of the plants more room to grow.

- When we grow food ourselves, we take control of our food source. Our respect for the people who grow food increases; it teaches us how to value our local organic farmer's markets and support them.

- By growing our own, we get to eat freshly picked food, and the prana (life force) in home-grown food is very high.

• Creating a vegetable garden and working with soil is a good way to get grounded. Being around things that are growing and changing daily keeps us in touch with the weather and the seasons—and the beauty of it all. We learn so much about life.

I hope this encourages you to start a back yard garden so that you can enjoy the prana-filled produce you will receive—and the joy from the process!

Food Guidelines for Basic Constitutional Types

Reprinted with permission from *The Ayurvedic Cookbook* by Amadea Morningstar with Urmila Desai (Lotus Press, 1990).

NOTE: Fruit and fruit juices are best consumed by themselves for all doshas.

Fruit:

VATA		PITTA		KAPHA	
NO	YES	NO	YES	NO	YES
Dried Fruits	Sweet Fruits	Sour fruits	Sweet fruits	Sweet & sour	Apples
Apples	Apricots	Apples (sour)	Apples (sweet)	fruits	Apricots
Cranberries	Avocado	Apricots (sour)	Apricots (sweet)	Avocado	Berries
Pears	Bananas	Berries (sour)	Avocado	Bananas	Cherries
Persimmon	All berries	Bananas	Berries (sweet)	Coconut	Cranberries
Pomegranate	Cherries	Cherries (sour)	Coconut	Dates	Figs (dry)
Prunes	Coconut	Cranberries	Dates	Figs (fresh)	Mango
Quince	Dates	Grapefruit	Figs	Grapefruit	Peaches
Watermelon	Figs (fresh)	Grapes (green)	Grapes (sweet)	Grapes*	Pears
	Grapefruit	Kiwi#	Mango	Kiwi*	Persimmon
	Melons (sweet)	Lemons	Melons	Lemons	Pomegranate
	Oranges	Limes (in excess)	Oranges (sweet)	Limes	Prunes
	Papaya	Papaya	Pears	Melons	Quince
	Peaches	Peaches	Pineapples	Oranges	Raisins
	Pineapples	Pineapples (sour)	(sweet)	Papaya	Strawberries*
	Plums	Persimmon	Plums (sweet)	Pineapples	
	Raisins (soaked)	Plums (sour)	Pomegranate	Plums	
	Rhubarb	Rhubarb	Prunes	Rhubarb	
	Soursop	Soursop	Quince (sweet)	Soursop	
	Strawberries	Strawberries	Raisins	Watermelon	
			Watermelon		

* These foods are OK in moderation.   # These foods are OK occasionally.

Vegetables

VATA		PITTA		KAPHA	
NO	**YES**	**NO**	**YES**	**NO**	**YES**
Frozen, dried, or raw vegetables	Cooked vegetables	Pungent vegetables	Sweet & bitter vegetables	Sweet & juicy vegetables	Raw, pungent & bitter vegetables
Beet greens*	Artichoke	Beets	Artichokes	Artichokes*	Asparagus
Bell peppers	Asparagus	Beet greens	Asparagus	Cucumber	Beets
Broccoli#	Beets	Carrots#	Bell peppers	Olives (black or	Beet greens
Brussels sprouts	Carrots	Chili peppers	Broccoli	green)	Bell peppers
Burdock root	Cucumber	(hot)	Brussels sprouts	Parsnip#	Chili peppers
Cabbage	Daikon	Daikon#	Burdock root	Potatoes (sweet)	Broccoli
Cauliflower	Fenugreek	Eggplant#	Cabbage	Pumpkin	Brussel sprouts
Celery	greens*	Fenugreek greens	Corn (fresh)	Rutabagas	Burdock root
Corn (fresh)#	Green beans	Garlic	Cauliflower	Squash (Acorn,	Cabbage
Eggplant	(well-cooked)	Horseradish	Chili peppers	Butternut,	Carrots
Jerusalem	Horseradish#	Kohlrabi#	(mild)	Spaghetti,*	Cauliflower
artichokes*	Leeks (cooked)	Leeks (cooked)#	Cucumber	Winter)	Celery
Jicama*	Mustard greens	Mustard greens	Celery	Tomatoes	Corn (fresh)
Kohlrabi	Okra (cooked)	Olives (green)	Green beans	Zucchini	Daikon
Leafy greens*	Olives (black &	Onions (raw)	Jerusalem		Eggplant
Lettuce*	green)	Onions	artichoke		Fenugreek greens
Mushrooms	Onion (cooked)	(cooked)*	Jicama		Garlic
Onions (raw)	Parsnip	Pumpkin#	Leafy greens		Green beans
Parsley*	Potato (sweet)	Radish	(esp. collards and		Horseradish
Peas	Pumpkin	Spinach#	dandelion)		Jerusalem
Potatoes (white)	Radish	Tomatoes	Lettuce		artichoke
Spaghetti	Rutabaga	Turnip greens	Mushrooms		Jicama
Squash#	Squash (Acorn,	Turnips	Okra		Kohlrabi
Spinach*	Butternut, Scal-		Olives (black)*		Leafy greens
Sprouts*	lopini, Summer,		Parsley		Leeks
Tomatoes	Winter, Yellow		Parsnip		Lettuce
Turnips	Crookneck)		Peas		Mushrooms
Turnip greens*	Watercress		Potatoes (sweet		Okra
	Zucchini		or white)		Onions
			Rutabagas		Parsley
			Squash (Acorn,		Peas
			Butternut,		Potatoes (white)
			Scallopini,		Radish
			Spaghetti,		Spinach
			Summer, Winter,		Sprouts
			Yellow		Squash (Scallopini,
			Crookneck)		Summer, Yellow
			Sprouts		Crookneck)
			Watercress*		Turnip greens
			Zucchini		Turnips
					Watercress

* These foods are OK in moderation.   # These foods are OK occasionally.

Grains

VATA		PITTA		KAPHA	
NO	YES	NO	YES	NO	YES
Cold, dry, puffed cereals	Amaranth*	Amaranth#	Barley	Oats (cooked)	Amaranth*
Barley#	Oats (cooked)	Buckwheat	Oats (cooked)	Rice (brown or white)	Barley
Buckwheat	All Rice (including brown rice)	Corn	Rice (basmati or white)	Wheat	Buckwheat
Corn	Wheat	Millet	Rice cakes		Corn
Granola	Wild rice	Oat bran*	Wheat		Granola (low-fat)
Millet		Oat granola	Wheat bran		Millet
Oat bran		Oats (dry)	Wheat granola		Oat bran
Oats (dry)		Quinoa			Oats (dry)
Quinoa		Rice (brown)#			Quinoa
Rice cakes#		Rye			Rice (basmati, small amount with clove or peppercorn)
Rye					Rice cakes#
Wheat bran (in excess)					Rye
					Wheat bran#

Animal Foods

VATA		PITTA		KAPHA	
NO	YES	NO	YES	NO	YES
Lamb	Beef#	Beef	Chicken or turkey (white meat)	Beef	Chicken or turkey (dark meat)
Pork	Chicken or turkey (white meat)	Duck	Egg whites	Duck	Eggs (not fried or scrambled with fat)
Rabbit	Duck	Egg yolks	Fish (freshwater)*	Fish (freshwater)#	Rabbit
Venison	Duck eggs	Lamb	Rabbit	Lamb	
	Eggs	Pork	Shrimp*	Pork	
	Fish (freshwater)	Seafood		Seafood	
	Seafood	Venison		Shrimp	
	Shrimp			Venison#	

* These foods are OK in moderation.   # These foods are OK occasionally.

Legumes

VATA		PITTA		KAPHA	
NO	**YES**	**NO**	**YES**	**NO**	**YES**
Black beans	Aduki beans*	Black lentils	Aduki beans	Black lentils	Aduki beans
Black-eyed peas	Black lentils*	(Urad dal)	Black beans	(Urad dal)	Black beans
Brown or green	(Urad dal)	Red (Masoor)	Black-eyed peas	Brown or green	Black-eyed peas
lentils	Mung beans*	lentils	Brown or green	lentils	Channa dal
Channa dal	Red (Masoor)	Tur dal	lentils	Kidney beans	Chickpeas
Chickpeas	lentils*		Channa dal	Mung beans*	(Garbanzo
(Garbanzo	Soy cheese*		Chickpeas	Soy beans	beans)
beans)	Soy milk (liquid)*		(Garbanzo	Soy milk (cold)	Lima beans
Kala channa*	Tepery beans*		beans)	Soy cheese	Kala channa
Kidney beans	Tofu*		Kala channa	Soy flour	Navy beans
Lima beans	Tur dal*		Kidney beans	Soy powder	Pinto beans
Navy beans			Lima beans	Tempeh	Red (Masoor)
Pinto beans			Mung beans	Tofu (cold)	lentils
Soy beans			Navy beans		Soy milk (hot)*
Soy flour			Pinto beans		Split peas
Soy powder			Soy beans		Tepery beans
Split peas			Soy cheese		Tofu (hot)*
Tempeh			Soy flour*		Tur dal
White beans			Soy milk (liquid)		White beans
			Soy powder *		
			Split peas		
			Tempeh		
			Tepery beans		
			Tofu		
			White beans		

Nuts

VATA		PITTA		KAPHA	
NO	**YES**	**NO**	**YES**	**NO**	**YES**
	Almonds*	Almonds		Almonds	
	Brazil nuts*	Brazil nuts		Brazil nuts	
	Cashews*	Cashews		Cashews	
	Coconut*	Hazelnuts		Coconut	
	Hazelnuts*	Macadamia nuts		Hazelnuts	
	Macadamia nuts*	Peanuts		Macadamia nuts	
	Peanuts#	Pecans		Peanuts	
	Pecans*	Pine Nuts		Pecans	
	Pine nuts*	Pistachios		Pine nuts	
	Pistachios*	Walnuts (Black		Pistachios	
	Walnuts (Black*	or English)		Walnuts (Black	
	or English*)			or English)	

* These foods are OK in moderation.   # These foods are OK occasionally.

Seeds

VATA		PITTA		KAPHA	
NO	**YES**	**NO**	**YES**	**NO**	**YES**
Psyllium#	Chia	Chia	Psyllium	Psyllium	Chia
	Flax	Flax	Pumpkin*	Sesame	Flax*
	Sesame	Sesame	Sunflower		Pumpkin*
	Pumpkin				Sunflower*
	Sunflower				

Sweeteners

VATA		PITTA		KAPHA	
NO	**YES**	**NO**	**YES**	**NO**	**YES**
White sugar	Barley malt syrup	Honey*	Barley malt syrup	Barley malt syrup	Raw honey
	Brown rice syrup	Jaggery (gur)	Brown rice syrup	Brown rice syrup	Fruit juice
	Fructose	Molasses	Maple syrup	Fructose	concentrates
	Fruit juice		Fruit juice	Jaggery (gur)	(esp. apple and
	concentrates		concentrates	Maple syrup	pear)
	Honey		Fructose	(in excess)	
	Jaggery (gur)		Sucanat*	Molasses	
	Maple syrup		Sugar cane juice	Sucanat	
	Molasses		White sugar*	Sugar cane juice	
	Sucanat			White sugar	
	Sugar cane juice				

* These foods are OK in moderation.   # These foods are OK occasionally.

Condiments

VATA		PITTA		KAPHA	
NO	**YES**	**NO**	**YES**	**NO**	**YES**
Chili peppers*	Black pepper*	Black sesame	Black pepper*	Black sesame	Black pepper
Ginger (dry)*	Black sesame	seeds	Cilantro leaves	seeds	Chili peppers
Ketchup	seeds	Cheese (grated)	(fresh)	Cheese (grated)	Cilantro leaves
Onion (raw)	Coconut	Chili peppers	Coconut	Coconut	(fresh)
Sprouts*	Cilantro leaves*	Daikon*	Cottage cheese	Cottage cheese*	Daikon
	(fresh)	Garlic	Dulse	Dulse	Garlic
	Cottage cheese	Ginger	(well-rinsed)	(well-rinsed)*	Ghee*
	Cheese (grated)	Gomasio	Ghee	Hijiki*	Ginger (esp. dry)
	Daikon	Horseradish	Hijiki (well-	Kelp	Horseradish
	Dulse	Kelp	rinsed)	Ketchup	Lettuce
	Garlic	Ketchup	Kombu	Kombu*	Mint leaves
	Ghee	Mustard	Lettuce	Lemon	Mustard
	Ginger (fresh)	Lemon	Mango chutney	Lime	Onions
	Gomasio	Lime	Mint leaves	Lime pickle	Radish
	Hijiki	Lime pickle	Sprouts	Mango chutney	Sprouts
	Horseradish	Mango pickle		Mango pickles	
	Kelp	Mayonnaise		Mayonnaise	
	Kombu	Onions		Papaya chutney	
	Lemon	(esp. raw)		Pickles	
	Lettuce*	Papaya chutney		Salt	
	Lime	Pickles		Seaweeds	
	Lime pickle	Radish		(well-rinsed)*	
	Mango chutney	Salt (in excess)		Sesame seeds	
	Mango pickle	Seaweed,		Soy sauce	
	Mayonnaise	unrinsed		Tamari	
	Mint leaves*	(in excess)		Yogurt	
	Mustard	Sesame seeds			
	Onion (cooked)	Soy sauce			
	Papaya chutney	Tamari*			
	Pickles	Yogurt			
	Radish	(undiluted)			
	Salt				
	Seaweeds				
	Sesame seeds				
	Soy sauce				
	Tamari				
	Yogurt				

* These foods are OK in moderation.   # These foods are OK occasionally.

Spices

VATA		PITTA		KAPHA	
NO	**YES**	**NO**	**YES**	**NO**	**YES**
Neem leaves*	Ajwan	Ajwan	Basil leaves	Almond extract*	Ajwan
	Allspice	Allspice	(fresh)*	Amchoor	Allspice
	Almond extract	Almond extract*	Black pepper*	Tamarind	Anise
	Amchoor	Amchoor	Cardamom*		Asafoetida (hing)
	Anise	Anise	Cinnamon*		Basil
	Asafoetida (hing)	Asafoetida (hing)	Coriander		Bay leaf
	Basil	Basil	Cumin		Black pepper
	Bay leaf	Bay leaf	Dill		Caraway
	Black pepper	Caraway*	Fennel		Cardamom
	Caraway	Cayenne	Mint		Cayenne
	Cardamom	Cloves	Neem leaves		Cinnamon
	Cayenne*	Fenugreek	Orange peel*		Cloves
	Cinnamon	Garlic (esp. raw)	Parsley*		Coriander
	Cloves	Ginger	Peppermint		Cumin
	Coriander	Horseradish	Rose water		Dill
	Cumin	Mace	Saffron		Fennel*
	Dill	Marjoram	Spearmint		Fenugreek
	Fennel	Mustard seeds	Turmeric		Garlic
	Fenugreek*	Nutmeg	Vanilla*		Ginger (esp. dry)
	Garlic	Onion (esp. raw)	Wintergreen		Horseradish
	Ginger	Oregano			Mace
	Horseradish*	Paprika			Marjoram
	Marjoram	Pippali			Mint
	Mint	Poppy seeds*			Mustard seeds
	Mustard seeds	Rosemary			Neem leaves
	Nutmeg	Sage			Nutmeg
	Onion (cooked)	Savory			Onion
	Orange peel	Star anise			Orange peel
	Oregano	Tarmarind			Oregano
	Paprika	Tarragon*			Paprika
	Parsley	Thyme			Parsley
	Peppermint				Peppermint
	Pippali				Pippali
	Poppy seeds				Poppy seeds
	Rosemary				Rosemary
	Rose water				Rose water
	Saffron				Saffron
	Sage				Sage
	Savory				Savory
	Spearmint				Spearmint
	Star anise				Star anise
	Tamarind				Tarragon
	Tarragon				Thyme
	Thyme				Turmeric
	Turmeric				Vanilla*
	Vanilla				Wintergreen
	Wintergreen				

* These foods are OK in moderation.   # These foods are OK occasionally.

Dairy

VATA		PITTA		KAPHA	
NO	YES	NO	YES	NO	YES
Goat's milk (powdered)	All dairy*	Butter (salted)	Butter (unsalted)	Butter	Ghee
		Buttermilk (commercial)	Cheese (mild and soft)	Cheese (all kinds)	Milk (goat's)
		Cheese (hard or Feta)	Cottage cheese	Buttermilk (commercial)	Yogurt (diluted, 1:4 pts or more with water)
		Sour cream	Ghee	Ice cream	
		Yogurt	Ice cream	Milk (cow's)	
			Milk (cow's or goat's)	Sour cream	
			Yogurt (diluted, 1:2–3 pts water)	Yogurt (undiluted)	

Oils

VATA		PITTA		KAPHA	
NO	YES	NO	YES	NO	YES
	All oils (esp. sesame)	Almond	Avocado*	Apricot	In very small amounts:
		Apricot	Coconut*	Avocado	Almond
		Corn	Olive*	Coconut	Corn
		Safflower	Sesame*	Olive	Sunflower
		Sesame	Sunflower*	Safflower	
			Soy walnut*	Sesame	
				Soy	
				Walnut	

* These foods are OK in moderation.   # These foods are OK occasionally.

Index

Amrita Sondhi is a certified yoga instructor and Ayurvedic cooking teacher; she is also owner of Movementglobal (*movementglobal.com*), a cutting-edge clothing line specializing in sustainable fibers. Her first book, *The Modern Ayurvedic Cookbook*, was published in 2006. She lives on Bowen Island, BC.

MARQUIS

Marquis Book Printing Inc.

Québec, Canada

2012